T0355378

THE

PUBLICATIONS

OF THE

Lincoln Record Society

FOUNDED IN THE YEAR

1910

VOLUME 76

ISSN 0267-2634

FOR THE YEAR ENDING 31ST AUGUST 1985

THE
ROLLS AND REGISTER
OF
BISHOP OLIVER SUTTON

EDITED BY

ROSALIND M. T. HILL

M.A., B.LITT., F.S.A.

Formerly Professor of Medieval History, Westfield College,
University of London

Volume VIII

Institutions, collations and sequestrations,
all archdeaconries except Lincoln and Northampton

Published for
The Lincoln Record Society
by
The Boydell Press
1986

© Lincoln Record Society 1986

First published 1986
for the Lincoln Record Society
by The Boydell Press
an imprint of Boydell & Brewer Ltd
PO Box 9, Woodbridge, Suffolk IP12 3DF and
Wolfeboro, New Hampshire 03894–2069, USA

ISBN 0 901503 40 1

British Library Cataloguing in Publication Data
Catholic Church. *Diocese of Lincoln. Bishop*
    The rolls and register of Bishop Oliver Sutton. —
    (The Publications of the Lincoln Record Society;
    v. 76)
    Vol. 8: Institutions, collations and sequestrations,
    all archdeaconries except Lincoln and
    Northampton.
    1. Lincoln. *(Diocese) Bishop 1280–1299 (Sutton)* —
    Sources
    I. Title   II. Hill, Rosalind M. T.
    III. Lincoln Record Society   IV. Series
262'.0242534   BX1495.L/
ISBN 0-901503-40-1

Printed and bound in Great Britain by
Short Run Press Ltd, Exeter, Devon

CONTENTS

CORRIGENDA TO VOLUMES I TO VII

The editor of this edition, and successive general editors, are indebted to members of the Society, and other users of the volumes, who have contributed to this list. References are in all cases, unless otherwise indicated, to the indexes of these volumes.

Volume I

Albemarle *read* Aumale
Asfordeby Leics. *read* Asserby.
 Lincs.
Barna *read* Barua (Barrow,
 Lincs.)
Bisham *add* Berks.
Brampton Master Adam of, *read*
 Barmpton co. Durham
Branston *delete* Lincs., *add* Leics,
Cheyle, Geoffrey de, *delete*
Easington *delete* Northants
Edelington *see* Edmonton; *delete*
 Edlington Lincs.
add Edmonton Middlesex 217
Ellington *delete* Kent
Fiskerton *add* or Lincs.
for Greton unid. *read* Creeton
 Lincs.
Greendale *delete* Devon (probably
 Grindale Yorks.)

Haxby, Axby *read* Castle Ashby
 Northants.
Helegeye, Healing Helingeye,
 read Hilgay, Norfolk
Markingfield *delete*; *add* Mark-
 field, Leics, John of, 220
Nafferton *delete* Northumb.
Pagula *add* Paull, Yorks
Panton, 220, *read* Ponton, Great
Paunton *see* Panton, Ponton
Santon *delete* Cumb. *add* ? Lincs.
Scheyle Cheylc *add* Keal Lincs.
Stow cont. *delete*
Stow, vicarage of, *add* Stow
 Green, next Threekingham
Viterbo *delete* Rome
Winwick *delete* Lancs.
Wormington, Wermington *delete*
 Glos. *add* ? Northants

Volume II

Chalcombe *read* Chacombe
Chaucombe *add* see Chacombe
Cheal *read* Cheal Lincs.
De Montibus *delete*
Fifehead *delete* Dorset
Haugh *read* Hough-on-the-Hill
Hochecote *see* Edgcote
Hulcote *read* Edgcote
Marchington *read* Staffs.
Neubotle, Newbottle *delete*
 Bridge

Ripton Abbot's *read* Hunts
Snotiscombe *see* Snorscumb
Somersham *read* unid.
Swaffham *delete* Cambs
Tutbury *read* Staffs.
Thwangcaistr *read* Caistor Lincs.
Woodend, *read* Woodhead

Volume III

add Ardeley Ardley Erdeleye
Herts, 143
add Basle *read* Switzerland
Bosworth *delete* unid. *add*
Husband's
Bibbeworth *read* unid.
Castlethorp *delete* in Broughton
parish
add Erdeleye *read* Ardeley
add Hacham *see* Haugham

Harby *add* Leics. or Northants.
Haugham *add* Hacham
Parteneye *see* Partney
Plungar *add* Leics.
Sixhills, *read* Lincs.
Stathern *delete* from places in
Plungar
Stoke Willoughby *read* Scott
Willoughby
Syston *read* Lincs.

Volume IV

Albirbury *read* Alberbury Salop
Bibbeworth *read* unid.
Boreham Wood *delete* and also
cross-reference under
Borham John of, 85
Chatton *delete* Northants
Edlington Lincs. *delete*; *add*
Edlington see Edmonton; *add*
Edmonton, Edlington,
Middlesex, 197

Greendale *delete* Devon and in
vol.v
Hautebarg *read* Alkborough
Lincs.
Kirby *delete* Lonsdale, *add* Kendal
Paulerspury *add* 81

Volume V

Ailby Alesby *delete*
Albury John of, *delete*
Aldesby *read* unid.
Aldredeby unid. *delete*
Alesby *delete* Ailby and; Aylesby
add 55–6, 156–7, 163
Cheal, Scheyle *add* Keal
Gostewick *read* unid. Guestwick
delete
Reston *delete* Riston Lincs.; *add* see
Ruston; and Ruston Norfolk
109–10
Stoneley, prior of *add* 215; Stow
prior of, *add* ? Stoneley

add Edelington iuxta Totenham *see*
Edmonton
Easington *read* co. Oxon. *add*
Flitton see Flitton; *delete* Fleet,
Flitte, dean of 204
Frowlesworth *read* Leics.
Harcourt *delete* Salop
add Moggerhanger Morhangr'
Beds, 19; Morhanger *add* see
Moggerhanger
Oadby? *delete*

Volume VI

add Ardele Edrele Herts. 155

add Bonthorpe, Brunthorpe Lincs. 135–7; Brunthorpe *read* see Bonthorpe

Bodington *delete* Salop (probably Ruddington, Notts)

Blewbury Blebiri *add* Berks

add Burnham Deepdale, Debdale Norfolk, *see* Geoffrey rector of

Calthorpe *read* see Cawthorpe; *add* Cawthorpe, Calthorp, Lincs., brother T. of, 93

Carleton, Great *read* Lincs.

Caythorpe *delete* Calthorp, brother T. of

Debedale *read* see Burnham Deepdale; Deepdale *read* see Burnham Deepdale

add Edelington see Edmonton; *add* Edmonton, Edelinton Middlesex, 155

Elham *delete*; *add* Elmingham, Ralph of, 119

Erdele *read* see Ardley; delete Yardley

Luttegereshale *read* Ludgershall

Panton *delete*; *add* Paunton see Ponton; *add* Ponton, Paunton, Lincs. 91, 126

Pittesford *read* Pisseford unid.

Warmington *delete* Warwicks.

Volume VII

p. 105 n. 2 Brenyston is certainly Branston Lincs. Richard of Thistleton is incorrectly identified

Acthorpe *read* a lost vill in S. Elkington Lincs.

Ailby, Aleby Lincs. *add* Aleby see Ailby; Alesby see Aylesby; Aylesby Lincs.

Aisthorpe *delete* Alan, Master, *read* vicar

Alcotesle *read* see Abbotsley; Abbotsley *add* Alcotesle, 3, 91

Alnemouth *add* Alnemue with cross reference

Belchford 45, *delete*

Bracewell, *read* see Brightwell, Baldwin; *add* Brightwell, Baldwin 57

Braithwell *add* Braycheswelle 11, with cross reference

Branston Leics. *delete read* Branston, Brenyston Lincs. 105, with cross reference

Brington *delete* 105 n.

Burton, West *delete* Rutland

Bycherest *read* unid.

Calthorpe *delete* Oxon. *read* see Cawthorpe; Cawthorpe, Little Calthorpe, Clathorp, Lincs 87, 90, 92, 121; *add* Clathorpe *see* Cawthorpe

Cokesdwald *read* see Cuxwold; *delete* Coxwold; *add* Cuxwold Cokeswald Cokewald Lincs. Walter of, 69, 79

add Comberton, Cumbrington Worcs. William of, 96; with cross reference

delete Culmington

add Fylingdales Filineham Yorks 79

Grasby *delete* ? Gryeby, Thomas of *add* Graby, Grybey Lincs., Thomas of 43

Gryebey *read* see Graby

Greendale *delete* Devon

Halsington *read* unid.

Halwynefeld *read* unid.
Hardwick ? John of, *for* 16 *read* 116
Harrington *add* Northants.
Hellifield *delete*
add Hothorpe, Huthorp
  Northants., Hugh of, 112
Howthorpe *delete*
Huthorp *read* see Hothorpe
Loughborough *add* Lutteburg;
  Loughborough, Nicholas of,
  add 77
Lutteburg *add* see Lough-
  borough
Marefield *read* Leics.
Mareham *read* Lincs.
Markingfield *delete*; Markfield,
  add Merkenfeld, John of 107;
  Merkenfeld *see* Markfield

Morbonne *read* Morbourne
Scarborough, *add* Scoresburgh,
  18, 43; Scorborough *delete*; *add*
Scoresburgh see Scarborough
Stebenach *delete* Stepney and;
  delete Stepney; *add* Stevenage,
  Stibenach, 60–1
add Swineshead, Swinesheved
  Beds., 110, 118; *delete*
  Swineshead Lincs.
delete Winkesley
add Winchelsea, Wychelse,
  Wynchelse, Sussex, John of,
  40, 53, 59
add Wychelse see Winchelsea;
  Wynchelse *read* see Winchelsea

Note: Professor C. J. Holdsworth has added to the history of Bishop Sutton's family in *Rufford Charters* vol. i (Thoroton Society Record Series XXIX, 1972), pp. cvii–cxvi.

The Rolls and Register of Oliver Sutton, Bishop of Lincoln 1290–1299

ARCHDEACONRY OF STOW 1280–99

[*membrane 1.*] INSTITUTIONES ET CARTE FACTE PER DOMINUM OLIVERUM LINCOLN' ELECTUM A DIE CONFIRMATIONIS SUE VIDELICET A V KALENDAS MARTII ANNO DOMINI M.CC. SEPTUAGESIMO NONO. IN ARCHIDIACONATU STOWE.

GAINSBOROUGH. V. John of Hill (Hulle) ch. p. by the Master of the Templars in England to the vicarage of Gainsborough vacant by the death of Alexander. Inst. Theydon Mount, May 10, 1280.

INCIPIT ANNUS PRIMUS CONSECRATIONIS DOMINI OLIVERI EPISCOPI XIIII KALENDAS JUNII ANNO DOMINI M.CC. OCTOGESIMO.

THORNHOLM. Thomas of Hedon, canon of Thornholm, appointed by the bishop to be prior thereof in succession to Laurence who had resigned. An election on postulation made on July 15, 1280 of Simon prior of Markby was quashed for incorrect procedure on July 23. Thomas was appointed Stow Park, July 25, 1280.

HAXEY. V. Roger of Landmoth (Landemoth') ch. p. by the P. and C. of Newburgh to the vicarage of Haxey vacant by the death of Hugh. Inst. Launde Priory, July 31, 1280.

SUDBROOKE. R. William Braund subd. p. by the A. and C. of Barlings to the church of Sudbrooke vacant by the death of Alrenand. Inst. Eynsham, Feb. 8, 1281.

WADDINGHAM ST MARY. R. William of Moulton pr. p. by Sir Thomas son of Lambert of Moulton pr. p. by Sir Thomas son

1

of Lambert of Moulton knight to the church of St Mary at Waddingham vacant by the death of Sir Alexander of Algarkirk. Inst. Buckden Apr. 30, 1281.

GATE BURTON. R. Master William of Littleport subd. p. by the P. and C. of Spalding to the church of Gate Burton vacant by the death of Master Ranulph of Nassington. Inst. London, O.T., May 18, 1281.

ANNUS PONTIFICATUS DOMINI OLIVERI SECUNDUS ET INCARNATIONIS M.CC. OCTOGESIMUS I.

FISKERTON. R. Sir Geoffrey of Thornley (Thornlauwe) d. p. by the A. and C. of Peterborough to the church of Fiskerton vacant by the res. of Elias of Beckingham. Inst., with a papal dispensation, London, May 20, 1281.

SCOTHERN. V. Roger of Osbournby ch. p. by the A. and C. of Barlings to the vicarage of Scothern vacant by the death of Richard. Inst. Nettleham, July 29, 1281.

ROXBY. R. Henry Sparry subd. p. by the P. and C. of Drax to the mediety of the church of Roxby vacant by the death of Roger. Inst. London, Oct. 17, 1281.

LEA. R. Robert of Haxby subd. p. by the P. and C. of Spalding to the church of Lea vacant by the res. of Robert of Littlebury. Inst. London, O.T., Oct. 19, 1281.

FRODINGHAM (Froxingham). V. Master Henry Le Meger, d. p. by Michael of Northampton who was in actual occupation as rector (*detinentem ecclesiam ut rector*) to the vicarage of Frodingham. No reason given for vacancy. Henry resigned the living of St. Mary extra Castrum, Northampton, and the bishop instituted him without acknowledging Michael's right of presentation, and assigned a manse to him with the consent of the Earl of Cornwall as patron. Inst. Edlesborough, Nov. 6, 1281.

RAVENTHORPE (Ragnilthorp'). V. Richard of Appleby ch. p. by the P. and C. of Thornholm to the vicarage of Raventhorpe vacant by the death of Geoffrey. Inst. Chalcombe, Nov. 30, 1281.

XIIII KALENDAS JUNII SANCTI DUNSTANI ANNUS PONTIFICATUS DOMINI OLIVERI TERTIUS ET INCARNATIONIS DOMINI M.CC. OCTO-GESIMUS SECUNDUS.

CAMMERINGHAM. V. William of Halton ch. p. by Julian, proctor-general of the A. and C. of Blanchland, to the vicarage of Cammeringham vacant by the death of Ralph. Inst. Newstead-by-Stamford, June 1, 1282.

TORKSEY.[1] William of Rasen, canon of Torksey, appointed by the bishop as prior thereof in succession to John of Owmby (Ouneby) who had died. An attempt made on July 25 to elect William was quashed for incorrect procedure. No date [?late July, 1282].

[*membrane 2.*] ROXBY. R. Henry of Selby subd. re-presented by the P. and C. of Drax to the mediety of the church of Roxby, from which he had resigned in order to clear his conscience, with the injunction that he should follow the advice of his confessor in disposing of the fruits which he had wrongfully received. Inst. Thornholm, Oct. 2, 1282.

[*endorsed*] APPLEBY (Cantaria de Appelby).[2] *Inspeximus* under his seal by the bishop of a charter of Laurence, prior, and the convent of Thornholm, by which, in return for a grant by Master Walter of Kir(k)by, vicar of Appleby, of a hundred and fifty marks sterling annually, invested in certain lands, tenements and services in Risby and Appleby, they are to establish a perpetual chantry, to be served by a secular priest for five days a week in Appleby and two days in the chapel of St. Michael in Manton, for the souls of the said Master Walter, his parents, the canons of Thornholm and their relations and friends, the parishioners of Appleby, and all faithful departed. They are to be compelled to observe this obligation by the Archbishop of Canterbury, the Bishop, Dean and Chapter of Lincoln, the Archdeacon of Stow and his official. Charter dated Thornholm, June 24, 1272, under their seal. *Inspeximus* dated Thornholm, Oct. 4, 1282.

---

[1] No heading is given.
[2] This entry is endorsed, with a pointing hand which indicates that it should be on the front of the roll.

SAXBY. R. John of Lathbury (Lathebiry), clerk in minor orders p. by the P. and C. of St. Katherine's outside Lincoln to the church of Saxby vacant by the death of Thomas of Bradwell. Ordained subd. Dec. 12, Inst. Wycombe, Dec. 19, 1282, and had letters patent under the small seal.

FOSSE. Alice of Rye, appointed by the bishop to the office of prioress of Fosse in succession to Ala who had been removed from office about the time of St. Gregory's Mass (Mar. 12). An attempt to elect her was quashed for incorrect procedure. Milton, Apr. 1, 1283.

––––––––

XIIII KALENDAS JUNII DIE SANCTI DUNSTANI ANNUS INCARNATIONIS M.CC. OCTOGESIMO III ET PONTIFICATUS DOMINI OLIVERI QUARTUS.

––––––––

NORMANBY. R. Robert de Ferrariis of Fotheringhay (Fodring') subd. p. by the A. and C. of Peterborough to the church of Normanby vacant because Nicholas of Loddington (Lodington') had been inst. to Paston. Inst. Peterborough, June 17, 1283, saving to the A. and C. an annual pension of ten marks. Had letters patent.

HEMSWELL (Helmeswell'). R. John of Helpston subd. p. by Edmund Earl of Cornwall to the church of Helmswell vacant by the death of Michael of Northampton. Inst. Peterborough June 17, 1283.

WILLOUGHTON (Willeweton'). V. William of Manningford ch. p. by the Master of the Templars in England to the vicarage of Willoughton vacant by the death of Peter. Inst. Peterborough, June 18, 1283.

GRAYINGHAM (Greyingham). R. Roger of Nottingham clerk in minor orders, p. by Sir Robert de Ros knight to the mediety of the church of Grayingham vacant because John of Helpston had been inst. to Hemswell. Ordained subd. and inst. Lincoln, Sept. 18, 1283.

TORKSEY. V. Roger of Sixhills (Sixil) subd. p. by the P. and C. of Torksey to the vicarage thereof vacant by the death of William. Ordained d. Lincoln, Sept. 18, and inst. Lincoln, Sept. 1, 1283.

GLENTWORTH. V. Peter of Huntingdon ch. p. by the A. and C. of Newhouse to the vicarage of Glentworth vacant by the death of William. Inst. Buckden, Dec. 5, 1283.

PILHAM. R. Nicholas of Kingsbury (Kynnesbir') ch. p. by Edmund Earl of Cornwall to the church of Pilham vacant by the res. of Master John de Kernik'. Inst. Stow Park, Jan. 23, 1284.

FOSSE (Fossa).
Alice of Laxton, sub-prioress of Fosse, elected to the office of prioress vacant because Alice of Rye had insisted, in great distress and against the bishop's efforts to persuade her to remain, on resigning her office. Election confirmed [Fosse] May 16, 1284.

Memorandum quod episcopo declinante ad monasterium de Fossa ob certam causam, ac domina Alicia de Rye priorissa ejusdem domus petente instanter sicut multotiens prius fecerat ab officio suo totaliter absolvi, cum non posset induci quoquomodo in officio priorisse gratis vellet ulterius continuare, episcopus ejusdem Alicie instancia et lacrimatione mirabili plurimum motus, cessionem suam maximo affectu ut videbatur oblatam admisit et ipsam ab officio et regimine domus absolvit, suadens conventui quod ipse pro labore et dispendio sumptuum evitandis ad electionem de priorissa faciendam statim procederent, propter quod constante quod non tenebantur ad alicujus licenciam petendam ad electionem faciendam illico processerunt, et facto modico intervallo episcopus duos de clericis suis quidnam fecerant dicte moniales examinaturos in capitulum intromisit, a quibus didicit quod omnes de conventu qui[1] voluerunt, potuerunt et debuerunt interesse tunc presentes, unica sola excepta, in dominam Agnetem de Laxinton' subpriorissam dicte domus per viam scrutinii consenserant, ipsamque elegerant suo modo, quam quidem electionem supleto prius de gracia speciali si quid contra formam juris in processu fuisset attemptatum, episcopus confirmavit, et factis aliis que subsequenter incumbebant, salvo jure archidiaconi cui prejudicare nullatenus intendebat, dictam Agnetem electam et confirmatam per unum de suis fecit installari, curam spiritualium quatenus sexui muliebri congruebat necnon temporalium domus eidem plenius committendo. Fecit etiam moniales et sorores domus repromittere dicte priorisse canonicam obedienciam quam et

---

[1] sic, recte 'que'.

ipse idem recepit et dicta priorissa antequam recessit. Datum XVII Kalendas Junii anno M.CC. octogesimo quarto.

XIIII KALENDAS JUNII DIE SANCTI DUNSTAN I ANNUS DOMINI M.CC.LXXX QUARTUS ET PONTIFICATUS DOMINI OLIVERI QUINTUS.

WADDINGHAM, ST. PETER'S (Wadingham Sancti Petri). R. William of Beverley (Beverlaco) subd. p. by the P. and C. of Thornholm to the church of St. Peter at Waddingham vacant by the death of William of Owston (Osolveston'). Presentation opposed in the King's court before the justices John of Reigate (Reygate) and Geoffrey Aguyllum by Robert Benet of Waddingham who presented another clerk. A royal writ (given in full and dated York, Oct. 3, 1284 witnessed by John of Reigate) directed the bishop to accept the prior's candidate. William was inst. Milton, Oct. 19, 1284.

BLYBOROUGH. R. William de Byblesworth' subd. re-presented by the P. and C. of Durham to the church of Blyborough vacant because the said William had failed to be ordained pr. within a year of institution. Inst. Milton near Harpford bridge,[1], Nov. 16, 1284.

SPRINGTHORPE. R. Thomas of Whissendine, clerk in minor orders p. by Edmund Earl of Cornwall to the church of Springthorpe vacant by the death of John. Ordained subd. and inst. Brampton near Huntingdon, Dec. 23, 1284.

TORKSEY, ST. MARY'S. V. Thomas called Penne ch. p. by the P. and C. of Torksey to the vicarage of St. Mary's, Torksey, vacant by the res. of Roger of Sixhills. Inst. Daventry, Feb. 28, 1285.

WADDINGHAM, ST. MARY'S.[2] R. Richard of Fleet (Flete), clerk in minor orders p. by Sir Thomas son of Lambert of Moulton (Moleton') knight, to the church of St. Mary, Waddingham, vacant by the death of Sir William of Moulton. Granted custody Dec. 26, 1284. Ordained subd. and inst. Brampton near Huntingdon, Mar. 10, 1285 and had letters patent.

[1] Milton in Oxfordshire.
[2] See presentation to Stainton, below, p. 8.

RISBY. V. Hugh of Goxhill (Gousel) ch. p. by the P. and C. of Thornholm to the vicarage of Risby vacant by the death of John. Inst. Ware, Apr. 21, 1285.

BRATTLEBY (Brotelby). R. William of Moulton (Moleton') d. re-presented by Robert Foucher to the church of Brattleby vacant because the said William had failed to be ordained pr. within a year of institution. Presentation disputed by the A. and C. of Lessay (Exaqueo) in the diocese of Coutances, who presented another clerk. A royal writ (given in full, dated Westminster, May 6, 1285, and witnessed by T. de Weylaund) directed the bishop to accept Robert Foucher's candidate. William was inst. London, O.T., May 10, 1285, saving to the chapter of Lincoln Cathedral an annual pension of five marks.

[*membrane 3.*] XIIII KALENDAS JUNII DIE SANCTI DUNSTANI ANNUS DOMINI M.CC. OCTOGESIMUS QUINTUS ET PONTIFICATUS DOMINI OLIVERI SEXTUS.

Institutio Hugonis Durandi in ecclesia de Ingham est in dorso rotuli.[1]

AISTHORPE (Asthorpe). R. Sir Simon of Worth, canon of Lincoln, p. by Peter Bozun lord of Aisthorpe to the church thereof vacant by the res. of William of Moulton (Multon'). Inst. Melton Mowbray, July 12, 1285.

SCOTTER (Scoter). R. John called Colman ch. p. by the A. and C. of Peterborough to the church of Scotter vacant by the res. of Robert of Hungerford. Inst. Liddington, July 14, 1285.

WINTERTON (Wyntrington'). V. Master Geoffrey of Holme subd. p. by the P. and C. of Malton to the vicarage of Winterton vacant by the death of William. Ordained d. and inst. Brampton near Huntingdon Dec. 22, 1285.

[*endorsed*] [INGHAM. R. Master Durand of Lincoln subd. p. by the P. and C. of Bullington to the church of Ingham vacant by the res. of Master Thomas of Louth (Luda). Inst., in the person of Robert of Kibworth, his proctor, Buckden, Jan. 21, 1286, and had letters patent.]

---

[1] See below, at the end of the entry for this year.

XIIII KALENDAS JUNII ANNO DOMINI M.CC. OCTOGESIMO SEXTO DIE SANCTI DUNSTANI INCIPIT ANNUS PONTIFICATUS DOMINI OLIVERI EPISCOPI LINCOLN' SEPTIMUS.

WADDINGHAM ST. PETER'S (Wadingham). R. Richard of Saham *or* Soham (Sahum) clerk in minor orders p. by the P. and C. of Thornholm to the church of St. Peter, Waddingham, vacant because William of Beverley (Beverlaco) had been inst. to the mediety of Gedling in the diocese of York. Granted custody until the next ordinations. Ordained subd. (with letters dimissory) by the Archbishop of York, June 8, 1286, and inst. York, June 9, 1286. Had letters patent.

TORKSEY (Torkes'). Joel of Lincoln, subprior of Torksey, elected moderately successfully (*satis canonice — per electionem in substantialibus usquequaque rite celebratam*) to the office of prior thereof vacant by the res. of William of Rasen and the refusal of William of Keelby (Keleby) canon of Thornton to stand for election. Election confirmed Louth, July 14, 1286.

CAENBY (Cavenby). R. Master William of Clixby (Clisseby) pr. p. by the Λ. and C. of Barlings to the church of Caenby vacant because Robert of Clixby had been inst. to the church of Great Carlton (Magna Karleton') near Louth. Inst. Brackley, May 3, 1286.

STAINTON[1] (Steynton' juxta Wadingham). R. Richard of Fleet (Flete) ch. re-presented by Sir Thomas son of Lambert of Moulton (Multon') knight to the church of Stainton vacant because the said Richard had not been ordained pr. within a year of institution. Inst. Buckden, Sept. 3, 1286, and had letters patent.

KETTLETHORPE (Ketelsthorpe'). R. Robert Cross (de Cruce) ch. p. by Nicholas Cross to the church of Kettlethorpe vacant by the death of Gerard of Lincoln. Granted the church *in commendam* for a period, then inst. Fingest, Dec. 14, 1286.

TORKSEY. R. Stephen of Howden, clerk in minor orders p. by the P. and C. of Torksey to the church of St. Peter at Torksey vacant by the death of Master Thomas. Granted custody Sept. 22, 1286. ordained subd. and inst. Thame, Dec. 21, 1286.

---

[1] Earlier called St. Mary's, Waddingham. See above, p. 6.

SNARFORD (Snartesford'). R. Richard of Barton, ch. p. by the
P. and C. of Elsham to the church of Snarford vacant because
Master Robert of Barton had joined the Augustinian canons
at Elsham. Granted the church *in commendam* for six months.
Then inst. Fingest, Jan. 2, 1287, and had letters patent.

WILLINGHAM-BY-STOW (Wyvelingham). R. Master Henry de
La Wyle, clerk in minor orders, p. by Lady Alice de Lacy
(Lasci), acting for Henry de Lacy Earl of Lincoln while he was
abroad, to the church of Willingham, vacant by the death of
Richard Makerel. Ordained subd. Wycombe, Mar. 1, 1287,
and inst. Wooburn, Mar. 2, 1287.

BLYTON. Master Richard Bidun subd. p. by the P. and C. of
Thornholm to the portion which Richard of Langar held in
the church of Blyton, vacant by the death of the said Richard.
Ordained d. Mar. 30, 1286 and pr. Mar. 1, 1287. An examination of the rolls of Bishops Hugh of Wells and Robert
Grosseteste showed that the rector of this portion was bound
to perform the actual office of vicar (i.e. to serve the church
and reside). Inst. Wycombe, Mar. 3, 1287, the institution
being attested by Master John Le Fleming, canon of Lincoln,
Sir William of Stockton, Robert of Thorpe and John de
Scalleby, who added his sign.

HACKTHORN (Hagthorn'). R. Philip of Norton, clerk in minor
orders and under age, p. by John of Dean (Dene) to the
mediety of the church of Hackthorn vacant by the death of
Geoffrey of Norton. Custody of the church and candidate
granted to Richard of Stockton, guardian of the Cathedral
choir-boys. Ordained subd. and inst. Bradwell, Mar. 22, 1287.

GATE BURTON. R. Sir Richard of Winchcomb ch., canon of
Lincoln, p. by the P. and C. of Spalding to the church of Gate
Burton (Gayte Burton') vacant because William of Littleport
had been inst. to the vicarage of Weston in Holland. Inst.
Banbury, Apr. 2, 1287, and had letters patent.

XIIII KALENDAS JUNII DIE SANCTI DUNSTANI ANNO DOMINI M.CC.
OCTOGESIMO SEPTIMO INCIPIT ANNUS PONTIFICATUS DOMINI
OLIVERI EPISCOPI LINCOLN' OCTAVUS.

WEST HALTON. R. Master Robert de Lacy (Lascy) ch. p. by Henry de Lacy Earl of Lincoln to the church of West Halton vacant by the death of John of St. Mary (de Sancta Maria). Inst., in the person of Geoffrey of Hemingford (Hemmingford') his proctor, Liddington, July 12, 1287.

WHITTON (Wytten'). V. Thomas of Spalding, canon of Welbeck, p. by the A. and C. thereof to the vicarage thereof vacant by the death of Master Richard of Coates. The presentation was made in virtue of a papal privilege granted by Martin IV (given in full and dated Orvieto Aug. 23, 1284) by which the Premonstratensians of Welbeck were empowered to present two members of their own communities to serve the vicarages of Cuckney, Watton, Whitton, Coates, Etwell and Duckmanton. The bishop to the Archdeacon of Stow (letter given in full) quoting this privilege and telling him to make sure that the rights and privileges of the see of Lincoln were in no way infringed. Thomas was inst. Stow Park, Aug. 1, 1287, and had letters patent (given in full).

Vacante vicaria de Wytten' per mortem Magistri Ricardi de Cothes ultimi vicarii ejusdem, ac fratre Thoma de Spaldinge canonico monasterii de Wellebeck' per....[1] abbatem et conventum loci ejusdem ad ipsam virtute cujusdam privilegii apostolici presentato, facta prius inquisitione etc., ad dictam vicariam est admissus Kalendis Augusti anno octavo apud Parcum Stowye et vicarius perpetuus cum onere personaliter ministrandi una cum alio canonico sacerdote ydoneo prout tenor privilegii exigit infrascripti, et secundum formam statuti legati continue residendi, prestita episcopo a dicto fratre Thoma canonica obediencia juxta solitum morem, salvis etiam in omnibus juribus episcopalibus et consuetudinibus ac Lincoln' ecclesie dignitate, canonice institutus in eadem. Alioquin, si per dictos religiosos in contrarium temere presumptum fuerit in hac parte, privilegii pretacti beneficium prorsus amittant. Unde scriptum fuit....[1] Archidiacono Stowye sub hac forma:... O etc. Quia fratrem Thomam de Spaldinge canonicum monasterii de Wellebeck' per..8..[1] abbatem et conventum loci ejusdem ad vicariam ecclesie de Wytthen' vacantem nobis presentant[2] virtute cujusdam privilegii apostolici cujus tenor talis est. — Martinus etc. dilectis in Christo filiis abbati et conventui monasterii de Wellebeck' Premonstratensis ordinis Ebor' diocesis salutem et apostolicam benedictionem. Religionis vestre meretur

---

[1] Blank in MS.
[2] The grammar is confused. One would expect 'presentatur'.

honestas ut petitiones vestras quantum cum Deo possumus ad exauditionis graciam admittamus. Hinc est quod nos vestris supplicationibus inclinati ut ecclesiis vestris de Cukenay, de Watthon', de Wytthen', de Cotes, de Etewell' et de Dukemanton, Ebor, Lincoln' et Lychefelden' diocesum, quas in usus proprios vos asseritis optinere, in quibus ordinate sunt vicarie et perpetui vicarii instituti, liceat vobis cedentibus vel decedentibus ipsarum ecclesiarum vicariis per duos de vestris canonicis sacerdotes ydoneos facere deserviri, quorum unum diocesano episcopo presentetis qui ei de spiritualibus, vobis autem de temporalibus et ordinis observencia debeat respondere, dummodo ipsis sacerdotibus tantum de ipsarum tantum de ipsarum ecclesiarum proventibus reliquatis quod diocesano de suis juribus respondere valeant et universa onera ipsis ecclesiis incumbentia sustinere, auctoritate vobis presentium indulgemus. Nulli igitur etc. Si quis etc. Datum apud Urbem Veterem X Kalendas Septembris pontificatus nostri anno quarto. ...prout requirit forma apostolice littere prescripte admissum, ipsumque vicarium perpetuum cum onere personaliter ministrandi una cum alio concanonico sacerdote ydoneo monasterii predicti et secundum formam statuti legati continue residendi, prestita nobis a dicto fratre Thoma obediencia juxta solitum morem canonice instituimus in eadem. Alioquin si per dictos religiosos in contrarium temere presumptum fuerit hujus privilegii beneficium prorsus amittant, vobis mandamus quatinus dictum fratrem Thomam corporalem possessionem dicte vicarie habere faciatis modo pretacto. Valete. Datum apud Parcum Stowye, Kalendas Augusti, pontificatus nostri anno octavo ... Universis etc. Datum apud Parcum Stowye, Kalendas Augusti, anno domini M.CC. octogesimo septimo.

[*membrane 4.*] HEMSWELL. R. William of Wendover (Wendovere) clerk in minor orders p. by Oliver of Wendover to the church of St. Helen, Hemswell, vacant by the death of Hugh. Granted custody Oct. 12, 1287. Ordained subd. and inst. Huntingdon, Dec. 20, 1287.

WINTERINGHAM. R. Robert Marmiun, clerk in minor orders and under age, p. by John Marmiun to the church of Winteringham vacant by the res. of Master Roger Marmiun. Custody granted to the said Master Roger until Robert came of age to receive custody, Sept. 18, 1287. Ordained subd. and inst. Huntingdon, Dec. 20, 1287.

FILLINGHAM. R. Master Thomas Le Fleming (Flemeng') clerk in minor orders p. by Master John Le Fleming, proctor-

general in England of the A. and C. of Lessay, to the church
of Fillingham vacant by the res. of Sir Pagan of Liskeard
(Liskered). Ordained subd. and inst. Huntingdon, Dec. 20,
1287.

[*endorsed*] [NO HEADING.[1] Letters patent in which the bishop
first of all issues an *inspeximus* of letters of the A. and C. of
Lessay (given in full and dated Lessay Aug. 8, 1290) quoting
letters patent of Bishop Hugh of Wells, given under his seal
and that of the chapter of Lincoln Cathedral, most of whose
members act as witnesses, concerning the churches of Fillingham, Brattleby, Riseholme and Great Carlton, of which
Lessay Abbey held the patronage. In these letters Bishop
Hugh grants to the A. and C. an annual pension of twenty
marks from the church of Fillingham, while alloting a payment to the chapter of two and a half marks from Riseholme
and five marks from Brattleby on their first vacancy, and
reserving the right to deal with the church of Great Carlton.
Bishop Hugh's letter is dated Lincoln, Sept. 9, 1232. The A.
and C. of Lessay now propose to reduce their pension
claimed from the church of Fillingham from twenty marks to
six, and to allot these six marks to the foundations of a
chantry for the soul of William of Newark, Archdeacon of
Huntingdon, who had been a benefactor of this house.
    Bishop Sutton and the chapter of Lincoln ratify this
arrangement under their seals in a tripartite agreement,
adding certain details, viz. that the chantry is to be established
at Newark and that the right of presentation is to rest with the
executors of Newark, and after their deaths with the town of
Newark, or, failing that, with the dean and chapter of Lincoln.
One copy of the agreement is to remain in the chapter
muniments, a second with the executors of William of Newark,
and a third in the church of Fillingham. Witnessed by Master
Adam the precentor, Richard of St. Frideswide Archdeacon
of Buckingham, Gilbert the subdean, Durand Archdeacon of
Stow, Thomas of Burland, John Le Fleming, William called
Hopiton', William of Langworth, Robert of Kilworth, Jocelyn
of Kirmington and Sir Richard of Rothwell, canons of
Lincoln, and others. Lincoln, Sept. 28, 1291.

    Universis sancte matris ecclesie filiis ad quos presentes
littere pervenerint, Oliverus etc. salutem in omnium salvatore.
Litteras religiosorum virorum abbatis et conventus de
Exaqueo ordinis Sancti Benedicti Constantien' diocesis

---

[1] This entry, which refers to the church of Fillingham, has been endorsed
in a hand which appears to be fourteenth-century.

recepimus et inspeximus tenorem qui sequitur continentes —
Universis sancte matris ecclesie filius Petrus permissione
divina abbas monasterii Sancte Trinitatis de Exaqueo ordinis
Sancti Benedicti Constantien' diocesis recepimus et inspeximus
tenorem qui sequitur continentes: Universis sancte matris
ecclesie filiis Petrus permissione divina abbas monasterii
Sancte Trinitatus de Exaqueo ordinis Sancte Benedicti
Constantien' diocesis ac ejusdem loci conventus salutem in
salutis auctore. Noverit universitas vestra quod felicis recordationis dominus Hugo Lincoln' Episcopus pensionem
nostram quam in ecclesia de Fylingham Lincoln' diocesis quod
de nostro patronatu existit a tempore cujus non extat
memoria percipere consueverimus augmentavit annuam
prestationem viginti marcarum nobis et dicto monasterio
nostro nomine simplicis benficii assignando, prout in littera
ejusdem domini super hiis confecta plenius continetur sub
hac forma: Omnibus Christi fidelibus ad quos presens
scriptum pervenerit Hugo Dei gracia Lincoln' Episcopus
salutem in domino. Noverit universitas vestra quod cum
dilecti nobis Robertus abbas et conventus de Exaqueo super
ecclesiis de Fylingham, Brotelby, Risum et Carleton' ad eorum
patronatum spectantibus sponte, simpliciter et absolute de
assensu et voluntate venerabilis fratris Hugonis Constantien'
episcopi dictorum abbatis et conventus diocesani nostre se,
subjecerint ordinationi per Anketillum priorem de Bosgrave
procuratorem suum ad hoc litteratorie constitutum, eodem
etiam abbate tunc presente, nos de assensu et voluntate
dilectorum filiorum Willelmi decani et capituli nostri Lincoln'
de predictis ecclesiis in hunc modum duximus ordinandum,
videlicet quod abbas et conventus de Exaqueo habeant in
ecclesia de Filingham cum primo vacaverit nomine perpetui
beneficii viginti marcas eo computato si quid de ea prius
percipere consueverunt per manus eorum qui in ipsa ecclesia
pro tempore canonice fuerint instituti percipiendas in duobus
anni terminis, videlicet in festo Sancti Martini decem marcas
et in festo Pentecostis decem marcas, ita quidem quod si dicte
ecclesie rectores dictos terminos vel aliquem de eis non
observaverint solvent monachis memoratis viginti solidos
nomine pene pro termino non observato. Ordinamus etiam
quod quotiens eadem ecclesia vacaverit dicti abbas et conventus salvis sibi predictis viginti marcis presentent nobis et
successoribus nostris ad ipsam clericum idoneum a nobis
persona in ea instituendum, qui omnia onera illius ecclesie
ordinaria debita et consueta sustinebit. Iterum ordinamus
quod due marce et dimidia de ecclesia de Risum et quinque
marce de ecclesia de Brotelby cum primo vacaverint cedant in
augmentum commune canonicorum ecclesie nostre Lincoln'

annuatim percipiende per manus eorum qui pro tempore dictas rexerint ecclesias ad dictorum abbatis et conventus presentationem per nos et successores nostros in eisdem instituendi qui personaliter ibidem in officio sacerdotali ministraturi de oneribus ordinariis debitis et consuetis pro ecclesiis ipsis respondebunt. Ecclesia vero de Magna Carleton' cum pertinentiis ordinationi nostre reservamus in perpetuum. Preterea volumus et concedimus quod sepedicti abbas et conventus annuam pecuniam quam in ecclesiis predictis percipere consueverunt percipient donec hec ordinatio nostra per supradictarum viginti marcarum perceptionem plene fuerit effectui mancipata. Si autem ecclesias de Brotelby et Rysum vel unam earum infra prenotatum terminum vacare contigerit, dilecti filii supradicti decanus et capitulum cum beneficium inde sibi superius concessum receperint sepedictis monachis pro ecclesia de Brotelby de una marca et pro ecclesia de Rysum de tribus solidis interim tantummodo respondebunt salvis in omnibus episcopalibus consuetudinibus et Lincoln' ecclesie dignitate. Quod ad perpetuam optineat firmitatem presenti scripto sigillum nostrum una cum sigillo predicti capituli nostri Lincoln' duximus apponendum. Hiis testibus, Willelmo decano Roberto archidiacono Johanne precentore, Willelmo cancellario, Waltero Thesaurario et Johanne subdecano Lincoln, Roberto Leyc' Willelmo Stowe Johanne de Bedeford' Matheo Buckingham, Adam Oxon' et Gilberto Huntyndon' archidiaconis, Willelmo de Avalun, Magistris Gocelino de Cicestr', Roberto de Gravele, Willelmo de Beningworth Theobaldo et Ricardo de Kantia, Galfrido Scoto, Thoma de Norton' et Warino de Kirketon' capellanis, Magistris Willelmo de Lincoln', Roberto de Brevel et Waltero de Well, Radulphe de Warravill', Petro de Hungaria et Willelmo de Winchecumb' diaconis., Theobaldi de Bossell', Magistris Amaurico de Buggeden et Ricardo de Wendover' et Ricardo de Oxon' et Thoma de Askeby subdiaconis, canonicis Lincoln'. Datum per manum nostram in capitulo Lincoln' quinto idus Septembris pontificatus nostri anno vicesimo secundo. Quam quidem litteram tradimus Magistro Thome de Flemyng' nunc rector ecclesie de Fylyngham memorate. Nos vero attendentes ipsam ecclesiam de Filingham tanta appensatione annua seu prestatione nimium onerari ac ipsam diminuere et ad suum antequum statum reformare et reducere cupientes eandem pensionem viginti marcarum usque ad sex marcas dicte ecclesie de Filingham et dicto suo rectori ac ceteris rectoribus ejusdem qui pro tempore fuerint consensu unanimi sponte, simpliciter et absolute per presentes remittimus et perpetuo relaxamus, dictasque sex marcas residuas ac earundem annuam prestationem ipsas a nobis et dicto monasterio nostro totaliter abdicando assignari concedimus, et ex nunc tenore presentium assignamus ad sustentationem unius capellani pro anime bone memorie quondam Magistri Willelmi de Newerk' archidiaconi Huntingdon de cujus bonis fatemur nos habundanter habuisse et in utilitatem domus seu monasterii nostri convertisse in perpetuum celebraturi, ubi executores testamenti dicti Magistri Willelmi duxerint ordinandum, ac presenti scriptura renunciantes pure et expresse pensioni prefato tam in toto quam in qualibet sui parte ac etiam omnibus juribus, possessionibus, actionibus petitionibus, defensionibus nobis et dicto monasterio nostro in eodem vel ad eandem aut ejusdem occasione competentibus aut in posterum competituris, necnon et litteris et munimentis predicti domini Hugonis de quibus supra fit mentio pariter et cujuscumque alterius superioris ordinarii vel delegati qualitercumque pro nobis in hac parte habitis et confectis. Ita videlicet quod prefate littere vel alique earum sive in nostris sive in cujuscumque alterius manibus fuerint quatenus dictam pensionem contingunt nulli sunt nec nobis proficiant in futurum, jure patronatus dicte ecclesie ac ceteris articulis in dicta littera dicto rectori tradita contentis ipsam pensionem non contingentibus quod et quos nobis integre reservamus et retinemus per has litteras minime derogatis. Et si prefata nostra assignatio sex marcarum in aliqua sui parte minoris efficacie aliquorum judicio censeatur, ad ipsius plenariam firmitatem volumus et petimus et nostrum presentibus prebemus assensum ut venerabilis pater dominus Lincoln Episcopus qui pro tempore fuerit cum capitulo suo dictam ecclesiam de Filingham sublata prestatione viginti marcarum predicta, quam ut superius resignamus, in dictis sex marcis tantum pensionariam remanere decetero, easdemque sex marcas ad predictam sustentationem modo quo superius assignamus prestandas et salvandas foredeclaret, ordinet, statuat seu discernat vel alio modo ipsam assignationem corroboret et sub hac forma vel alia ad efficacem et perpetuam finem perducat. In cujus rei testimonium sigilla nostra apposuimus huic scripto. Ordinationem in hac parte dilecti nostri Magistri Johannis Le Flemeng Lincoln' canonici cui nos et dictum monasterium nostrum submisimus et quam post submissionem hujusmodi in scriptis sub effectu premissi tenoris recepimus per omnia et in omnibus secuti. Datum apud Exaquium in capitulo nostro, et hora capituli, anno domini millesimo CC nonagesimo, die martis ante festum Sancti Laurencii martiris. — Nos vero pie ac laudabili voluntati et proposito dictorum abbatis et conventus, honorem divinum et exonerationem prefate ecclesie de Filingham a gravi pensione seu prestatione predicta, habito respectu ad proventum ejusdem ecclesie annuum valorem nimium et sine justa causa hactenus onerate suo commodo preservando temporali Magistro Thoma Le Flemeng nunc rectore ejus expressum prebente consensum favorabiliter condescendere cupientes, de consensu capituli nostri Lincoln' ordinamus, statuimus et decrevimus quod cessante ex nunc solutione dictarum viginti marcarum nomine simplicis beneficii vel annue pensionis predictis religiosis ut prius facienda unusquisque rector prefate ecclesie de Filingham qui est vel qui pro tempore fuerit ad sustentationem unius capellani imperpetuum celebraturi in ecclesia de Neuwerk' pro anima bone memorie quondam Magistri Willelmi de Neuwerk' Archidiaconi Huntingdon', eidem capellano celebranti seu celebraturo fideliter sine qualibet diminutione persolvat in majori ecclesia Lincoln' annuatim in festis Beati Michaelis et Annunciationis Virginis Gloriose pro equali portione sex marcas de quibus supra fit mentio sub debito juramenti corporaliter a quolibet rectore prestandi in institutione seu quacumque admissione sua sub quocumque titulo juris vel gracie aut qualicumque colore admissus fuerit ad ecclesiam de Filingham antedictam. Si vero quispiam de rectoribus in ecclesia supradicta futuris vel sub alio titulo seu gracia quacumque dispensationis vel alia ejus possessionem incumbens contra hanc ordinationem nostram veniendo tanquam immemor exonerationis ecclesie seu et grandis beneficii per hoc sibi prestiti predictas sex marcas maliciose reservavit seu distulerit in solidum sine diminutione qualibet capellano predicto solvere terminis supradictis, preter reatum perjurii manifesti senteciam majoris excommunicationis pro tante ingratitudinis vitio et offensa tam gravi ipsorum quem- libet singulis vicibus decrevimus et volumus incurrere ipso facto. Ordinamus insuper et statuimus decernendo quod executores prefati archidiaconi vel eorum quivis quamdiu vixerint seu vixerit ad prefatam cantariam in ecclesia de Neuwerk ut premittitur imperpetuum faciendam presentent vel presentet domino archidiacono Notyngham qui pro tempore fuerit ydoneum capellanum. Post mortem autem omnium executorum ad communitatem ville de Neuwerk' si voluerit, alioquin ad decani et capituli ecclesie Lincoln' presentationem spectare volumus hujusmodi capellani quotiens casus contigerit in futurum, quod si communitas ville predicte seu decanus et capitulum Lincoln' in forma predicta postquam prefatam cantariam vacaverit ad eam neglexerit presentare, archidiaconus predictus libere illa vice post lapsum unius mensis a tempore vacationis cum contigerit sine reclamatione cujuslibet ordinet de eadem in forma predicta facienda. Et ut premissa robur habeant perpetue firmitatis, de consilio et consensu capituli ecclesie nostre Lincoln' requisito et interveniente expresso ordinationem nostram predictam et omnia et singula suprascripta auctoritate pontificali in capitulo nostro predicto confirmamus, ratificamus et approbamus ad perpetuam rei memoriam has litteras nostras super confirmatione, ratificatione et approbatione ordinationis nostre predicte facientes fieri tripartitas, quarum unam penes dictum capitulum nostrum Lincoln', aliam penes ecclesiam de Filingham et tertiam penes executores prefati Magistri Willelmi volumus remanere. Et nos capitulum Lincoln' ecclesie omnibus predictis consensum prebemus et assensum, sigillum nostri capituli una cum sigillo predicti domini Oliveri patris nostri presentibus facientes apponi in testimonium premissorum. Que omnia et singula presente patro nostro predicto in capitulo predicto de verbo ad verbum audivimus et intelleximus recitari. Hiis testibus, Magistris Adam precentore, Ricardo de Sancta Fredeswida Archidiacono Buckyngham, Gilberto subdecano, Durando Archidiacono Stowe, Thoma de Birland', Johanne de Flemyng', Willelmo dicto Hopiton', Willelmo de Langwath', Roberto de Kevelingworth, Goscelino de Kirmington' et domino Ricardo de Rowell' canonicis et aliis. Datum in capitulo nostro Lincolnien' die veneris proxime ante festum Sancti Michaelis, anno domini millesimo ducentesimo nonagesimo primo.]

SCAMPTON. R. John de Schaddewrth' clerk in minor orders, p. by the A. and C. of Bardney to the church of Scampton vacant by the death of Master Thomas of Caistor (Castre). Granted custody for a period, then ordained subd. and inst. Bedford, Feb. 21, 1288, and had letters patent.

HACKTHORN ('Hakethorn'). R. Philip of Norton d. represented by John of Dean (Dene) and Alice his wife to the mediety of the church of Hackthorn vacant because the said Philip had not been ordained pr. within a year of institution. Inst. Buckden, Mar. 21, 1288, and had letters patent.

XIIII KALENDAS JUNII DIE SANCTI DUNSTANI ANNO DOMINI M.CC. OCTOGESIMO OCTAVO INCIPIT ANNUS PONTIFICATUS DOMINI OLIVERI EPISCOPI NONUS

SPRIDLINGTON. V. Robert of Chafford ch. p. by the P. and C. of Bullington to the vicarage of St. Alban's church

Spridlington vacant by the death of Richard. Inst. Liddington, June 25, 1288.

NETTLEHAM (Nettelham). R. Robert Meadows (de Pratellis) ch. collated by the bishop to the church of Nettleham vacant by the resignation, at Biggleswade, Sept. 15, 1288, of William of Chillenden (Chilingden'). Collated the same day, Weston near Baldock. Had letters patent under the bishop's seal. Collation witnessed by Masters Durand of Lincoln, Jocelyn of Kirmington, canons of Lincoln and Sir Robert of Thorpe, Roger of Sixhills, Robert of Kibworth and John de Scalleby, chaplains.

BUSLINGTHORPE. R. John of Buslingthorpe ch. p. by Sir Richard of Buslingthorpe knight to the church of Buslingthorpe vacant by the res. of Master Simon. Inst. Buckden, Nov. 18, 1288, and had letters patent.

FRIESTHORPE. R. Alan of Drayton ch. p. by the D. and C. of Lincoln to the church of Friesthorpe vacant by the death of Master Hugh of Retford. Inst. Buckden, Nov. 27, 1288.

RISBY, near ROXBY (Riseby). V. Master Robert of Alkborough (Hautebarge) clerk in minor orders p. by the P. and C. of Thornholm to the vicarage of Risby vacant by the death of Sir H....[1] Ordained subd. Sept. 18, 1288 (place not given) Ordained d. and inst. Huntingdon, Dec. 18, 1288.

EPWORTH (Eppewrth'). R. Master William of Nottingham subd. p. by the P. and C. of Newburgh to the church of Epworth vacant by the death of Master Henry of Skipton. Inst. Buckden, Jan. 21, 1289, and had letters patent.

SCOTTON. R. Robert de Neville, clerk in minor orders and under age p. by Sir Robert de Neville knight to the church of Scotton vacant by the res. of Sir William d'Aubeney (de Albiniaco). Custody of the church and candidate granted to Master Robert of Radclive, M.A. (*magister artium*) until Robert de Neville came of age. Then ordained subd. and inst. Wycombe, Mar. 5, 1289, and had letters patent.

MANTON (Malmeton'). R. John de Neville clerk in minor orders p. by Sir Robert de Neville knight to the church of

[1] The initial alone is given.

Manton vacant by the death of Sir William d'Aubeney.[2] Made proof of age, and was ordained subd. and inst. Wycombe, Mar. 5, 1289, and had letters patent.

XIIII KALENDAS JUNII DIE SANCTI DUNSTANI ANNO DOMINI M.CC. OCTOGESIMO NONO INCIPIT ANNUS PONTIFICATUS DOMINI OLIVERI EPISCOPI LINCOLN' DECIMUS

FILLINGHAM. R. Master Thomas Le Fleming subd. represented by Master John Fleming, canon of Lincoln and proctor-general in England of the A. and C. of Lessay, to the church of Fillingham vacant because the said Thomas had not been ordained pr. within a year of institution. Inst. May 25, 1289 (place not given) and had letters patent.

HEMSWELL. R. Roger of Marlow (Merlawe) ch. p. by Edmund Earl of Cornwall to the church of All Saints, Hemswell, vacant by the death of John. Inst. Liddington, Sept. 5, 1289, and had letters patent.

RISEHOLME (Rysum). R. Nicholas of Exning (Ixening') ch. p. by Master John Le Fleming, canon of Lincoln and proctor-general in England of the A. and C. of Lessay, to the church of Riseholme vacant by the death of Master Thomas of Shoreham (Schorham). Inst. Buckden, Feb. 3, 1290.

[*membrane 5*] TORKSEY (Thorkesaya). V. Walter of Horston ch. p. by the P. and C. of Torksey to the vicarage of Torksey vacant by the res. of Thomas Pen. Inst. Blisworth, Mar. 3, 1290.

SAXILBY. V. Stephen of Winthorpe ch. p. by the A. and C. of Newhouse to the vicarage of Saxilby vacant by the death of Walter of Sotby. Inst. Brackley, Mar. 5, 1290, and had letters patent.

HARPSWELL (Henpeswell'). R. Master Thomas de Perariis subd. p. by Master Thomas of Louth (Luda) to the church of Harpswell vacant by the death of Alexander of Hotham (Hothum). Inst. Canons' Ashby, Mar. 8, 1290, and had letters patent.

---

[2] In the previous entry, which may refer to an earlier presentation, he is described as having resigned the church of Scotton.

[*f. 246*] QUARTO DECIMO KALENDAS JUNII DIE SANCTI DUNSTANI ANNO DOMINI M.CC. NONAGESIMO INCIPIT ANNUS PONTIFICATUS DOMINI OLIVERI EPISCOPI LINCOLN' UNDECIMUS.

BOTTESFORD (Botenesford'). R. Master Thomas Malherbe subd. p. by the P. and C. of Thornholm to the church of Bottesford vacant by the death of Sir Alexander of Hotham (Hothum) and the withdrawal of Master William of Louth (Luda) who was first presented. Presentation opposed by the prior of the Hospitallers in England, who presented John of Lincoln pr., and by the A. and C. of Selby who presented Nicholas of Garthorpe (Gerelthorp') subd. Two royal writs (given in full, witnessed by J. de Metyngham, and dated at Westminster respectively May 6 and July 10, 1290) directed the bishop to accept the candidate of the P. and C. of Thornholm. Master Thomas was therefore inst. (in the person of Master Benedict of Utterby (Uttreby) his proctor), Sleaford, July 21, 1290.

HIBALDSTOW. V. Robert of Wighton ch. p. by the subdean of Lincoln[1], the precentor[2] *ratione custodie puerorum*, Salomon canon of Lincoln[3] and the Prioress and C. of Gokewell to the vicarage of Hibaldstow vacant by the death of Hugh. Inst. Louth, Aug. 30, 1290.

ALTHORPE. R. Roger Delisle (de Insula) clerk in minor orders p. by the Master of the Templars in England to the church of Althorpe vacant by the death of Master Adam of Filby. Ordained subd. (with letters dimissory) by the Bishop of Bath and Wells. Granted custody for a period then inst. Ely, Oct. 3, 1290.

FRODINGHAM (Frothingham). R. Master Robert of Sotwell pr. p. by Edmund Earl of Cornwall to the church of Frodingham vacant by the death of Michael of Northampton and the fact that John d'Osevile, first to be presented, had become Archdeacon of Ely. Inst. Buckden, Oct. 18, 1290.

[*f. 246v*] UPTON. V. Robert of Stainsby (Stavenesby) pr. p. by the Prioress and C. of Heynings to the vicarage of Upton vacant by the death of Richard. Inst. by the Archdeacon of

[1] Gilbert of Stratton.
[2] Adam of Barmpton.
[3] Probably Solomon of Northbourne, prebendary of Welton Ryval.

Huntingdon, acting on the bishop's instructions, Lincoln, Dec. 18, 1290

HARPSWELL (Herpeswell'). R. Master Thomas de Perariis pr. re-presented by Master Thomas of Louth (Luda) to the church of Harpswell vacant because the said Master Thomas de Perariis had not been ordained pr. until a year and eight days after his institution. Inst. Northampton, Mar. 17, 1291. Had letters patent.

———

XII DIE[1] SANCTI DUNSTANI VIDELICET XIIII KALENDAS JUNII ANNO DOMINI M.CC. NONAGESIMO PRIMO INCIPIT ANNUS PONTIFICATUS DOMINO OLIVERI EPISCOPI LINCOLN' DUODECIMUS.

———

BELTON. R. Roger Delisle subd. by Lady Gerina of Beltoft to the church of Belton vacant by the death of Thomas of Middleton. Presentation disputed by Sir Roger of Beltoft knight who p. Ralph of Fulbeck. A royal writ (given in full, witnessed by J. de Metyngham, Westminster, May 17, 1291) directed the bishop to accept Lady Gerina's candidate. She thereupon withdrew (with his consent) her first choice, Sir Richard Delisle, and substituted Roger. This presentation was thereupon challenged by Sir Roger de Mowbray, Lord of the Isle of Axholme, who presented William of Melton, but subsequently withdrew this presentation in a letter patent written in French and sealed with the seal of the Bishop of Bath and Wells. Roger Delisle produced a privilege of Pope Nicholas IV (given in full and dated at Orvieto, Mar. 3, 1291) allowing him to hold one benefice in plurality with his church of Althorpe, and was inst. Sleaford, June 22, and had letters patent.

BOTTESFORD (Botenesford'). R. Master Thomas called Maleherb' of Louth d. re-presented by the P. and C. of Thornholm to the church of Bottesford vacant because the said Master Thomas had not been ordained pr. within a year of institution. Inst. Figheldean, Sept. 11, 1291, and had letters patent.

HACKTHORN (Hakthorn'). R. Simon of Dean (Dene), clerk in minor orders p. by John son of William of Dean to the

———

[1] There is the picture of the face of a hook-nosed man attached to the capital 'D', which is further ornamented by a leafy scroll.

mediety of the church of Hackthorn vacant by the death of John of Norton. Ordained subd. and inst. Grantham, Sept. 22, 1291.

KIRTON-IN-LINDSEY. V. Hugh of Bicester (Burnecestr') ch. p. by Master Gilbert of Stratton, subdean and prebendary of Kirton-in-Lindsey, and Salomon of Northbourne prebendary of Welton Ryval, to the vicarage of Kirton vacant by the death of Thomas. Inst. Nettleham, Oct. 1, 1291.

FISKERTON. R. Robert of Wardington ch. p. by the A. and C. of Peterborough to the church of Fiskerton vacant by the death of Geoffrey. Inst. Wooburn near Wycombe, Feb. 16, 1292.[1]

[*f. 247v*] XIII DIE SANCTI DUNSTANI VIDELICET QUARTODECIMO KALENDAS JUNII ANNO DOMINI M.CC. NONAGESIMO SECUNDO INCIPIT ANNUS PONTIFICATUS DOMINI OLIVERI DEI GRACIA EPISCOPI LINCOLN' TERTIUSDECIMUS.

HEMSWELL. R. William de Briwere (Brueria) ch. p. by Edmund Earl of Cornwall to the church of All Saints at Hemswell vacant because Roger of Marlow (Merlawe) had received the living of Harwell in the diocese of Salisbury. Inst. Nettleham, May 30, 1292, and had letters patent.

TORKSEY. William of Rasen, sub-prior of Torksey, elected to the office of prior vacant by the res. of Joel. No licence obtained, as this was the custom. Election submitted to the bishop for confirmation Stow Park, July 26, 1292, and found to be substantially canonical, a few slips having been caused by the simplicity of the electors. Confirmed July 27, 1292.

HATHERN[2] (Hauthirn').

HACKTHORN. R[3]. Simon of Dean (Dene) subd. re-presented by John of Dean to the church of Hackthorn vacant because

---

[1] This entry is followed by one relating to Hackthorn, with a note 'Ista institutio debet sedere ex alia parte folii'. Since the entry relates to the following year it has been transcribed in its proper place.
[2] This entry belongs properly to the Archdeaconry of Leicester and has been transcribed among its records. See p. 52.
[3] This entry has been transferred from the previous folio, upon which it was wrongly entered.

the said Simon had not been ordained pr. within a year of institution. Biggleswade, Nov. 30, 1292.

CAMMERINGHAM. V. Ralph of Bottesford ch. p. by William, guardian of the manor of Cammeringham and proctor of the A. and C. of Blanchland[4], to the vicarage of Cammeringham vacant by the death of William. Inst. London, O.T., Apr. 13, 1293.

———

[*f. 248*] DIE SANCTI DUNSTANI VIDELICET XIIII KALENDAS JUNII ANNO DOMINI M.CC. NONAGESIMO TERTIO, INCIPIT ANNUS PONTIFICATUS DOMINI OLIVERI LINCOLN' EPISCOPI QUARTUSDECIMUS.

———

BURTON. R. Master Walter of Fulbeck, clerk in minor orders p. by Sir Robert de Schadwurth' knight and Margery his wife, and by John of Fulbeck, to the church of Burton vacant by the death of Ralph. Ordained subd. (by licence of the Bishop of London) and inst. London, O.T., May 23, 1293.

CONESBY (Cuningesby). Roger of Crosby ch. p. by Sir John Bek, knight, to the chapel of Conesby Darcy vacant because Ralph had been inst. to the vicarage of Cammeringham. Inst. Rowsham, July 15, 1293.

NETTLEHAM (Nettelham). R. Roger of Sixhills pr. collated by the bishop to the church of Nettleham vacant because Robert Meadows (de Pratellis) had been inst. to the living of Chalfont. Inst. London, O.T., Oct. 10, 1293.

INGHAM. R. Master William of Lowther (Louther), clerk in minor orders p. by the P. and C. of Bullington to the church of Ingham vacant by the death of Hugh Durand. Ordained subd. and inst. Wycombe, Dec. 19, 1293, and had letters patent.

FILLINGHAM. R. Thomas of Foxley (Foxele) ch. p. by Master John Le Fleming, canon of Lincoln and proctor of the A. and C. of Lessay to the church of Fillingham vacant by the lapse of a semester since the church was granted *in commendam* to Master Thomas Le Fleming, who had now been inst. to Burton. Inst. Wooburn near Wycombe, Dec. 22, 1293, and had letters patent.

[4] Incorrectly described as being 'in Normannia'.

SAXBY. R. Richard of Burton ch. p. by the P. and C. of St. Katherine's outside Lincoln to the church of Saxby vacant by the death of John. Inst. (in the person of John of Scalleby his proctor), Dorchester-on-Thames, Jan. 30, 1294, and had letters patent.

MARTON. V. Walter of Scrayingham ch. p. by the P. and C. of St. Katherine's outside Lincoln to the vicarage of Marton vacant because Richard of Burton had been inst. to the church of Saxby. Inst. Banbury, Mar. 13, 1294.

[*f.248v*] DIE SANCTI DUNSTANI VIDELICET XIIII KALENDAS JUNII ANNO DOMINI MILLESIMO DUCENTESIMO NONAGESIMO QUARTO INCIPIT ANNUS PONTIFICATUS DOMINI OLIVERI DEI GRACIA LINCOLN' EPISCOPI QUINTUSDECIMUS

ROXBY. R. Master John of Crowcombe (Craucumb'), clerk in minor orders p. by the P. and C. of Drax to the mediety of the church of Roxby vacant by the death of Henry Sperry. Granted custody for a period, then ordained subd. (by licence of the Bishop of London) and inst. London O.T., June 12, 1294, and had letters patent.

REEPHAM. R. William de la Dune, clerk in minor orders p. by King Edward as guardian of the lands and heir of Sir John de Neville knight to the church of Reepham vacant by the res. of Sir Ralph of Hingham (Hengham). Granted custody for a period, then ordained subd. (by licence of the Bishop of London), London O.T., June 12, 1294. Inst. at the Carmelites' house, London, June 18, 1294, and had letters patent.

SCAWBY (Scallesby). R. Robert of Kington (Kynton') subd. p. by the P. and C. of Thornholm to the church of Scawby vacant by the death of Master Peter Org'. Granted custody for a period. Inst. London, New Temple, July 31, 1294. Had letters patent.

APPLEBY. V. Robert of Middleton ch. p. by the P. and C. of Thornholm to the vicarage of Appleby vacant by the death of Master Walter. Inst. Hillingdon, Aug. 2, 1294, and had letters patent.

CAENBY (Cavenby). R. John of Burwell ch. p. by the A. and C. of Barlings to the church of Caenby vacant by the death of

Master William of Clixby (Clisseby). Inst. Dunstable, Sept. 18, 1294.

LITTLE CARLETON. R. Roger of Haxey (Haxay) ch. p. by Sir Ralph Paynell knight to the church of Little Carleton vacant by the death of Geoffrey. Inst. Northampton, Oct. 24, 1294, and had letters patent.

FISKERTON. R. Master Henry Sampson the younger d. p. by the A. and C. of Peterborough to the church of Fiskerton vacant because Robert had received other preferment. Inst. Louth Jan. 20, 1295, and had letters patent.

[*f. 249*] FALDINGWORTH. R. Robert de Neville, clerk in minor orders p. by Sir Thomas de Neville knight to the church of Faldingworth vacant by the death of Ralph. Granted custody for a period. Then ordained subd. and inst. Lincoln, Feb. 26, 1295.

GREETWELL. R. Thomas of Headon (Hedon'), clerk in minor orders p. by the Prioress and C. of Hampole to the church of Greetwell vacant by the death of Ralph de Cressy. Had custody for a period. Then ordained subd. and inst. Lincoln, Feb. 26, 1295, and had letters patent.

ALKBOROUGH (Hautebarg'). V. John of Swanton (Swaneton') d. p. by the P. and C. of Spalding to the vicarage of Alkborough vacant by the death of Richard. Inst. Horncastle, Mar. 6, 1295.

TORKSEY. Geoffrey of Beckering canon of Kyme, elected or postulated to the office of prior of Torksey, vacant by the res. of William of Rasen. No licence sought, as this was not the custom. Geoffrey asked to be allowed to keep his rights of fraternity at Kyme. Election confirmed [Liddington], Apr. 13, 1295.

INGHAM. R. Master William of Lowther subd. re-presented by the P. and C. of Bullington to the church of Ingham vacant because the said Master William had not been ordained pr. within a year of institution. Inst. Spaldwick, Apr. 24, 1295, and had letters patent.

HEAPHAM. R. Master William Chambers (de Camera) subd. p. by Edmund Earl of Cornwall to the church of Heapham vacant by the death of Adam. Inst. Spaldwick, May 5, 1295, and had letters patent.

[f. 249v] DIE SANCTI DUNSTANI EPISCOPI VIDELICET QUARTODECIMO KALENDAS JUNII ANNO DOMINI M.CC. NONAGESIMO QUINTO INCIPIT ANNUS PONTIFICATUS DOMINI OLIVERI EPISCOPI LINCOLN' SEXTUSDECIMUS.

BOTTESFORD (Botenesford'). R. Master William of Langworth (Langwath') subd. p. by the P. and C. of Thornholm to the church of Bottesford vacant by the death of Master Thomas Maleherb', and the renunciation of Master Thomas of Louth (Luda) first presented. Inst. Spaldwick, Oct. 16, 1295, and had letters patent.

BELTON-IN-AXHOLME. R. Roger of Beltoft, clerk in minor orders, p. by his father, Sir Roger of Beltoft knight to the church of Belton vacant by the death of Roger Delisle (de Insula). Presentation disputed by Sir Roger de Mowbray (Mubray) knight. A royal writ (given in full, witnessed by J. de Metingham and dated Westminster Nov. 16, 1295) directed the bishop to accept Sir Roger of Beltoft's candidate. Roger was therefore ordained subd. and inst. Huntingdon, Dec. 17, 1295.

ALTHORPE. R. Nicholas of Misterton ch. p. by Walter of Langton, master, and the brethren of St. Leonard's Hospital, York, to the church of Althorpe vacant by the death of Roger Delisle. Presentation opposed by the Master of the Templars in England. A royal writ (given in full, witnessed by J. de Metingham and dated Westminster Nov. 7, 1295) directed the bishop to accept the candidate of St Leonard's Hospital. Inst. (in the person of Robert the Frenchman (Le Fraunceys) his proctor) Fingest, Dec. 27, 1295.

OWSTON (Ouston'). R. Sir Stephen de Mauley d. p. by the P. and C. of Newburgh to the church of Owston vacant by the death of Master John Clarel. Master Simon de Clairvaux, first presented and granted the church *in commendam*, resigned by letters patent. Master[1] Stephen produced a privilege of Pope Nicholas IV (given in full and dated Orvieto May 21, 1291) allowing him to hold in plurality the Archdeaconry of Cleveland and the churches of Bainton and Lyth, or one other church in place of either of these. Stephen resigned the church of Lyth and was inst. to Owston, Newark, Mar. 15, 1296, and had letters patent.

---

[1] This seems to have been his correct title, although he is first called 'dominus'.

TORKSEY (Torkeseye). William of Rasen, canon of Torksey, elected to the office of prior in succession to Geoffrey of Beckering (Bekering) who had resigned. No licence was sought, this being the custom. Election confirmed Stow Park, May 13, 1296. A letter was sent to the P. and C. of Kyme, from which house Geoffrey had originally been postulated, concerning his re-admission. This letter was recorded among the memoranda.[1]

[*f. 250v*] DIE SANCTI DUNSTANI ARCHIEPISCOPI VIDELICET QUARTO-DECIMO KALENDAS JUNII ANNO DOMINI M.CC. NONAGESIMO SEXTO, INCIPIT ANNUS PONTIFICATUS DOMINI OLIVERI DEI GRACIA LINCOLN' EPISCOPI SEPTIMUSDECIMUS.

SCOTTON. Martin son of William Smith of Scotton ch. p. by Sir Robert de Neville knight to the chantry in the chapel of St. Mary in the parochial church of Scotton, on the south side vacant by the death of Robert Haldan. Inst. Kyme, July 6, 1296.

INGHAM. R. Roger of Bolingbroke (Bullingbrok') subd. p. by the P. and C. of Bullington to the church of Ingham vacant by the death of Master William of Lowther. Inst. Sempringham July 22, 1296, and had letters patent.

COATES (Cotes). V. William of Chesterfield (Cestrefeld') canon of Welbeck Abbey, p. by the A. and C. of Welbeck to the vicarage of Coates vacant by the death of Henry. The presentation was made in virtue of a papal privilege (not given in full) which allowed the said A. and C. to present two members of their own order, of whom the bishop chose one for institution, to the appropriated churches of Cuckney (Cukeneye), Watton, Whitton (Whyten'), Coates (Cotes), Etwall (Ettewell') and Duckmanton (Dukemanton'). Inst. Sleaford, Aug. 11, 1296. Letters on his behalf were written to the A. and C. of Welbeck, and he had letters patent. (Same place and date).

[*f. 251*] LAUGHTON (Laghton'). R. Roger of Sixhills ch. p. by the P. and C. of Thornholm to the church of Laughton vacant because Master William of Langworth (Langwath') had

---

[1] L.R.S. 60, p. 152.

been inst. to the church of Bottesford, and Walter of Malling had withdrawn. Inst. Stow Park, Oct. 9, 1296, and had letters patent. 'Et est sciendum quod Magister Walterus de Malling' ad dictam ecclesiam prius presentatus habuit eandam ecclesiam commendatam prout plenius patet in rotulo de commendis.'[1]

FILLINGHAM. R. Richard of Bottisham (Bodekesham) ch. p. by Master John Le Fleming, proctor-general in England of the A. and C. of Lessay to the church of Fillingham vacant by the res. of Thomas of Foxley (Foxele). Inst. Stow Park, Oct. 11, 1296, and had letters patent.

NETTLEHAM. R. John of Bayton d. collated by the bishop to the church of Nettleham vacant because Roger of Sixhills had been inst. to Laughton (Lacton'). Inst. Stow Park, Oct. 24, 1296, and had letters patent.

GLENTHAM. V. Bartholomew of Dunham ch. p. by the D. and C. of Lincoln to the vicarage of Glentham vacant by the res. of Richard of Stamford. Inst. Buckden, Nov. 1, 1296, and had letters patent.

FLIXBOROUGH (Flikesburgh). R. Master John of Glentham, clerk in minor orders p. by Sir Richard d'Arcy knight to the church of Flixborough vacant by the death of Master William de Montfort and the lapse of a semester since it was granted *in commendam* first to Master Jocelyn of Kirmington and then to Robert of Burton. Ordained subd. and inst. Huntingdon, Dec. 22, 1296.

SAXILBY. V. Thomas of Cave pr. p. by the A. and C. of Newhouse to the vicarage of Saxilby vacant by the death of Stephen. Inst. London O.T., Jan. 23, 1297.

[*f. 251v*] REDBOURNE. V. Peter of Immingham ch. p. by the A. and C. of Selby to the vicarage of Redbourne vacant by the death of Simon. Inst. London, O.T., Jan. 23, 1297.

———

QUARTODECIMO KALENDAS JUNII VIDELICET DIE SANCTI DUNSTANI ANNO DOMINI M.CC. NONAGESIMO SEPTIMO INCIPIT ANNUS PONTIFI- CATUS DOMINI OLIVERI DEI GRACIA LINCOLNIEN' EPISCOPI OCTAVUS- DECIMUS.

———

[1] This roll is now lost.

FRODINGHAM (Frothingham). R. Richard of Cornwall (Cornubia) subd. by Edmund Earl of Cornwall to the church of Frodingham vacant by the res. of Master Richard of Sotwell (Sottewell'). Inst. Nettleham, Oct. 17, 1297.

FOSSE. Agnes of Scothern (Schotethorn') sub-prioress of Fosse, appointed by the bishop to the office of prioress vacant by the res. of Alice of Laxton (Lexington). An attempt to elect her was quashed for incorrect procedure. Nettleham, Nov. 22, 1297.

HACKTHORN. V. Richard of Houghton (Houton') subd. p. by the P. and C. of Bullington to the vicarage of Hackthorn vacant by the death of John. Ordained d. and inst. Lincoln, Mar. 22, 1298.

NETTLEHAM. R. John of Bayton d. re-collated by the bishop to the church of Nettleham vacant because the said John had not been ordained pr. within a year of institution. Inst. Nettleham, Mar. 27, 1298.

SUDBROOKE. R. John of Carcroft (Kercroft') ch. p. by the A. and C. of Barlings to the church of Sudbrooke vacant by the death of William Brond. Inst. St. Katherine's outside Lincoln, Mar. 30, 1298.

[f. 252–253] CAMMERINGHAM. V. John de Ringeden' ch. p. by William Sampson, proctor-general of the A. and C. of Blanchland to the vicarage of Cammeringham vacant by the death of Ralph. Inst. Liddington, May 9, 1298.

————

QUARTODECIMO KALENDAS JUNII VIDELICET DIE SANCTI DUNSTANI ANNO DOMINI M.CC. NONAGESIMO OCTAVO INCIPIT ANNUS PONTIFICATUS DOMINI OLIVERI EPISCOPI LINCOLN' NONUSDECIMUS.

————

FILLINGHAM (Cantaria de Filingham). Copy of the letters relating to the foundation at Newark by the A. and C. of Lessay of a chantry for the soul of William of Newark Archdeacon of Huntingdon.
Printed above, pp. 11–12.

[f. 253v] FILLINGHAM. Note under the seals of the bishop and of Jocelyn of Kirmington, Archdeacon of Stow, that Richard of Bottisham (Bodekesham) rector of Fillingham, being peremptorily cited to appear before the bishop or his commissaries to take the oath (which he had not taken at the time of his institution) to pay six marks a year to the chantry of Master William of Newark, appeared before Master Jocelyn of Kirmington Archdeacon of Stow, the bishop's commissary, in the conventual church of the canons of Huntingdon on June 7, 1298, and took the necessary oath. Witnessed by Master Nicholas of Whitchurch the official-principal, John de Scalleby pr. and certain canons of Huntingdon.

REEPHAM. R. William of Melton, clerk in minor orders p. by King Edward as guardian of the lands and heir of Sir John de Neville to the church of Reepham vacant because William de La Dune had been inst. to Washingborough. Ordained subd. (with letters dimissory) by the Bishop of Lichfield and Coventry, May 31, 1298. Inst. (in the person of John de Scalleby his proctor), Theydon Mount, June 17, 1298.

CAENBY. R. Geoffrey of Langworth (Langwath') ch. p. by the A. and C. of Barlings to the church of Caenby vacant by the death of John of Burwell. Inst. Ardley, Apr. 3, 1299.

APPLEBY. R. Hugh of Ravenser, clerk in minor orders p. by the P. and C. of Thornholm to the vicarage of Appleby vacant by the death of Ralph. Ordained subd. by the Bishop of Lincoln and d. (with letters dimissory) by the Archbishop of Canterbury. Inst. Buckden, Apr. 7, 1299.

FISKERTON. R. Richard of Stamford subd. p. by the A. and C. of Peterborough to the church of Fiskerton vacant because Master Henry Sampson the younger had been inst. to Bringhurst and Master Richard of Hertford (first presented) had withdrawn. Inst. Buckden, May 2, 1299.

———

[f. 254] QUARTODECIMO KALENDAS JUNII VIDELICET DIE SANCTI DUNSTANI ANNO DOMINI M.CC. NONAGESIMO NONO INCIPIT ANNUS PONTIFICATUS DOMINI OLIVERI EPISCOPI LINCOLN' VICESIMUS.

———

HEYNINGS. Margaret of Marton elected to the office of prioress of Heynings in succession to Margery of Pocklington who had resigned. Licence to elect had been obtained from the patrons, Sir Philip of Linley (Linle) knight, Geoffrey of

Fountains (Funtayns) and Walter of Stow. Election presented to the bishop Oct. 12, 1299, and confirmed Oct. 13, both at Stow Park.

WROOT (Wrot). R. Robert ch. p. by the A. and C. of St. Mary's York to the church of Wroot, vacant by the death of John. Inst. Nettleham, Nov. 10, 1299. Note that the said Robert had been promoted to all holy orders by the Bishop of St. Andrew's in Scotland without letters dimissory, and that Bishop Sutton ratified these orders and imposed a salutary penance before instituting him.

INGLEBY[1] (Fundatio capellanie sive cantarie de Engelby). Registration, and collation with the original document, by Thomas Colston, notary-public, of an agreement made and sealed in cyrograph, May 3, 1232, between the A. and C. of Newhouse, of the one part, and William of Ingleby, of the other, with the consent of Matthew of London, vicar of Saxilby. By this agreement, William of Ingleby and his heirs are to have the right to nominate to the Abbot of Newhouse suitable chaplains whom the abbot shall present to the arch-deacon, to minister in Ingleby chapel, at the expense of the said William. During vacancy of the said chapel, the people of Ingleby are to attend the mother church of Saxilby. The A. and C. of Newhouse quitclaim to the said William and his heirs all the lands belonging to the said chapel. Witnessed by Peter de Campania, William de Vere, Herbert of Ingleby, Ralph Blund, Ralph son of Herbert, John of Keelby, Walter of Welwick and Adam of Croxton.

[1] This entry is written in a fifteenth-century hand. The scribe appears to have taken advantage of half a blank folio. Ingleby is, however, in the Arch-deaconry of Stow.

ARCHDEACONRY OF LEICESTER

The roll containing the institutions for this archdeaconry from the beginning of Sutton's episcopate to the summer of 1286 has been lost. The beginning of the remaining portion is badly torn.

[*membrane 1*]
[MELTON MOWBRAY.] This appears to be part of an ordinance of Bishop Sutton, setting up in the church of Melton Mowbray,

which was appropriated to the P. and C. of Lewes, a perpetual vicarage, on the death of Richard of Higham now vicar. The vicar is to maintain two chaplains at his own expense. The P. and C. are to have the lands belonging to the church, the greater tithes and the tithe of lambs, mortuary dues paid in live animals, and thirty shillings paid annually as tithe by the A. and C. of Garendon. The vicar is to have the lesser tithes, the altarage and a manse. The P. and C. are to repair the chancel and pay all extraordinary expenses as well as thirteen marks annually to Lincoln Cathedral and two marks to the Archdeacon of Leicester. The vicar is to pay the procurations and maintain the books, vestments and church furnishings. Witnessed by Masters Henry of Nassington, official-principal, John Le Fleming, Thomas of Sutton, canons of Lincoln, Robert of Kilworth, John of St. Leofard, Sir John of Bennington dean of Framland, Robert of Thorpe and others. Under the bishop's seal, Liddington, Aug. 14, 1286. The prior took the oath of obedience under protest, and it was agreed that if this proved to be contrary to Cluniac privileges it should be declared null and void.

... resignavit ... [vi]carie dudum ordinate in ea ac nostre Lincoln' ... ac loci archidiaconi red ... eandem ecclesiam de Melton' ... pristinum affectantes, et ut id graciose facere ... postulantes, se et eorum monasterium nostre ordinationi tam super ipsa ecclesia de Melton' quam vicaria ejusdem pure, sponte et absolute in omnibus ad ... oppositioni religiosorum ipsorum pio compatientes affectu, ac factis predecessorum nostrorum inducti, consensu nostri capituli Lincoln' prehabito, ordinationem ... usus concedimus, religiosis pretactis et monasterio eorundem perpetuo possidendam, ordinantes et ordinando tenore presentium statuentes quod in dicta ecclesia ... sit perpetua vicaria, dictique prior et conventus ac eorum successores futuris temporibus successive post mortem Ricardi de Hecham nunc vicarii ejusdem ecclesie de Melton' ... ydoneum nobis et successoribus nostris canonice presentent instituendum suo perpetuo in eadem vicaria, qui duos capellanos, unum diaconum et unum subdiaconum, competentes et honestos ipsius vicarii sumptibus exhibendos secum continuo habeant residentes ad divina obsequia in eadem ecclesia perpetuo sustinenda. Habeant autem dicti prior et conventus integre et pacifice totam terram pertinentem ad ecclesiam de Melton' cum pratis, pascuis et pasturis, et omnibus aliis ad dictam terram ecclesie pertinentibus. Percipiant etiam iidem prior et conventus totam decimam

---

[1] Blank in MS.

garbarum et feni et totam decimam agnorum, et mortuaria in vivis animalibus ac pecoribus consistentia, et triginta solidos annuos de abbate et conventu de Gerwedon' quos ecclesia consueverat ab eisdem percipere nomine decimarum. Et vicarius qui pro tempore fuerit percipiet totum alteragium dicte ecclesie de Melton', scilicet totam decimam lane, omnesque alias minutas decimas, oblationes et obventiones undecumque ad dictam ecclesiam nomine altaragii pertinentes exceptis decima agnorum et mortuariis consistentibus in vivis pecoribus ut superius est expressum, et habebit mansum prope ecclesiam ab omni onere et servicio liberum et quietum quod nunc vicarius ipsius ecclesie et sui predecessores habebant secundum domini Henrici ordinationem predictam. Sustinebunt auctoritate dicti prioris et conventus onera reficiendi, reparandi ac etiam de novo construendi cancellum dicte ecclesie cum necesse fuerit, ac etiam omnia onera extraordinaria. Ad hec post recompensationem dampnorum que ex dicta appropriatione ac nostra ordinatione contingere possent in hac parte ordinamus et statuimus quod dicti prior et conventus solvant annuatim imperpetuum in signum reverencie et honoris et conservationem indempnitatis de dictis bonis ecclesiasticis suis usibus assignatis tresdecim marcas argenti ecclesie nostre Lincoln' in ipsa ecclesia per suum proprium nuncium sacriste ejusdem loci tradendas die Nativitatis Beati Johannis Baptiste in usus vicariorum ac clericorum ministrantium in ipsa ecclesia convertandas prout super hoc duxerimus ordinandum. Item quod solvant perpetuo annuatim archidiacono loci qui pro tempore fuerit pro dampnis suis imposterum recompensandis preter annuam procurationem quam vicarius ei solvet duas marcas argenti vel suo certo nuncio ad ecclesiam de Melton' dicto die Sancti Johannis, vicarius autem qui pro tempore fuerit ac ipsa vicaria sustinebit omnia ordinaria debita et consueta dictam ecclesiam de Melton' contingentia, scilicet inveniendi, reficiendi et reparandi libros, vestimenta, calices et alia vasa, ceteraque omnia ornamenta ecclesiastica in ecclesia memorata. Hec autem ordinamus et statuimus et perpetuo manere volumus illibita, salvis in omnibus episcopali et Lincoln' ecclesie dignitate et nobis ac successoribus nostris auctoritate et potestate interpretandi et declarandi si quid dubium super dicta ordinatione personatus et vicarie forsan emerserit in futurum, et etiam compellendi dictos priorem et conventum ac vicarium suosque successores ad plenam observationem hujusmodi nostre ordinationis, interpretationis et declarationis ejusdem si quam fieri contingat de plano et absque strepitu judiciali per sequestrationem et subtractionem fructuum et proventuum dicte ecclesie de Melton' aliisque modis quibus

nobis visum fuerit expedire. Acta sunt hec apud Lidington'
XIX Kalendas Septembris anno domini M.CC. octogesimo
sexto et pontificatus nostri septimo, in presencia testium
subscriptorum, videlicet Magistrorum H. de Nassington' tunc
officialis nostri, Johannis le Flemeng' et Th. de Sutton'
canonicorum Lincoln', Roberti de Kivelingwrth', Johannis de
Sancto Leofardo, ac dominorum Johannis de Benington' tunc
decani de Framelund' et Roberti de Thorp' capellani et
aliorum plurimorum. Et ad perpetuam hujusmodi rei
memoriam sigillum nostrum presentibus est appensum. ...
Preter vero contenta in littera memorata ordinavit quod prior
et conventus de Lewe' ordinationem suam predictam quantum
ad duas marcas archidiacono loci pro dampnis suis imposterum
recompensandis annuatim solvendas a religiosis memoratis
per litteram suam patentem ratificarent, quod expressius
concesserunt. Deinde altercato aliquamdiu super juramento
canonice obediencie a priore predicto ratione prefate ecclesie
prestando, priore asserente secum super prestatione hujusmodi
juramenti esse per sedem apostolicam dispensatum, tandem
post varia idem prior juravit pro ecclesia de Melton' predicta
episcopo, successoribus suis et officialibus eorundem canonicam
obedienciam in forma consueta, protestatione premissa quod
si ante festum Omnium Sanctorum proxime sequens posset
docere per privilegium sedis apostolice se ad prestationem
hujusmodi juramenti non teneri, per dictum juramentum
nullatenus arcaretur, sed pro non prestito haberetur, alioquin
juramentum hujusmodi robur haberet perpetue firmitatis.
Postmodum scriptum fuit forma: O.....[1] officiali .....[1]
archidiaconi Leyc' sub hac O. etc. Quia ecclesia de Melton'
Mubray vacantem religiosis viris ....[1] prior et conventui de
Lewes ejusdem patronis caritatis intuitu concessimus in usus
suos proprios perpetuo possidendam salva portione vicarie in
ea antiquitus ordinata vobis mandamus quatinus eosdem
religiosos in corporalem possessionem dicte ecclesie inducatis
seu faciatis induci. Valete, Datum apud Lidington' XIX
Kalendas Septembris pontificatus nostri anno septimo —
Sequitur ratificatio in dorso rotuli.
[*Endorsed*]
[Letters patent of John, Prior of Lewes, and the convent
thereof, under their common seal, accepting the arrangement
made by Bishop Sutton about the church of Melton Mowbray,
and promising to fulfil their obligations.
Lewes Oct. 13, 1286. Copies of both these documents were
sent to Lincoln for safe-keeping, by the hand of Master
Durand, Oct. 26, 1286.

[1] Blank in MS.

Universis sancte matris ecclesie filiis ad quos presentes littere pervenerint, frater Johannes prior humilis Lewen' et ejusdem loci conventus salutem in domino. Noverit universitas vestra quod cum venerabilis pater dominus O. Dei gracia Lincoln' episcopus ecclesiam de Melton' Moubrey nobis nostrisque successoribus caritatis intuitu in proprios usus perpetuo possidendam nuper sui gracia concessisset, ac inter cetera juxta submissionem nostram quam ei super hoc litteratorie fecimus tempore appropriationis hujusmodi ordinasset quod nos pro recompensatione dampnorum que ex dicta appropriatione ac sua ordinatione contigere possent in hoc parte imperpetuum solvamus annuatim in signum reverencie et honoris, et observationem indempnitatis de dictis bonis ecclesiasticis nostris usibus assignatis, tredecim marcas argenti matrici ecclesie Lincoln' in ipsa ecclesia per nostrum proprium nuncium sacriste ejusdem loci tradendas die Nativitatis Sancti Johannis Baptiste, in usus vicariorum et clericorum ministrantium in ipsa ecclesie convertendas prout dictus pater super hoc duxerit ordinandum. Item, quod solvamus, perpetuo annuatim archidiacono loci qui pro tempore fuerit, pro damnis suis imposterum recompensandis preter annuam procurationem quam vicarius noster ei solvet duas marcas argenti vel suo certo nuncio ad ecclesiam de Melton' dicto die Sancti Johannis. Nos vero attendentes ordinationem predictam per tam pium patrem tam salubriter quam rationabiliter factam, ipsam quoad dictas quindecim marcas prefatis die et locis ex causis predictis solvendas necnon et quoad omnes alios ipsius articulos acceptamus devote et approbamus expresse unanimiter per presentes, promittentes bona fide nos et successores nostros dicte ordinationi in omnibus perpetuo parituros, ac volentes et expresse consentientes quod si in solutione prefate pecunie in toto vel in parte suis locis et termino defecerimus vel contra ipsam ordinationem in aliquo in futurum venerimus modo quovis, dictus pater et sui successores de plano et sine strepitu judiciali, per sequestrationem et subtractionem fructuum et proventuum ecclesie de Melton' ad ipsius ordinis observationem nos et successores nostros libere possint compellere aliisque modis quibus eis visum fuerit expedire. In cujus rei testimonium sigillum nostrum commune presentibus est appensum. Datum in capitulo nostro apud Lewes die dominica proxima post festum Sancti Dionysii, anno domini M.CC.LXXX sexto. ... Ista vero ratificatio et submissio prioris et conventus de Lewes ex alia parte rotuli conscripta misse fuerunt VII Kalendas Novembris anno septimo per Magistrum Durandum apud Lincoln' ut ibidem per decanum et capitulum custodirentur.]

BILLESDON. V. Gregory of Kimcote (Kinemundecote) ch. p. by the A. and C. of St. Mary de Pratis, Leicester, to the vicarage of Billesdon vacant because Thomas had received other preferment. Inst. Lidddington, Aug. 23, 1286.

GRACEDIEU (Gracia Dei) ...[1] appointed by the bishop as prioress of Gracedieu in succession to Agnes de Grifle who had died. Licence to elect had been obtained from Sir Theobald de Verdun, patron. The election, held on Sept. 29, 1286, was quashed for incorrect procedure. Northampton, St. Andrew's Priory, Oct. 3, 1286.

EASTWELL (Estewell'). R. Master Robert of Hathern (Hawethurn) subd. p. by the A. and C. of St. Mary de Pratis to the church of Eastwell vacant by the death of Master Gilbert. Inst. Barnet, Oct. 12, 1286, and had letters patent.

ST. MARY DE CASTRO, LEICESTER (Sancte Marie Leycestr'). V. Henry of Aylestone ch. p. by the A. and C. of St. Mary de Pratis to the vicarage of St. Mary de Castro vacant by the death of Hugh. Inst. Fingest, Nov. 15, 1286.

SWITHLAND (Swythelund'). R. Gilbert of Rothbury (Roubir'), clerk in minor orders, p. by Fulk, prior of Ware and proctor-general in England of the A. and C. of St. Evroult, to the church of Swithland vacant by the death of Peter. Ordained subd. and inst. Thame Dec. 21, 1286.

VIII

XIIII KALENDAS JUNII DIE SANCTI DUNSTANI ANNO M.CC. OCTO-GESIMO SEPTIMO INCIPIT ANNUS PONTIFICATUS DOMINI OLIVERI EPISCOPI OCTAVUS.

GREAT DALBY (Dalby Chaucumb'). V. Thomas of Wistow (Wystowe) ch. p. by the P. and C. of Chalcombe to the vicarage of Great Dalby vacant by the death of Peter. Inst. Theydon Mount, June 26, 1287.

COLD OVERTON. R. John of Dalby ch. p. by Sir Nicholas de Seagrave (Segrave) knight to the church of Cold Overton vacant by the res. of Richard of Toynton. Inst. Eynsham, June 28, 1287.

[1] Her name is not given; she is called simply 'dicta electa'.

GREAT GLEN. V. Robert of Edwinstowe ch. nominated by the bishop to the A. and C. of Alcester for presentation to the vicarage of Great Glen, vacant by the death of John of Stonesby (Stonnesby). The procedure followed was that laid down in the ordinance drawn up by Bishop Gravesend in 1266.[1] No inquiry was made, since the facts were well known to the bishop. Inst. Daventry, July 1, 1287.

WIGSTON MAGNA (Wygingeston'). R. Roger Buteturt subd. p. by the P. and C. of Lenton to the church of Wigston Magna vacant because the said Roger had not been ordained pr. within a year of institution. Inst. (in the person of William of Ellingham (Elingham) his proctor, July 11, 1287. Place not given.

REDMILE (Redemild). R. Master Robert of Redmile d. p. by the P. and C. of Belvoir to the church of Redmile vacant because Roger de Beaufoy (Bello Fagio) had been inst. to the church of Morcott. Inst. Torksey, July 25, 1287.

ALL SAINTS, LEICESTER. V. Robert of Barsby (Barnesby) ch. p. by the A. and C. of St. Mary de Pratis to the vicarage of All Saints, vacant by the death of Henry of Kenton (Kinton'). Inst. Louth, Sept. 8, 1287.

WYMESWOLD (Wymundwold'). V. Henry of Rotherham, canon of Beauchief p. by the A. and C. thereof to the vicarage of Wymeswold vacant by the res. of Walter of Warwick. The presentation was made in virtue of a papal privilege, the relevant clause of which is quoted, and was accepted by the bishop without prejudice for the future. Lincoln, Oct. 24, 1287.

... In parochialibus etiam ecclesiis quas habetis liceat vobis quatuor vel tres de canonicis vestris ponere, quorum uno diocesano episcopo presentatis, ut ei de plebis cura, vobis vero de temporalibus et ordinis observancia debeat respondere ... eodemque privilegio diligentius examinato, licet iidem religiosi a beneficio dicti privilegii quantum ad contenta in clausula suprascripta ceciderant per hoc quod post impetrationem privilegii quemdam clericum ad dictam vicariam presentarant, episcopus tamen volens eis facere graciam specialem prefatum fratrem Henricum ad dictam vicariam admisit, ipsumque vicarium perpetuum cum onere personaliter ministrandi et continue residendi juxta formam in dicto privilegio

[1] L.R.S. 20, pp. 146–7.

contentam canonice instituit in eadem. Contra ipsum et
religiosis predictos si secus actum foret procedendi prout
justicia suaderet potestate sibi specialiter reservata, prestitoque a
dicto vicario juramento de continua residencia facienda et de
obediendo episcopo et officialibus suis in canonicis mandatis,
scriptum fuit etc.

[Endorsement] [Copy of the bishop's letter to the Archdeacon
of Leicester or his official, telling him of the institution of
Henry of Rotherham to the vicarage of Wymeswold, as
above, in virtue of the privilege granted by Urban III.
Lincoln, Oct. 24, 1287. Also a copy of a letter under the
bishop's seal, confirming the institution, as above, of the said
Henry of Rotherham. Lincoln. Oct. 24, 1287.

EDMONDTHORPE (Thorp' Eymere). R. William of Alconbury
(Alkemundebir') d. re-presented by Edmund Earl of Lancaster
to the church of Edmondthorpe vacant because the said
William had not been ordained pr. within a year of institution.
Inst. Ramsey, Nov. 13, 1287, and had letters patent.

FRISBY-ON-THE-WREAK. V. Hugh of Weston ch. p. by the P. and
C. of Launde to the vicarage of Frisby vacant by the death of
Thomas. Inst. Buckden, Dec. 15, 1297.

WITHCOTE (Wytecok'). R. John of Musgrave, clerk in minor
orders, p. by the A. and C. of Owston to the church of Withcote
vacant because Robert of Redmile had been inst. to Redmile.
Custody until the next ordinations granted Nettleham, Oct.
(*mense Octobris*) 1287. Ordained subd. and inst. Huntingdom, Dec.
20, 1287.

WYMONDHAM (Wymundham). R. Master Hugh Hamelyn subd.
p. by Edmund Earl of Lancaster to the church of Wymondham
vacant by the res. of Nicholas. Had custody for a period. Then
inst. Buckden, Dec. 22, 1287.

SHEEPY (Schepeye). R. Master John Launcelyn clerk in minor
orders, p. by William Burdet of Sheepy to the mediety of the
church thereof vacant by the res. of William de la Leye.
Presentation disputed by William of Sheepy (another). A royal
writ (given in full and witnessed by T. de Weland', Westminster,
Jan. 16, 1288) directed the bishop to accept William Burdet's
candidate, who was ordained subd. and inst. Bedford, Feb. 21,
1288.

APPLEBY (Appelby). R. John de Areyns, subd. collated by the
bishop to the church of Appleby vacant by the death of Henry

Luvel and the failure of Sir Richard de Vernun knight (who presented Sir Hugh of Cave) and the P. and C. of Lytham to come to an agreement in the King's court within a reasonable time. Bedford, St. Paul's, Feb. 22, 1288, in the presence of Master John le Fleming, Robert of Thorpe chaplain, Richard Burdon and others.

[*Endorsement*] [Note that at Nettleham on July 11, 1288, the bishop received a royal writ (given in full and witnessed by R. de Hengham, Westminster, July 4, 1288) directing him to accept the candidate of the P. and C. of Lytham, but that nothing could be done on this occasion because of the collation of John de Areyns.]

NOSELEY (Novesle). R. Nicholas Taylhast' ch. p. by Richard prior of Ware, proctor-general in England of the A. and C. of St. Evroult, to the church of Noseley vacant by the death of Lawrence de Ripariis. Inst. Newnham, Feb. 26, 1288, and had letters patent.

DISEWORTH. V. Robert of Balbegrave ch. p. by the Prioress and C. of Langley to the vicarage of Diseworth vacant by the death of Richard. Newnham, Feb. 29, 1288.

NETHER BROUGHTON (Bructon'). R. Henry de Besancon (Bisancon) clerk in minor orders p. by the P. and C. of Lenton to the church of Nether Broughton vacant by the death of Hugh of Skeffington. Ordained subd. and inst. Buckden, Mar. 13, 1288, and had letters patent.

PEATLING. V. Walter of Peatling d. p. by Richard prior of Ware, proctor-general in England of the A. and C. of St. Evroult to the vicarage of Peatling vacant because Thomas of Leicester had been inst. to the church of Muston. Inst. Huntingdon, Mar. 25, 1288.

SOMERBY (Somerdeby). V. Rowland of Tong ch. p. by the Prioress and C. of Langley to the vicarage of Somerby vacant by the death of Walter. Inst. Buckden, Apr. 15, 1288.

STOCKERSTON (Stokfaston'). R. Master William of Upping- ham ch. p. by Sir William Murdak knight to the church of Stockerston vacant by the death of Hugh de Neville. Presen- tation opposed by Thomas de Beyville and Alice his wife, who failed to appear in the King's court. A royal writ (given in full, witnessed by T. de Weylaund' and dated Westminster Apr. 20,

1288) directed the bishop to accept Sir William's candidate. William was inst. Theydon Mount, May 8, 1288.

IX.

XIIII KALENDAS JUNII DIE SANCTI DUNSTANI ANNO DOMINI M.CC. OCTOGESIMO OCTAVO INCIPIT ANNUS PONTIFICATUS DOMINI OLIVERI EPISCOPI LINCOLN' NONUS.

KEGWORTH. R. Thomas de Neville subd. p. by Sir John of Seagrave knight, empowered to present to churches in the patronage of Sir Nicholas of Seagrave knight, to the church of Kegworth vacant by the lapse of six months since it was granted *in commendam* to Sir Gilbert of Seagrave ch. Inst. Dorchester-on-Thames, May 27, 1288.

THURLASTON. R. John de Campania d. p. by Sir Robert de Campania knight to the church of Thurlaston vacant by the death of Thomas of Keythorpe. Inst. Kidlington, May 30, 1288.

NORTON-JUXTA-TWYCROSS. R. Roger of ?Baumber (Bayne-burg'), clerk in minor orders p. by the P. and C. of Belvoir to the church of Norton-juxta-Twycross vacant by the death of Thomas of Drewton (Dreuton'). Ordained subd. and inst. Hertford, Sept. 18, 1288.

WANLIP (Anelep). R. William the Welshman (Le Waleys), clerk in minor orders p. by Sir William the Welshman knight to the church of Wanlip vacant by the res. of Walter the Welshman. Custody of the church and candidate granted to Master Gilbert of Birstall (Burstal') clerk during the bishop's pleasure. After coming of age William was ordained subd. and inst. Hertford, Sept. 18, 1288, and had letters patent.

NOSELEY. R. Simon of Rothwell (Rowell') ch. p. by Richard prior of Ware, proctor-general in England of the A. and C. of St. Evroult, to the church of Noseley vacant by the res. of Nicholas Taylhast. Inst. Buckden, Nov. 10, 1288, and had letters patent.

REDMILE. R. Master Robert of Redmile d. re-presented by the P. and C. of Belvoir to the church of Redmile vacant because the said Robert had not been ordained pr. within a year of institution. Inst. Huntingdon, Dec. 18, 1288, and had letters patent.

STAPLEFORD. R. Richard of Loughborough (Luchteburg'), clerk in minor orders to the church of Stapleford vacant by the death of Vincent de Petra Castri. Name of patron not given. Granted custody from Sept. 24 until the next ordinations, then ordained subd. and inst. [Huntingdon] Dec. 18, 1288.

HINCKLEY (Hinkele). V. William of Stamford ch. p. by Hervey, proctor-general in England of the A. and C. of Lyre, to the vicarage of Hinckley vacant because Master Gilbert had been inst. to the church of Nuneaton in the diocese of Lichfield and Coventry. Inst. Buckden, Dec. 17, 1288.

WIGSTON MAGNA (Wykingeston'). R. Master Roger Buteturte subd. re-presented by the P. and C. of Lenton to the church of Wigston Magna vacant because the said Roger had not been ordained pr. within a year of institution. Inst. (in the person of William of Ellingham (Elingham) his proctor). Buckden, Dec. 20, 1298.

SILEBY. R. Edmund La Zouch (Zuch') ch. p. by Sir Nicholas of Seagrave knight to the church of Sileby vacant by the res. of Henry of Seagrave. Inst. Buckden Jan. 9, 1289, and had letters patent.

LUTTERWORTH. R. Master Henry of Bray subd. p. by the Bishop of Bath and Wells, acting for Sir Theobald de Verdun, knight, to the church of Lutterworth vacant by the death of John of Wheathampstead, and the withdrawal of Sir William of Hamilton first presented. Master Henry, examined, admitted that he had custody of the churches of Cottesbach, Ballykelly in Ireland, ?Alverstoke, and Naunton, and that he had been inst. to the church of Woodford Halse. He resigned his interests in the churches of Woodford Halse, ?Alverstoke [Eldestok] and Naunton, and was inst. Jan. 21, 1289 (place not given). A pension of forty shillings annually was reserved to the master and brethren of Lutterworth Hospital.

WITHCOTE (Wythecok'). R. Robert of Cranoe (Cravenhowe) ch. p. by the A. and C. of Owston to the church of Withcote vacant because John of Musgrave (Musegrave) had been inst. to Rushden (Rissenden) in the deanery of Baldock. Inst. Feb. 25, 1289 (place not given).

COSSINGTON (Cusington'). R. Richard Le Hostage of Lough-borough clerk in minor orders p. by Sir Hugh Le Despencer knight to the church of Cossington vacant by the death of Stephen. Ordained subd. and inst. Wycombe, Mar. 5, 1289, and had letters patent.

OWSTON (Osolveston'). Ernald, prior of, Fineshade (Finnes-heved') elected or postulated to the office of abbot of Owston in succession to Robert of Lincoln who had died. Licence to elect was obtained from the King as patron. Election confirmed Wooburn near Wycombe, Mar. 26, 1289. Solemn benediction at Marlow Monialium Mar. 27, according to the form contained in the memoranda rolls of this year.[1]

·X.
XIIII KALENDAS JUNII DIE SANCTI DUNSTANI ANNO DOMINI M.CC. OCTOGESIMO NONO INCIPIT ANNUS PONTIFICATUS DOMINI OLIVERI EPISCOPO LINCOLN' DECIMUS.

LAUNDE (Landa). William of Somerby provided by the bishop to the office of prior of Launde, vacant by the death of William of Martival. Licence to elect was obtained from Sir Ralph Basset, patron. The election ended in dispute, both William of Somerby and Hugh of Dingley (Dingele) claiming to be elected, and the bishop had to settle the matter. No place or date (?summer, 1289).

SOUTH CROXTON. R. Robert of Stathern ch. p. by the A. and C. of Croxton to the church of South Croxton vacant by the death of Master John of Grantham (Graham). Inst. Lincoln, Aug. 16, 1289, and had letters patent.

BROOKSBY (Brokesby). R. Gilbert of Glen ch. p. by John de Vilers to the church of Brooksby vacant by the death of Ralph Barry and the res. of Thomas de Boothby (Botheby) who was first presented. Granted custody for a period, then inst. Buckden, Sept. 8, 1289.

BOTTESFORD (Botelesford'). R. Master William of Fillongley (Filingele) clerk in minor orders p. by Lady Isabel de Ros,

[1] The following entry, concerning the church of Woodford, is marked 'vacat'.

lady of Belvoir, to the church of Bottesford vacant because Master Peter de Ros had been appointed precentor of York Minster. Granted custody June 17, 1289. Ordained subd. and inst. Lincoln Cathedral, Sept. 24, 1289, and had letters patent.

STONESBY (Stonnesby). V. Robert of Morborne (Morburn') ch. p. by Geoffrey of Cheal (Cheyle). W. of Morton and Robert of St. Alban's, monks of Crowland deputed to present in the name of the A. and C. thereof, to the vicarage of Stonesby vacant by the death of Simon. Inst. Stow Park, Oct. 1, 1289.

HINCKLEY (Hinkele). Henry d'Aunay (de Alneto) monk of Lyre Abbey, p. by Peter de Deserto, proctor of the A. and C. of Lyre, to the office of prior of Hinckley vacant by the death of William de Arena, according to the form recorded in the beginning of this roll.[1] Admitted Lincoln, Nov. 20, 1289.

MARKFIELD (Merkefeld'). R. Philip of Northampton (Norht') clerk in minor orders p. by Lady Helen La Zouch (Zuch') to the church of Markfield vacant by the death of Robert of Bowden (Budon'). Given custody Nov. 20, 1289. Ordained subd. and inst. Stamford, St. Leonard's, Dec. 17, 1289.

NORTH KILWORTH (Northkivelingwrth'). R. William of Wakerley (Wakerle) clerk in minor orders p. by the A. and C. of St. Mary de Pratis to the church of North Kilworth vacant by the death of Master Alan. Presentation opposed by Sir Stephen Rabaz knight who afterwards withdrew by letters patent, without prejudice to future claims. Granted custody Jul. 16, 1289. Ordained subd. and inst. Stamford, St. Leonard's, Dec. 17, 1289.

SHANGTON (Schauketon'). R. Walter of Ketton (Keten') clerk in minor orders p. by the A. and C. of Lilleshall to the church of Shangton vacant by the death of Master Geoffrey of Lilleshall. Ordained subd. and granted custody for a period. Inst. Uffington, Dec. 18, 1289.

EDMONDTHOPRE (Thorp' Eymere). R. John of Calais (Caleys) clerk in minor orders p. by Edmund Earl of Lancaster to the church of Edmondthorpe vacant because William of Alconbury (Alkemundebir') had been inst. to Irchester (Irenchester). Ordained subd. and inst. Northampton, Feb. 25, 1290.

---

[1] Now lost.

SPROXTON. R. Master Robert of Redmile clerk in minor orders p. by the A. and C. of Croxton to two parts of the church of Sproxton vacant by the death of Master Alan. Ordained subd. and inst. Northampton, Feb. 25, 1290.

EXTON.[1] V. William of Freeby (Fretheby) ch. p. by the A. and C. of St. Mary de Pratis to the vicarage of Exton vacant by the death of Alexander. Inst. Liddington, Mar. 31, 1290.

AB KETTLEBY (Abbeketelby). R. Master John de Aneta subd. p. by the P. and C. of Launde to the church of Ab Kettleby vacant by the death of John of Melton. Inst. Kir(k)by, Apr. 15, 1290, and had letters patent.

[*Membrane 2*] COTES.[2] R. Milo of Leicester d. p. by Robert of Somerby, preceptor of Dalby, proctor of the Prior of the Hospitallers in England, to the chapel of Cotes vacant by the death of Robert of Cotes. Inst. Leicester, Apr. 24, 1290.

GLENFIELD (Clenefeld'). R. Master Richard of Bowden (Budon') ch. p. by Richard prior of Ware, proctor-general of the A. and C. of St. Evroult, to the church of Glenfield vacant by the death of Master Laurence. Inst. Hinckley, Apr. 26, 1290, and had letters patent.

WITHERLEY (Wytherdele). R. William, clerk in minor orders, nephew of William of Hotham a Dominican, collated by John Bishop of Winchester in virtue of a papal provision of which he was executor to the church of Witherley, in the gift of the A. and C. of Lyre. No reason was given for vacancy. Admitted Banbury, May 9, 1290.

Memorandum quod cum Willelmo clerico nepoti fratris Willelmi de Hothum de ordine fratrum predicatorum de beneficio ecclesiastico competenti cum cura vel sine cura consueto ab olim clericis secularibus assignari, ad cujuscumque collationem vel presentationem spectante dummodo ad collationem non pertineret exemptorum si quod in diocese Lincoln' vacaret, vel quam primum ad id offeret se facultas, provisio a sede apostolica concessa fuisset, ac venerabilis pater dominus J. Dei gracia Wynton' episcopus executor sibi super hoc deputatus per litteras quas patentes episcopo Lincoln' inhibuisset ne quodcumque beneficium ecclesiasticum predicto clerico competens cum cura vel sine cura ad ipsius episcopi vel

---

[1] In Rutland.
[2] By Prestwold.

cujuscumque alterius persone ecclesiastice collationem vel
presentationem spectans, beneficiis exemptorum dumtaxat
exceptis si quod in civitate vel diocese Lincoln' ad tunc vacaret,
vel quam cito ad id offeret se facultas cuiquam conferret vel
ad id quemquam admitteret, hujusmodi beneficium secundum
formam mandati apostolici sibi directi donationi sue, immo
verius apostolice, reservando, dictoque episcopo Linc' con-
ferendi hujusmodi beneficium seu ad id quemquam admittendi
et quibuscumque personis ecclesiasticis presentandi juxta
formam prescriptam interdicendo penitus potestatem,
postmodum vacante ecclesia de Wytherdale in diocese Linc'
ad presentationem abbatis et conventus de Lira Ebroyc'
diocesis pertinente, dictus dominus Wynton' Episcopus
eandem ecclesiam Willemo clerico nepoti fratris Willelmi de
Hothum auctoritate apostolica contulit memorato, Episcopo
Linc' per suas litteras patentes mandando ut eundem Willelmum
clericum in corporalem possessionem ipsius ecclesie induceret
et defenderet inductum, contradictores per censuram ecclesiasticam appellatione preposita[1] compescendo. Quo quidem
mandato VII idus Maii anno domini M.CC. nonagesimo apud
Bannebir' dicto Linc' Episcopo presentato et ab eodem
admisso, idem Episcopus Linc' recepto prius ab eodem
Willelmo juramento de obediendo sibi et officialibus suis in
canonicis mandati s etc., officiali Archidiaconi Leyc' eisdem
die, anno et loco dedit protinus in mandatis ut prefatum
Willelmum clericum in corporalem possessionem prefate
ecclesie de Wytherdele sibi collate ut premittitur induceret et
defenderet inductum, contradictores per censuram ecclesiasticam appellatione postposita compescendo.

BURTON OVERY. R. Nicholas Taylhast ch. p. by Richard prior
of Ware, proctor-general in England by the A. and C. of St.
Evroult, to the church of Burton Overy vacant because
Richard of Bowden (Budon') had been inst. to Glenfield
(Clenfeud'). Inst. Kidlington, May 12, 1290.

[f. 280] QUARTODECIMO KALENDAS JUNII DIE SANCTI DUNSTANI
ANNO DOMINI M.CC. NONAGESIMO INCIPIT ANNUS PONTIFICATUS
DOMINI OLIVERI EPISCOPI LINCOLN' UNDECIMUS.

SYSTON (Sytheston'). R. Walter of Clerkenwell ch. p. by King
Edward as guardian of the lands and heir of William de

---

[1] sic, normally 'postposita'.

Ferrariis to the church of Syston vacant by the death of Master Stephen. Inst. London, O.T., May 21, 1290.

HALLATON (Halgton'). R. Master Robert of Radcliffe (Radeclive), clerk in minor orders p. by Master Roger de Martival to the mediety of the church of Hallaton vacant by the death of Master Roger of Tilton. Ordained subd. and inst. Hertford, May 27, 1290. Had letters patent.

BELTON. V. William of Rotherby (Retherby) ch. p. by the Prioress and C. of Gracedieu to the vicarage of Belton vacant by the death of Richard. Inst. Liddington, June 14, 1290.

BRADLEY (Bradele). Walter of Drayton p. by William of Kir(k)by patron to the office of prior of Bradley in succession to Henry who had died. The bishop inquired why no election had taken place, and Walter produced two legal instruments (not quoted) of which the first reserved to the patron the right of presentation, and the second granted to the canons the right of free election subject to his consent. The bishop, finding that there were only two canons, summoned them, and by consent of Hugh declared Walter elected. After an enquiry made by the dean of Gartree had been certified, and the patron's consent obtained, Walter was admitted. Liddington, July 10, 1290.

Vacante prioratu de Bradele per mortem fratris Henrici ultimi prioris ejusdem dominus Willelmus de Kirkeby miles patronus ipsius prioratus fratrem Walterum de Drayton' canonicum ejusdem domus ad dictum prioratum presentavit. Episcopus vero volens scire utrum prior ad presentationem patroni nulla electione canonicorum premissa preficiendus esset vel alias per electionem assumendus, canonicis loci predicti tunc duobus numero tantum mandavit ut ad ipsum accederent pro informatione ipsius per ostensionem instrumentorum et modis aliis quibus melius posset fieri optinenda. Cujus pretextu dictus frater Walterus accessit ad episcopum exhibens duo instrumenta quorum unum fuit primi fundatoris ejusdem loci in quo patronus reservavit sibi jus presentandi episcopo priorem, et aliud instrumentum successoris seu heredis dicti fundatoris per quod concesserat canonicis dicti prioratus liberam facultatem eligendi sibi priorem nulla prius licencia eligendi petita, reservato sibi quod concensus suus post electionem requiretur, propter quod, predicta presentatione patroni non admissa, injunctum fuit dictis canonicis quod procederent ad electionem, adherendo instrumento posteriori per quod conceditur per quod conceditur eis libera facultas eligendi. Deinde dictus frater Walterus et frater Hugo concanonicus suus ad episcopum apud Lidington' accesserunt et idem frater Hugo dixit se in concanonicum suum fratrem Walterum predictum concensisse, nec fuit aliter ad aliquam electionem processum. Postea exhibita episcopo littera dicti domini Willelmi de Kirkeby patroni dicte domus super consensu exhibito persone dicti fratris Walteri, quia non constabat sibi de conditionibus et conversatione dictorum canonicorum, scriptum fuit decano de Gertre quod inquireret diligenter de eisdem et de inventis certificaret. Unde recepto certificatorio dicti decani cum inquisitio facta in pleno loci capitulo a viris fidedignis pro eodem fratre Waltero sufficienter operaretur, episcopus VI idus Julii anno domini M.CC. nonagesimo ipsum admisit et priorem instituit, curam et administrationem dicti loci in spiritualibus et temporalibus sibi committendo. Tandem jurata etc. scriptum fuit etc.

SHEEPY (Schepeye). R. William of Preston ch. p. by Sir Richard of Harcourt (Harecurt') knight to the mediety of the church of Sheepy vacant by the res. of Thomas of ?Thetford (Tefford'). Inst. Louth, Aug. 25, 1290, and had letters patent.

[f. 280v] THRUSSINGTON (Thurstanton'). R. Henry of Hales, clerk in minor orders, p. by the P. and C. of Sempringham to the church of Thrussington vacant because Nicholas of Bolingbroke had been inst. to the church of Grainthorpe. Had custody for a period. Then ordained subd. and inst. Stamford, Sept. 23, 1290.

SHARNFORD (Scharneford'). R. Richard of Wing, clerk in minor orders p. by the P. and monks[1] of Kirkby to the church of Sharnford vacant by the death of Matthew. Had custody for a period. Then ordained subd. and inst. Stamford, Sept. 23, 1290.

SADDINGTON (Sadington') R. Sir Robert of Kibworth (Kibbewurth') ch. p. by the A. and C. of St. Agatha's Easby to the church of Saddington vacant by the death of Philip. Presentation disputed by John de Moelles (Moeles) who p. Master Richard of Southill (Suthgivel). Case settled in the King's court. Writ (given in full, dated Westminster Nov. 22, 1290, and witnessed by J. de Metingham) directed the bishop to accept the candidate of the A. and C. Robert was inst. Baldock, Nov. 25, 1290.

---

[1] Sic.

HALLATON (Halgton'). R. Adam of Cranwell ch. p. by the P. and C. of Leeds to the mediety of the church of Hallaton vacant by the death of Master William de la Gare. Inst. Fingest, Jan. 1, 1291, and had letters patent.

GREAT BOWDEN (Magna Budon'). R. Robert of St. Alban's d. p. by King Edward to the church of Great Bowden vacant by the death of Walter of Kent. Master Nicholas de Luvetot, first presented as a minor, resigned when he came of age and was inst. to the church of Adlingfleet (Adelingflet'). Inst. Little Marlow, Jan. 22, 1291.

NORTH KILWORTH (Nortkyvelingwrth'). R. William of Wakerley ch. re-presented by the A. and C. of St. Mary de Pratis, Leicester, to the church of North Kilworth vacant because the said William had not been ordained pr. until a year and five days after institution. Inst. Banbury, Mar. 6, 1291, and had letters patent.

[*f. 281*] CROFT (Craft). R. Alan of Barkby pr. p. by the A. and C. of St. Mary de Pratis, Leicester, to the church of Croft vacant by the death of William of Brackley (Brakkele). Inst. Aston, Mar. 13, 1291, and had letters patent.

FRISBY-ON-THE-WREAK (Friseby). V. Richard of Ashby (Esseby) subd. p. by the P. and C. of Launde to the vicarage of Frisby vacant because Hugh had received other preferment. Ordained d. Northampton, Mar. 17, 1291 and inst. there Mar. 18.

STAPLEFORD. R. Richard of Loughborough (Lucteburg') d. p. by Edmund[1] son of King Henry III to the church of Stapleford vacant because the said Richard had not been ordained pr. within a year of institution. Inst. (by his proctor unnamed) Lincoln, Apr. 20, 1291, and had letters patent.

CHARLEY (Charle). Thomas of Evesham, canon of Ulverscroft, elected or postulated with the consent of Nicholas son of Nicholas of Seagrave (Segrave) custodian of the lands and heir of Sir William de Ferrariis the patron, to the office of prior of Charley vacant by the res. of Stephen of Keyham (Cayham). Election quashed for incorrect procedure. Thomas was appointed. Stow Park, May 9, 1291.

COTES. R. William Puleyn ch. by Peter of Haugham (Hagham) in the name of the P. of the Hospitallers in England to the

---

[1] Earl of Lancaster.

chapel of Cotes vacant by the res. of Milo. Inst Stow Park May 10, 1291, and had letters patent.

[*f. 281v*] QUARTODECIMO KALENDAS JUNII VIDELICET DIE SANCTI DUNSTANI ANNO DOMINI M.CC. NONAGESIMO PRIMO INCIPIT ANNUS PONTIFICATUS DOMINI OLIVERI EPISCOPI LINCOLN' DUODECIMUS.

THURNBY (Thirneby). V. John of Frisby subd. p. by the A. and C. of St. Mary de Pratis, Leicester, to the vicarage of Thurnby vacant because John the last vicar had been removed for bad behaviour. Ordained subd. and inst. Boston, June 16, 1291. He was however burdened with the obligation to pay to his predecessor an annual pension of forty shillings, and the bishop issued letters patent to this effect from Stow Park, May 17, 1291.

SHOBY (Sywaldby). R. William of Brocton ch. p. by the P. and C. of Launde to the church of Shoby vacant by the death of Thomas of Leicester (Leyc'). Inst. Spaldwick, July 7, 1291, and had letters patent.

TILTON. V. William of Weston ch. p. by the P. and C. of Launde to the vicarage of Tilton vacant by the death of Richard of Belton. Inst. Spaldwick, July 7, 1291.

FRISBY-ON-THE-WREAK. V. Robert of Swinford ch. p. by the P. and C. of Launde to the vicarage of Frisby vacant because Richard of Ashby (Esseby) had been inst. to the vicarage of Weston. Inst. Spaldwick, July 31, 1291.

[*f. 282v*] LEICESTER, ST. MARY DE PRATIS. William of Malvern canon of the house, elected to the office of abbot in succession to William of Shepshed who had died. Licence obtained from the King as patron. Election submitted to the bishop, Nettleham Sept. 27, 1291, and quashed for incorrect procedure Sept. 29, when the bishop appointed William of Malvern. Solemn benediction Nettleham, Sept. 30, on which day the bishop sent a letter (given in full) to the King reporting the appointment.

KIBWORTH HARCOURT (Kibwrth'). Master Geoffrey of Coddington pr. p. by the Warden, scholars and brethren of Merton College Oxford to the chapel of Kibworth Harcourt vacant by the death of Walter of Odiham. An inquiry showed that the chapel had ceased to exist but was represented by a portion of the tithes worth a hundred shillings a year. To this portion Master Geoffrey was admitted, Theydon Mount, Nov. 22, 1291.

Magistro Galfrido de Codington' presbitero presentato per custodem, scholares et fratres domus scholarium de Merton' in Oxonia ad capellam de Kibbewrth', factaque inquisitione per officialem Archidiaconi Leyc' super contingentibus statum capelle ejusdem per quam inter cetera acceptum est apud Kibbewrth' nunc[1] non est capella, set[2] antiquiter extitisse infra manerium nunc[1] scholarium predictorum ibidem, cui quedam portio decimarum separatarum valens per annum centum solidos fuit antiquiter assignata, ipsamque vacare per mortem Walteri de Odyham ultimi admissi ad eandem, idem Magister Galfridus ad capellam seu portionem hujusmodi X kalendas Decembris anno XII apud Theydon' est admissus. Jurataque etc. Scriptum est etc.

LEICESTER, ST. MARTIN'S. V. Robert of Barsby (Barnesby) ch. p. by the A. and C. of St. Mary de Pratis to the vicarage of St. Martin's vacant by the death of Richard. Inst. Wooburn, Dec. 21, 1291.

LEICESTER, ALL SAINTS (Omnium Sanctorum Leyc'). V. William of Leicester ch. p. by the A. and C. of St. Mary de Pratis to the vicarage of All Saints, vacant because Robert of Barsby had been inst. to St. Martin's. Inst. Wooburn, Jan. 14, 1292.

[f. 282v] SEALE (Scheyle). R. John de Montibus subd. p. by Edmund Earl of Lancaster to the church of Seale vacant by the death of Ralph of Burgh. Inst. in the person of John of Ditton his proctor, Fingest, Apr. 9, 1292.

STATHERN (Stakethirn'). Note that the ordinance concerning the chapel of Stathern is to be found among the memoranda.[3]

––––––

DIE SANCTI DUNSTANI VIDELICET QUARTODECIMO KALENDAS JUNII ANNO DOMINI M.CC. NONAGESIMO SECUNDO INCIPIT ANNUS

[1] Interlined.
[2] sic.
[3] L.R.S. 48, pp. 201–6.

PONTIFICATUS DOMINI OLIVERI DEI GRACIA EPISCOPO LINCOLN' TERTIUSDECIMUS.

———

LEICESTER, ST. JOHN'S HOSPITAL. Note of the appointment of Thomas of Bretford, nominated by the brethren and sisters of St. John's Hospital, to be master, Leicester, May 26, 1292.

STATHERN (Stakethirn'). William of Oakely (Okele) ch. p. by Richard de Bois Roard (Bosco Roardi) to his newly-founded chantry in honour of the Assumption of the Blessed Virgin, in the church of Stathern. Harby, May 27, 1292.

THORPE ARNOLD (Thorp' Arnald'). V. William of Frisby ch. p. by the A. and C. of St. Mary de Pratis to the vicarage of Thorpe Arnold vacant by the death of Henry. Inst. Lincoln, May 31, 1292.

EATON (Eyton'). V. David of Stretton ch. p. by the A. and C. of St. Mary de Pratis to the vicarage of Eaton vacant because William of Frisby (Fretheby) had been inst. to Thorpe Arnold. Inst. Louth, July 8, 1292.

[f. 283] NAILSTONE (Neyleston'). R. Walter of Maidstone, p. by Sir John of Hastings knight to the church of Nailstone vacant by the res. of Sir Hugh of Kendal. When examined as to his benefices Walter said that he had been collated by the Archbishop of York to a mediety of Kirkby Stephen, which was litigious, and that he held temporary possession from the Archbishop of Canterbury of the church of Newchurch. He promised to give up Newchurch and was inst. Laughton, Aug. 2, 1292.

SAXBY. R. William of Saddington (Sadington') ch. p. by Sir Thomas Brabazun clerk to the church of Saxby vacant by the death of Martin. Inst. Lincoln. Aug. 16, 1292, and had letters patent.

EDMONDTHORPE (Thorp' Eymere). R. John Brabazun subd. p. by Edmund Earl of Lancaster to the church of Edmondthorpe vacant by the res. of John of Calais (Caleys). Inst. Nocton, Aug. 23, 1292.

WILLOUGHBY WATERLESS (Wylgby). R. Roger Beler of Ingarsby (Ingewardeby) clerk in minor orders p. by Sir John d'Aungerville knight to the church of Willoughby Waterless vacant by the death of Oliver. Had custody for a period, then ordained subd. and inst. Northampton, Sept. 20, 1292, and had letters patent

CARLETON. R. Sir Gilbert of Rothbury (Roubir') ch. p. by Ralph prior of Ware, proctor general in England of the A. and C. of St. Evroult, to the church of Carleton vacant by the death of Master Nicholas. Granted the church *in commendam* for a period. Then inst. (in the person of Nicholas of Long Stratton, his proctor), Spaldwick, Oct. 19, 1292, and had letters patent.

HATHERN. Note that the institution of Hugh Duket to Hathern is to be found among the Stow institutions.[1]

SKEFFINGTON. R. James de Columbariis d. p. by Sir Theobald de Verdun knight to the church of Skeffington vacant by the death of ...[2] Inst. Spaldwick, Nov. 28, 1292 and had letters patent.

[*f. 283v*] ARNESBY (Ernesby). R. Edmund Roulond' clerk in minor orders p. by the P. and C. of Caldwell to the church of Arnesby vacant by the death of Nigel. Sir Alan of Elmesfeld' opposed the presentation but did not pursue his case although the church was vacant for a long time. Edmund was ordained subd. and inst. Dorchester-on-Thames, Dec. 20, 1292.

CRANOE (Cravenhou). R. Richard de Boyville clerk in minor orders p. by Thomas de Boyville to the church of Cranoe vacant by the death of William de Boyville. Ordained subd. and inst. Dorchester-on-Thames, Dec. 20, 1292.

ASHBY FOLVILLE (Esseby Folevile). R. Master Walter of Lowthorpe ch. p. by the P. and C. of Launde to the church of Ashby Folville vacant by the death of Walter Basset and the lapse of a semester during which the church was held *in commendam* by William of Stockton, canon of Lincoln. Inst. by the Archdeacon of Leicester, as commissary, Leicester, Jan. 13, 1293.

MIRABEL. John Sampson ch. p. by Sir William Murdak knight to the chapel of Mirabel vacant by the death of Adam. Inst. London, O.T., Mar. 13, 1293.

EASTWELL (Estewell'). R. Richard of Byrchele p. by the A. and C. of St. Mary de Pratis to the church of Eastwell vacant by the death of Master Robert of Hathern and the renunciation

[1] See p. 22.
[2] Blank in MS.

by letters patent of Master John of Caen (Cadomo), the first to be presented. Inst. London O.T., Mar. 13, 1293, and had letters patent.

BREEDON. William de Willeys p. by the P. and C. of Nostell to the office of prior in succession to Thomas of Oake(n) who had died. Licence obtained from Sir Robert of Tattershale knight, patron. An enquiry held at Hertford, Mar. 22, 1293, showed that it was customary for the P. and C. of Nostell to recommend two of their canons to the patron, of whom he chose one to present to the bishop for admission to office of prior. William was inst. Hertford, Mar. 23, 1293.

[f. 284] SOUTH KILWORTH. R. Master Robert of Kilworth ch. p. by the A. and C. of Sulby to the church of South Kilworth vacant by the death of Ralph. Inst. Biggleswade, Mar. 26, 1293, and had letters patent.

AYLESTONE. R. Master Gilbert of Seagrave ch. p. by King Edward as guardian of the lands and heir of Henry of Pembridge (Penebrugg') to the church of Aylestone vacant by the res. of John de La Zouch. Inst. Biggles-wade, Apr. 8, 1293, and had letters patent.

QUARTODECIMO KALENDAS JUNII VIDELICET DIE SANCTI DUNSTANI ANNO DOMINO M.CC. NONAGESIMO TERTIO INCIPIT ANNUS PONTIFICATUS DOMINI OLIVERI LINCOLNIEN' EPISCOPI QUARTUSDECIMUS.

KING'S NORTON. R. Robert of Barford (Bereford') clerk in minor orders p. by the A. and C. of Owston to the church of King's Norton vacant by the death of Simon. Had custody for a period, then ordained subd. (by licence of the bishop of London) and inst. London, O.T., May 23, 1293. Had letters patent.

COLE ORTON (Overton' Quatermars). R. Master John Clarel clerk in minor orders p. by Sir Ralph Basset as guardian of William son of William Maureward to the church of Cole Orton vacant by the res. of John Clarel the elder. Ordained subd. (as above) and inst. London, O.T., May 23, 1293.

FRISBY-ON-THE-WREAK. V. Thomas of Leamington (Lemmington') ch. p. by the P. and C. of Launde to the vicarage of Frisby vacant by the death of Robert. Inst. Louth, Sept. 7, 1293.

SEALE (Scheyle). R. Durand of Florence clerk in minor orders p. by Edmund Earl of Lancaster to the church of Seale vacant by the res. of John de Montibus. Ordained subd. and inst. Lincoln, Sept. 19, 1293.

[*f. 284v*] WISTOW (Wistanstowe). R. Gilbert de Reggate ch. p. by Sir John of Hastings knight to the church of Wistow vacant by the death of Master Salvagius. Inst. Acton, Dec. 13, 1293, and had letters patent.

COSSINGTON. R. Robert of Loughborough (Lucteburg') clerk in minor orders p. by Sir Hugh Le Despenser knight to the church of Cossington vacant by the res. of Richard of Loughborough. Granted custody for a period, then ordained subd. and inst. Wycombe, Dec. 19, 1293.

RATCLIFFE-ON-THE-WREAK (Radeclive). V. Richard of Dunton ch. p. by the P. and C. of Charley to the vicarage of Ratcliffe (Radeclive super Wrechek') vacant by the death of William. Inst. Wooburn, Dec. 24, 1293, and had letters patent.

———

DIE SANCTI DUNSTANI EPISCOPI VIDELICET QUARTODECIMO KALENDAS JUNII ANNO DOMINI MILLESIMO DUCENTESIMO NONAGESIMO QUARTO INCIPIT ANNUS PONTIFICATUS DOMINI OLIVERI DEI GRACIA LINCOLN-IEN' EPISCOPI QUINTUSDECIMUS.

———

COSTON. R. Henry of Barford (Bereford') clerk in minor orders p. by Sir Thomas Berkele knight to the church of Coston vacant by the death of Osbert of Barford. Granted custody for a period, then ordained subd. and inst. London O.T., June 12, 1294, and had letters patent.

DISHLEY (Dixle). R. William of Buxton (Buckstones) clerk in minor orders p. by the A. and C. of St. Mary de Pratis to the church of Dishley vacant by the death of Robert of Sutton. Ordained subd. and inst. Dunstable, Sept. 18, 1294.

STATHERN. R. Robert Le Chaumberlayn clerk in minor orders p. by Robert de Bois Road (Bosco Roardi) to the church of Stathern vacant by the death of Sir Richard. Ordained subd. and inst. Stow in Lindsey, Dec. 18, 1294, and had letters patent.

[*f. 285*] MORTON. R. Master Thomas of Nassington ch. p. by Master Roger de Martival to the church of Morton vacant by the death of Gilbert of Kirkeby. Held the church *in commendam* for a period then inst. by the Archdeacon of Leicester acting on the bishop's mandate, Noseley, Feb. 2, 1295.

BRADLEY (Bradele). John of Kirkeby canon of Launde elected to the office of prior vacant by the res. of Walter of Drayton. Licence obtained from Sir William of Kirby, patron. The canons of Bradley, three in all, brought documents under the priory seal as proof of election. The election was quashed for faulty and informal procedure. John was however appointed, Nettleham, Feb. 28, 1295.

COSBY (Cosseby). V. John of Corley (Cornleye) ch. p. by the A. and C. of St. Mary de Pratis to the vicarage of Cosby vacant by the res. of Roger. Inst. Liddington, Apr. 2, 1295.

COTES. R. William de Cap' (status not given) p. by the Prior of the Hospitallers in England to the church of Cotes vacant by the death of William Puleyn. Inst. at Uppingham, May 11, 1295.

DIE SANCTI DUNSTANI EPISCOPI VIDELICET QUARTODECIMO KALENDAS JUNII ANNO DOMINI M.CC. NONAGESIMO QUINTO INCIPIT ANNUS PONTIFICATUS DOMINI OLIVERI EPISCOPI LINCOLN' SEXTUSDECIMUS.

[*f. 285v*] SWITHLAND. R. Reginald of St. Evroult clerk in minor orders p. by Ralph Prior of Ware, proctor-general in England of the A. and C. of St. Evroult, to the church of Swithland vacant because Sir Gilbert of Roubir' had been inst. to Carleton. Ordained subd. (by licence of the Bishop of London) and inst. London, O.T., May 28, 1295.

CADEBY (Cateby). R. William of Cadeby clerk in minor orders p. by the P. and C. of Dunstable to the church of Cadeby vacant by the death of Robert. Ordained subd. (as above) and inst. London, O.T., May 28, 1295.

SHOBY (Sywaldby). R. Robert called Prudfot (status not given) p. by the P. and C. of Launde to the church of Shoby vacant by the res. of William of Brocton. Inst. London, O.T., May 30, 1295.

BARKBY. V. William of Brocton ch. p. by the A. and C. of St. Mary de Pratis to the vicarage of Barkby vacant by the res. of Robert Prudfot. Inst. London, O.T., May 30, 1295.

LONG CLAWSON (Claxton'). V. Richard of Denton p. by the P. and C. of Belvoir to the vicarage of Long Clawson vacant by the res. of Alexander Carbet and the renunciation of Geoffrey of Yaxley (Jakesle) who had been first presented. Inst. Caldwell, July 6, 1295.

REDMILE. R. Ralph of Dalton pr. p. by the P. and C. of Belvoir to the church of Redmile vacant by the death of Master Robert of Redmile. Presentation opposed by Isabel de Ros, lady of Belvoir, who p. William of Kelham (Kelum) but withdrew her presentation by letters patent under her seal (given in full and dated Belvoir, Sept. 5, 1295). William resigned his rights by letters patent (not given). Ralph was inst. Berkhamstead, Sept. 24, 1295, and had letters patent.

MELTON MOWBRAY. V. William of Melton ch. p. by the P. and C. of Lewes to the vicarage of Melton Mowbray vacant by the res. of Richard of Higham (Hecham). Inst. East Deeping, Oct. 29, 1295.

[f. 286] CLAYBROK'. V. Roger of Kilworth ch. p. by the Prioress and C. of Nuneaton to the vicarage of Claybrooke vacant by the death of Simon. Presentation opposed by Master William Wood, who obtained from the bishop an injunction against the said Prioress and C., but later agreed to an amicable settlement. (His letter to this effect, addressed to the bishop, is given in full and under his seal, and is dated London, Oct. 25, 1295.) Roger was inst. Oundle, Oct. 30, 1295.

Rogerus de Kevelingwurth' capellanus presentatus per ...[1] priorissam et conventum de Eton' ad vicariam ecclesie de Claybrok' vacantem per mortem Simonis ultimi vicarii ejusdem, facta prius inquisitione per ...[1] officialem R. Archidiaconi Leyc' per quam acceptum est eandem vicariam esse litigiosam per hoc quod Magister Willelmus de Bosco opposuit se et contendit contra dictas priorissam et conventum in curia regia, dicens se habere jus presentandi ad totam ecclesiam necnon et ad vicariam ejusdem. Deinde litigato super hoc aliquandiu inter partes, eodemque Magistro Willelmo per viam compositionis liti cedente, hoc idem episcopo[2] per

[1] Blank in MS.
[2] Interlined.

litteram suam patentem notificante in forma que sequitur:
Venerabili in Christo patri et domino O Dei gracia Lincoln'
episcopo suus humilis et devotus Willelmus de Bosco filius
domini Ernaldi de Bosco militis salutem cum omnibus
reverencia et honore debitis tanto patri. Noverit paternitas
vestra reverenda quod licet vacante nuper vicaria de Claybrok'
vestre diocesis crederem advocationem dicte ecclesie quam
religiose domine ..[1] priorissa et conventus de Nunneton' in
proprios usus canonice optinent et etiam advocationem dicte
vicarie ad me de jure pertinere, propter quod vobis auctoritate
regia in forma communi procureveram inhiberi ne, pendente
lite in curia domini regis inter me ex parte una et ipsas
dominas ex altera super advocatione hujusmodi, ad presentationem dictarum religiosarum aliquam personam admitteretis
ad vicariam memoratum, tandemque inspectis certis antecessorum meorum et aliis juribus quas et que eedem religiose
pro se optinent in hac parte evidenter perpendi quod dicte
religiose tam super advocatione et appropriatione dicte
ecclesie quam super jure presentandi ad vicariam ejusdem
ecclesie suo jure sunt sufficienter munite, idcirco prefate
inhibitioni regie ad meam procurationem et prosecutionem
vobis facte cujus effectui et omni juri et clamio quod mihi
aliquo modo vel colore competere potuit aut poterit in
advocatione dicte ecclesie vel vicarie seu presentatione aut
nominatione ad ipsas vel alteram earum pro me et heredibus
meis imperpetuum pure, sponte, simpliciter et totaliter
renuncio per presentes, vestre pie paternitati humiliter
supplicans et devote quatinus non obstante inhibitione regia
predicta seu aliqua mea reclamatione personam vobis ad
dictam vicariam per dictas religiosas presentatam admittere
velitis et quod vestrum est ulterius exequi circa ipsam. In cujus
rei testimonium sigillum meum presentibus est appensum.
Datum London' die martis proxima ante festum apostolorum
Simonis et Jude, anno domini M.CC. nonagesimo quinto. ...
admissus fuit III Kalendas Novembris anno XVI apud Undel
et vicarius perpetuus cum onere personaliter ministrandi et
continue residendi canonice institutus in eadem, Jurataque
etc. Scriptum etc.

KING'S NORTON (Westnorton). R. Richard of Langton ch. p.
by the A. and C. of Owston to the church of King's Norton
vacant because Robert of Barford had received other
preferment. Inst. London, O.T., Dec. 6, 1295, and had letters
patent.

---

[1] Blank in MS.

DALBY-ON-THE-WOLDS (Daleby). V. Roger of Ivel (Yvele) ch. p. by the Prior of the Hospitallers in England to the vicarage of Dalby vacant by the death of Henry. Inst. Biggleswade, Dec. 14, 1295.

ASFORDBY (Asfordeby). R. Philip of Swayfield pr. collated by the bishop to the church of Asfordby vacant by the death of Philip of Thorpe. Granted the church *in commendam* for six months, then inst. (in the person of John de Scalleby his proctor) Buckden, Dec. 15, 1295, and had letters patent.

[*f. 286v*] HIGHAM-ON-THE-HILL (Hegham). R. Master Roger of Bowden (Budon'), clerk in minor orders, p. by William de Arena, proctor-general in England of the A. and C. of Lyre, to the church of Higham vacant by the death of Master Nicholas. Granted custody for a period, then ordained subd. and inst. Huntingdon, Dec. 18, 1295, and had letters patent.

LANGLEY (Langeleye). Amicia, a nun of Langley, elected as prioress thereof in succession to Christina of Winton (Wynton') who had resigned. Election submitted to the bishop, Fingest, Jan. 19, 1296, and quashed for incorrect procedure. Amicia was appointed, Fingest, Jan. 20, 1296. The nuns declared that no licence was sought from Sir Robert of Tattershall the patron, since this was not customary, but Sir Robert, in assenting by letters patent to the admission of Amicia, said that such licence had been sought. ... Et est sciendum quod moniales predicte in suis depositionibus asserebant nullam licenciam eligendi fuisse petitam a domino Roberto de Tateshale milite patrono domus, quia nulla peti consuevit ut dicebant. Et dictus dominus Robertus per suam litteram patentem super consensu adhibito electioni facte de dicta sorore Amicia confectam asserebat licenciam fuisse petitam.

SLAWSTON. V. Baldwin de Langay ch. p. by the A. and C. of Owston to the vicarage of Slawston vacant because Richard had received other preferment. Inst. Naseby, Feb. 16, 1296.

HALLATON (Halugton'). R. William of Hakenesse, clerk in minor orders p. by Master Roger de Martival to the mediety of the church of Hallaton vacant by the death of (another) Master Roger and the lapse of a semester since Master Roger de Martival had received the church *in commendam*. Ordained subd. and inst. Rothwell, Feb. 18, 1296, and had letters patent.

BRAUNSTONE. R. Everard de Cessale, clerk in minor orders p. by Sir Roger de Morteyn knight to the church of Braunstone vacant by the death of Nicholas Hope. Ordained subd. and inst. Rothwell, Feb. 18, 1296, and had letters patent.

[*f. 287*] GREAT ASHBY (Magna Essebye). V. Walter of Greatworth (Grutwurth') ch. p. by the Prioress and C. of Catesby to the vicarage of Ashby Magna vacant by the res. of Alan. Inst Nettleham, Apr. 13, 1296.

SOUTH CROXTON. R. Geoffrey of Somerby ch. p. by the A. and C. of Croxton to the mediety of the church of South Croxton vacant by the res. of Robert of Stathern. Inst. Lincoln, May 17, 1296, and had letters patent.

———

DIE SANCTI DUNSTANI EPISCOPI VIDELICET QUARTODECIMO KALENDAS JUNII ANNO DOMINI M.CC. NONAGESIMO SEXTO INCIPIT ANNUS PONTIFICATUS DOMINI OLIVERI LINCOLN' EPISCOPI SEPTIMUS-DECIMUS.

———

AYLESTONE. R. Stephen of Seagrave, clerk in minor orders p. by Fulco de Pennebrok' to the church of Aylestone vacant because Master Gilbert of Seagrave had received other preferment. Granted custody for a period, then ordained subd. and inst. Lincoln, May 19, 1296, and had letters patent.

HIGHAM-ON-THE-HILL (Hegham). R. Robert Ridel of Hallaton (Halugton), clerk in minor orders p. by William de Arena, proctor-general in England of the A. and C. of Lyre, to the church of Higham vacant because Master Roger of Bowden had received other preferment. Granted custody for a period. Ordained subd. and inst. Lincoln, May 19, 1296, and had letters patent.

NEWBOLD VERDON (Neubold' Verdun'). R. Adam of Holywood (Sancto Bosco), clerk in minor orders p. by Sir Theobald de Verdun knight to the church of Newbold Verdun vacant by the res. of Robert Coudecok'. Ordained subd. and inst. Lincoln May 19, 1296, and had letters patent.

COSSINGTON (Cosington'). R. Nicholas of Loughborough (Lucteburg'), clerk in minor orders p. by Sir Hugh Le Despenser knight to the church of Cossington vacant because

Robert of Loughborough had received other preferment. Ordained subd. and inst. Lincoln, May 19, 1296, and had letters patent.

[*f. 287v*] WALTON-LE-WOLDS (Walton'). R. Robert of Loughborough ch. p. by Sir Richard of Loughborough to the church of Walton vacant by the death of Ralph of Harborough (Hareberg') and the lapse of six months since the church was granted *in commendam* to the said Sir Richard. Inst. Lincoln, May 19, 1296.

WYMONDHAM (Wymundham) John of Illston ch. p. by Sir William Hamelyn knight to the chantry-chapel which he had caused to be built and endowed in the church of Wymondham. Inst., after an inquiry by the official of the Archdeacon of Leicester had shown that the said chapel was decent, and properly endowed with lands and rents in Saxby, Edmondthorpe and Wymondham, worth ninety-one shillings, and that the King and Edmund Earl of Lancaster (the patron) had given their consent, Stow Park, May 7, 1296.[1]
    Appended to this are copies of the following:
(1)   Charter of Sir William Hamelyn, founding and endowing the chantry. This begins with a curiously archaic formula which suggests the work of a local scribe, out of touch with modern diplomatic. Given under Sir William's seal and witnessed by Sir Robert Tibetoft, Sir Richard Le Grey, Sir Roger Brabazun, Robert de Chevercurt, Robert of St. Peter, William of Purley, John Duraunt and others. No date. ?1293–6
(2)   Licence to evade the statute of Mortmain, granted by King Edward to Sir William Hamelyn by letters patent. Westminster, June 19, 1293.
(3)   Letters of Edmund, Earl of Lancaster, given under his seal confirming Sir William Hamelyn's endowment of the chantry, saving the customary services which are to be the responsibility of William and his heirs. Witnessed by Sir Walter de Helyun, seneschal of the earl's lands in England, Sir Laurence of St. Maur, Sir Roger Brabazun, Sir Walter of Wyther, knights Hugh of Vienne, John of Calais, Walter of Reading and John Basset, clerks, and others. Bear Park, Sept. 14, 1290.
(4)   *Inspeximus et confirmamus* by the bishop of Sir William Hamelyn's charter. Stow Park, May 7, 1296.

Memorandum quod dominus Willelmus Hamelyn miles pretendens se pro augmento cultus divine et pro salute anime

---

[1] This entry should appear among those of year XVI.

sue et Johanne uxoris sue, antecessorum, successorum et
parentum eorum, quandam capellam ecclesie de Wymundeham
conjunctam ex parte australi construi fecisse, seque in ea
perpetuam velle constituere cantariam, certis terris et redditu
ad hoc in puram elemosinam interveniente consensu regio et
domini Edmundi germani domini regis capitalis domini feodi
de quo sunt terre et redditus hujusmodi assignatis ad hujusmodi cantariam per episcopum approbandam et stabiliendam
perpetuis temporibus imposterum, Johannem de Ilveston'
capellanum episcopo presentavit, factaque inquisitione per
...¹ officialem R. Archidiaconi Leyc' de hujusmodi terris et
redditibus, quales, quanti et cujusmodi, valoris existerent, et
utrum aliquibus secularibus serviciis essent obnoxii, et an
absque alieno prejudicio in pios usus assignari valerent, de
consensu etiam regio et domini Edmundi an hujusmodi
assignationi adessent, rectorisque dicte ecclesie et patroni,
necnon decencia capelle predicte et persona ad eam presentata, per quam quidem inquisitionem acceptum fuit ad dictam
cantariam in prefata capella habendam quatuor bovatas terre
in campis de Saxby esse assignatas de dono domini Willelmi
Hamelyn que valent annuatim quadraginta solidos et sex
denarios, et in campis de Wymundham et de Thorpeymer'
quatuor bovatas terre que valent quadraginta solidos et sex
denarios annuatim. Et est dicte cantarie redditus annuus
assignatus in villa de Wymundham predicta X solidos, nec
sunt dicte terre et redditus aliquibus secularibus serviciis
obnoxii et absque alieno prejudicio in pios usus poterunt
assignari. Dominus rex et dominus Edmundus germanus suus
prefateque ecclesie de² Wymundeham² patronus hujusmodi
assignationi suum adhibent consensum, prout per litteras suas
in hac parte factas poterit apparere. Rector etiam ecclesie de
Wymundeham predicte ordinationi cantarie in capella
memorata habende consentit. Dicta vero capella decens est et
honesta. Dominus Johannes ad eam presentatus liber est et
legitimus, bone vite et conversationis honeste. Demum nonas
Maii anno domini M.CC. nonagesimo sexto, exhibitis episcopo
carta dicti domini Willelmi super assignatione predicta
necnon litterie regis et domini Edmundi predicti super
consensu in hac parte adhibito per eosdem, episcopus hujusmodi assignationem, concessionem et donationem terrarum
et redditus predictorum approbans et acceptans, et prefatum
Johannem de Ilveston' capellanum ad cantariam prefatam
admisit nonis Maii predictis apud Parcum Stowe, ipsumque
canonice instituit in eadem. Et super hos scriptum fuit, etc.

¹ Blank in MS.
² Interlined.

Tenor autem carte dicti domini Willelmi talis est: Dignum est scriptis commendare quod per longum tempus proponitur memoriter retineri. Hac igitur ratione inductus ego Willelmus Hamelyn omnibus Christi fidelibus notificare curavi me pro salute anime mee, Johanne[1] sponse[1] mee[1], antecessorum successorum, parentumque meorum animabus, ad honorem Dei et Beate Marie Virginis necnon et Beati Johannis Baptiste, ad augmentum cultus divini, dedisse, concessisse et hac presenti carta mea confirmasse, et de me et heredibus meis quietumclamasse in liberam, puram et perpetuam elemosinam. Deo et Beate Marie et capelle ejusdem Virginis ex parte australi ecclesie de Wymundeham fundate ad sustentationem unius presbiteri pro salute anime mee, Johanne sponse mee, antecessorum, successorum et parentum meorum animabus in predicta capella predicte Virginis perpetuo singulis diebus in anno divina celebraturi quatuor bovatas terre in villa et territorio de Saxby quas quidam Galfridus Murdak' quondam tenuit, et quatuor bovatas terre in villis et territorio de Wymundeham et Thorpeymere, unam scilicet quam habui de dono et concessione Radulphi Keynyn cum mesuagio pertinente, et unam bovatam et dimidiam quam habui de dono et concessione Ricardi Laundry, cum tofto quod Ricardus Griffin quondam tenuit in Wymondeham et sex acras terre de dominico meo in eadem villa, cum pratis, pascuis et pasturis et omnibus aliis libertatibus ad predicta tenementa spectantibus, habenda et tenenda omnia predicta tenementa perpetuis temporibus Deo et Beate Marie et capelle ejusdem Virginis, necnon et presbitero ibidem divina [f. 288] celebraturo ad perpetuam ipsius sustentationem in liberam, puram et perpetuam elemosinam cum omnibus libertatibus et aisiamentis in pratis, pascuis et pasturis, aquis, viis, semitis et omnibus aliis pertinenciis ad predicta tenementa spectantibus infra villam et extra, tam nominatis quam non nominatis. Volo etiam quod predictus presbiter per me vel heredes meos seu assignatos temporibus presentetur domino Lincoln' episcopo vel ejus vices gerenti. Et si ego, heredes vel assignati mei infra quadriganta dies ad predictam capellam presentare distulerimus a tempore vacationis, concedo quod dictus dominus episcopus vel vices ejus gerens possit idoneum presbiterum et non alium in inferioribus ordinibus constitutum in predicta capella instituere ea vice, absque prejudicio mei vel heredum mearum seu assignatorum tempore futuro, ita quod non liceat mihi, heredibus vel assignatis meis alium quam in sacerdotali ordine constitutum aliquo tempore ad predictam presentare capellam, qui quidem sacerdos statim a tempore

---

[1] Interlined.

sue admissionis continuam ibidem faciat residenciam personalem divina ut supradictum est celebrando. Nolo etiam quod predicti presbiteri per dominum episcopum vel vices ejus gerentem seu per me, heredes vel assignatos meos ad ipsam capellam successive admissi predicta tenementa vel partem ipsius possint cuicumque dare, vendere, assignare, legare vel alio modo alienare, vel in judaismo obligare seu ad firmam sine termino dimittere, sed ea omnia tenementa cum suis pertinenciis habeant in manu sua et teneant omnibus temporibus suis. Et sciendum quod si contingat quod presbiter ibidem divina celebraturus ex propria culpa suspendatur vel aliquo casu fortuito impediatur quominus servicium dicte capelle exerceatur, idem presbiter[1] presbiterum idoneum[1] loco sui sumptibus propriis inveniet ne dicta capella divinis defraudetur obsequiis, et idem capellanus capelle predicte fideliter ministrabit. Ego vero Willelmus Hamelyn, heredes vel assignati, dictam capellam sustinabimus, reparabimus, cooperiemus, et si necesse fuerit reedificabimus sumptibus nostris propriis, calicem, libros, vestimenta una cum luminari sufficienti et omnia alia ornamenta inveniemus in perpetuum. Ad que omnia et singula fideliter facienda volo et pro me et heredibus et assignatis concedo ordinario loci quotiens opus fuerit per censuram ecclesiasticam nos posse[1] cohercere. Si autem dictus capellanus absque sua culpa quominus ad tempus in dicta capella divinum obsequium exequi possit fuerit impeditus, videlicet quod si capella fuerit dirruta[2] vel discooperta vel aliqua in supradictis ad dictam capellam pertinentibus ob defectum mei, heredum seu assignatorum meorum defuerint, quod absit, idem capellanus interim in ecclesia parochiali divinum officium exequatur in forma prescripta quousque capella fuerit reparata vel reedificata vel dicta necessaria sibi competenter fuerint inventa. Predicti etiam capellani ad predictam capellam successive admissi in sua prima admissione coram domino episcopo vel vices ejus gerente prestito sacramento jurabunt quod omnia predicta tenementa, calicem, libros, vestimenta, luminaria et omnia alia ornamenta ad dictam capellam spectantia quantum in eis est salvo et fideliter custodient et facient custodiri. Et ego predictus Willelmus Hamelyn heredes seu assignati mei predicta mesuagia et prefata tenementa cum pratis, pascuis et pasturis, aquis, viis, semitis et cum omnibus aliis aisiamentis et libertatibus ad dicta tenementa spectantibus ut liberam, puram et perpetuam elemosinam sicut predictum est Deo et Beate Marie, Beato Johanni Baptiste et predictis capellanis ad

[1] Interlined.
[2] Sic.

dictam capellano successive admissis warantizabimus de omnibus scutagiis, wardis, releviis, eschaetis, maritagiis, auxiliis, sectis curiarum omnimodis comitatuum et wapentagiarum, murdis,[1] vigiliis communibus et de omnibus serviciis tam forinsecis quam aliis contra omnes homines tam christianos quam judeos in omnibus et per omnia adquietabimus et defendemus in perpetuum.[2] Si quis autem heredum vel assignatorum attemptaverit vel in aliquo forme prescripte ausu temerario contraire, vel cartam istam infringere presumpserit, nostram et indignationem omnipotentis Dei et Beate Marie Virginis et Beati Johannis Baptiste et omnium sanctorum et mei maledictionem se noverit incursurum.[3] Et ut hec mea duratio, concessio et quietaclamatio rata, stabilis et inconcussa permaneat in perpetuum huic scripto pro me, heredibus meis et assignatis sigillum meum apposui. Hiis testibus, domino Roberto Tibetoft, Domino Ricardo Le Grey. Domino Rogero Brabazun, Roberto de Chevercurt, Roberto de Sancto Petro, Willelmo de Purley, Johanne Duraunt et aliis. ... Item, tenor littere regis Talis est: Edwardus etc. Licet de communi consilio regni nostri statuerimus quod non liceat viris religiosis seu aliis ingredi feodum alicujus ita quod ad manum mortuam [*f. 288v*] deveniat sine licencia nostra et capitalis domini de quo res illa immediate tenetur, volentes/ tamen dilecto et fideli nostro Willelmo Hamelyn graciam facere specialem, dedimus ei licenciam quantum in nobis est quod ipse duo mesuagia et octo bovatas terre cum pertinenciis in Saxeby, Wymundham et Thorpeymere dare possit et assignare cuidam capellano divina celebranti in capella Beate Marie ex parte australi ecclesie de Wymundeham, habenda et tenenda eidem capellano et successoribus suis capellanis divina ibidem celebraturis imperpetuum, et eidem capellano quod ipse predicta mesuagia et terram a predicto Willelmo recipere possit tenore presentium similiter licenciam con- cedimus specialem, nolentes quod idem Willelmus vel heredes sui aut predictus capellanus seu successores sui ratione statuti predicti per nos vel heredes nostros inde occasionentur in aliquo vel graventur. Salvis tamen capitalibus dominis feodi illius serviciis inde debitis et consuetis. In cujus rei testimonium has litteras nostros fieri fecimus patentes. Teste meipso apud Westmonasterium decimo nono die Junii anno regni nostri XXI ... Item, tenor littere domini Edmundi talis est: Universis

---

[1] Sic for 'murdris'.
[2] Some of the contingencies seem highly improbable. The whole passage seems to have been borrowed from another charter to which it was more relevant.
[3] A formula borrowed from pre-Conquest diplomatic.

personis scriptum visuris vel audituris, Edmundus regis Anglie filius salutem in domino. Cum dominus Willelmus Hamelyn dederit, concesserit et assignaverit septem bovatas terre de feodo nostro et honore de Stapelford' Deo et Beate Marie et capelle in ejusdem honore fundate in ecclesia de Wymundeham ex parte australi ad sustentationem unius capellani pro salute anime sue, et Johanne quondam uxoris sue, necnon antecessorum et successorum suorum perpetuo celebrantis divina, quorum quidem septem[1] bovatarum terre quatuor jacent in villa et territorio de Saxby et alie tres jacent in villis et territoriis de Wymundham et Thorpeymere, nos volentes cultum divinum non minui sed augeri, predictas donationem, concessionem seu assignationem quantum in nobis est pro nobis et heredibus nostris ratas et gratas habemus, et eas tenore presentium confirmamus. Salvis nobis et heredibus nostris serviciis que pro predicta terra nobis hactenus fieri consueverunt per manus predicti domini Willelmi et heredorum suorum imperpetuum. In cujus rei testimonium huic scripto sigillum nostrum fecimus apponi. Hiis testibus, domino Waltero de Helyun tunc senescallo terrarum nostrarum in Anglia, Laurencio de Sancto Mauro, Rogero Brabazun, Thoma de Bray, Waltero de Wyther militibus, Hugone de Vienna, Johanne de Caleys, Waltero de Rading' et Johanne Basset clericis nostris et aliis. Datum apud Beurepeyr die Jovis in festo Exaltationis Sancte Crucis, anno regni Edwardi domini et fratris nostri karissimi octavodecimo: ... Item, tenor littere episcopi super approbatione et acceptatione concessionis et assignationis predictarum talis est: ... Universis etc. Oliverus etc. salutem in omnium salvatore. Universitati vestre certius innotescat quod nos quoddam scriptum dilecti in Christo filii domini Willelmi Hamelyn militis de Wymundeham nostre diocesis nobis absque ullo vitio sub sigillo suo exhibitum inspeximus sub hac forma: ... Dignum est, etc., ut supra ... Nos vero comperta juxta inquisitionem premissam prout negotii qualitas requirebat, pium ac decens esse et etiam expedire factum prescriptum adeo laudabiliter incohatum debita firmitate munire, et effectu prosequente complere, donationem, concessionem, assignationem et ordinationem prescriptas, consensu regio una cum consensu nobilis viri domini Edmundi comitis Leyc' capitalis domini terrarum et tenementorum concurrente, ad dicti domini Willelmi instanciam commendantes, approbantes et plenius acceptantes, illas quantum in nobis est auctoritate pontificali tenore presentium confirmamus. In cujus rei testimonium presens scriptum sigilli nostri appositione fecimus roborari.

---

[1] Interlined.

Datum apud Parcum Stowe nonis Mai anno domini M.CC. Nonagesimo sexto.

LONG WHATTON. R. Richard de Birchele ch. p. by the A. and C. of St. Mary de Pratis to the church of Long Whatton vacant by the death of Elias of Douai (Duaco). Granted the church *in commendam* for a period, then inst. Stow Park, June 20, 1296, and had letters patent.

EASTWELL. R. Walter of Barrow (Barwa) ch. p. by the A. and C. of St. Mary de Pratis to the church of Eastwell vacant because Richard de Birchele had been inst. to the church of Long Whatton. Inst. Nocton, July 5, 1296, and had letters patent.

DISHLEY. R. William of Buxton subd. re-presented by the A. and C. of St. Mary de Pratis to the church of Dishley vacant because the said William had not been ordained pr. within a year of institution. Inst. Sleaford, Aug. 11, 1296, and had letters patent.

[*f. 289*] BROUGHTON ASTLEY (Brocton', Broghton'). R. Roger de Baldington ch. p. by Sir Andrew of Astley (Astelee) knight to the church of Broughton Astley vacant by the res. of Master Walter of Hida. Inst. Stow Park, Oct. 13, 1296, and had letters patent.

KEGWORTH. R. Master Peter of Lek' p. by Sir John of Seagrave knight to the church of Kegworth vacant by the res. of Thomas de Neville. Inst. Buckden, Dec. 28, 1296, and had letters patent.

KIBWORTH HARCOURT (Kibwrth'). Master Bartholomew of Cowley (Covele) acolyte p. by the warden and scholars of Merton College, Oxford, to the chapel of Kibworth Harcourt vacant by the death of Master Geoffrey of Coddington. Inst. London O.T., Jan. 21, 1297.

RATCLIFFE-ON-THE-WREAK (Radeclive). V. William of Ratcliffe ch. by the P. and C. of Charley to the vicarage of Ratcliffe vacant by the death of Richard of Dunton. Inst. Buckden, Feb. 26, 1297.

FROWLESWORTH (Frolleswurth'). R. John Danvers, clerk in minor orders, p. by Thomas of Leicester to the church of Frowlesworth vacant by the death of Henry Danvers. Ordained subd. and inst. Brampton near Huntingdon, Mar. 9, 1297, and had letters patent.

SHEEPY (Schepeye). R. Geoffrey of Welford (Welleford') subd. p. by King Edward as guardian of the lands and heir of Sir Richard Harcourt knight to the mediety of the church of Sheepy vacant by the death of William Preston and the res. of Roger of Waltham who had been p. by the Bishop of Durham. Inst. Wooburn near Wycombe, Apr. 19, 1297, and had letters patent.

ROTHLEY (Rothele). V. Gilbert de Brueria ch. p. by Brian de Jay master of the Templars in England to the vicarage of Rothley vacant by the death of William of Warwick (Warewyk'). Inst. Berkhamstead, May 11, 1297.

––––––

[f. 289v] QUARTODECIMO KALENDAS JUNII VIDELICET DIE SANCTI DUNSTANI ANNO DOMINI M.CC. NONAGESIMO SEPTIMO INCIPIT ANNUS PONTIFICATUS DOMINI OLIVERI DEI GRACIA LINCOLN' EPISCOPI OCTAVUSDECIMUS.

––––––

HORNINGHOLD (Horningwold'). V. Thomas of Blaston ch. p. by Peter prior of Belvoir to the vicarage of Horninghold vacant by the death of Walter. Inst. May 22, 1297 (place not given).

GALBY. R. Master John of Stanton subd. p. by the master and brethren of the Hospital of Burton Lazars to the church of Galby vacant because of the unlicensed pluralism of Henry of Mersinton, and the fact that Sir Robert Burdet knight had not proceeded with his attempt to present another candidate. Inst. London, O.T., July 4, 1297, and had letters patent.

THRUSSINGTON (Thurstanton'). R. Thomas of Wolverton (Wiverton'), clerk in minor orders p. by the P. and C. of Sempringham to the church of Thrussington vacant by the res. of Henry of Hales. Ordained subd. and inst. Leicester, Sept. 21, 1297.

BARKBY (Barkeston'[1]). V. Robert of Croxton ch. p. by the A. and C. of St. Mary de Pratis to the vicarage of Barkby vacant by the death of William. Inst. Louth, Jan. 11, 1298.

COTES. R. Roger Mantil ch. p. by the Prior of the Hospitallers in England to the church of Cotes vacant by the res. of William of Gaddesby. Inst. Nettleham, Feb. 22, 1298.

[1] Corrected, in a later hand, to 'Barkeby'.

WITHCOTE. R. Ralph of Pilton subd. p. by the A. and C. of Owston to the church of Withcote vacant because Robert of Cranoe (Cravenhou) had been inst. to the church of Harrington. Inst. Nettleham, Mar. 1, 1298.

CHARLEY (Charle). Robert of Ratcliffe (Radeclive) canon of Charley elected to the office of prior thereof in succession to Thomas of Evesham who had joined the Cistercians and entered Garendon Abbey. Election submitted to the bishop, Lincoln, Mar. 18, 1298, and quashed by him for incorrect procedure and the unsuitablility of the candidate.[1]

[f. 290] CARLTON CURLIEU. R. Reginald of St. Evroult p. by Ralph prior of Ware, proctor-general in England of the A. and C. of St. Evroult, to the church of Carlton Curlieu vacant because Gilbert of Roubir' had been inst. to the church of Shillington. Haugh, Apr. 18, 1298.

———

QUARTODECIMO KALENDAS JUNII VIDELICET DIE SANCTI DUNSTANI ANNO DOMINI M.CC. NONAGESIMO OCTAVO, INCIPIT ANNUS PONTIFICATUS DOMINI OLIVERI EPISCOPI LINCOLN' NONUSDECIMUS.

———

SWINFORD. V. Richard of Shadwell (Schadewell') ch. p. by the Prior of the Hospitallers in England to the vicarage of Swinford vacant by the res. of Ranulph. Inst. London, O.T., June 30, 1298, and had letters patent.

CHARLEY. John of Bawtry elected to the office of prior of Charley vacant by the res. of Thomas of Evesham, who had joined the Cistercians at Garendon, and the rejection by the bishop of Richard of Ratcliffe (Redeclive) the first to be elected. Licence obtained from Sir William de Ferrariis as patron. Election quashed for irregular procedure, but John appointed as being the best candidate in the depressed state of the house (de alia persona dicte domui ipsius nimia paupertate et alio statu ejusdem inspectis non potuit ut videbatur melius consuli illa vice.) Banbury, Aug. 3, 1298.

[f. 290v] BRINGHURST (Brunghirst'). R. Master Henry Sampson the younger, p. by the A. and C. of Peterborough to the

———

[1] The two following entries, referring to Bolnhurst and Felmersham, are cancelled.

church of Bringhurst vacant by the death of William of Langton (Langeton'). Inst. Buckden, Aug. 15, 1298, and had letters patent.

SWITHLAND. R. Master Alexander of Bowden, clerk in minor orders p. by Ralph prior of Ware, proctor-general in England to the A. and C. of St. Evroult, to the church of Swithland vacant because Reginald of St. Evroult had been inst. to Carlton Curlieu. Ordained subd. and inst. Brampton near Huntingdon, Sept. 20, 1298.

KNIPTON (Gnipton'). R. Gilbert Avenel, clerk in minor orders p. by William Avenel to the church of Knipton vacant by the death of Hugh. Ordained subd. and inst. Brampton near Huntingdon, Sept. 20, 1298.

PECKLETON (Petlington'). R. Robert of Belchford (Beltesford') p. by William Motun to the church of Peckleton vacant by the death of John of Wootton (Wutton'). Inst. Nettleham, Nov. 23, 1298, and had letters patent.

OWSTON (Osolveston'). Richard of Boxworth (Bokeswrth') canon of Owston elected to be prior thereof in succession to Ernald who had died. Licence was obtained from the King as patron. Election submitted to the bishop for confirmation, Bassingham, Nov. 28, 1298, and confirmed Nov. 29. Solemn benediction of Richard as abbot, Dec. 28, 1298.

STAPLEFORD (Stapelford'). R. John called Whiteglove of Loughborough, clerk in minor orders p. by Thomas Earl of Lancaster to the church of Stapleford vacant by the res. of Richard of Loughborough. Ordained subd. and inst. Liddington, Dec. 20, 1298.

CONGERSTON (Cuningeston). R. Richard Charnels, clerk in minor orders p. by Ralph de Charnels to the church of Congerston vacant because Robert of Belchford had been inst. to Peckleton. Ordained subd. and inst. Liddington, Dec. 20, 1298.

THORNTON. V. Henry of Aylestone ch. p. by the A. and C. of St. Mary de Pratis to the vicarage of Thornton vacant by the death of Simon. Inst. Liddington, Jan. 7, 1299.

LITTLE DALBY. R. Robert Prudefot' pr. p. by the Prioress and C. of Langley to the church of Little Dalby vacant by the death of Hugh of Crick (Crek'). Presentation disputed by Sir

John Hamelyn knight. A royal writ (given in full, witnessed by J. de Metyngham and dated York, Jan. 24, 1299) directed the bishop to accept the prioress's candidate. Robert was inst. Liddington, Jan. 27, 1299.

LEICESTER, ST. LEONARD'S. V. William of Hauthon' ch. p. by the A. and C. of St. Mary de Pratis to the vicarage of St. Leonard's vacant by the death of Master John Halifax. Inst. Liddington, Feb. 8, 1299.

LEICESTER, ST. MARY DE CASTRO. V. Master Roger of Foston, ch. p. by the A. and C. of St. Mary de Pratis to the vicarage of St. Mary de Castro vacant because Henry of Aylestone had been inst. to the vicarage of Thornton. Inst. Liddington, Feb.8, 1299.

OWSTON (Osolveston'). V. Henry of Barkby ch. p. by the A. and C. of Owston to the vicarage vacant by the death of Richard. Inst. Liddington, Feb. 10, 1299.

LUTTERWORTH. Robert of Billesdon elected to the office of master of the Hospital of St. John Baptist at Lutterworth, vacant by the death of John of Hathern. Licence to elect obtained from the seneschal of Sir Theobald de Verdun acting on behalf of the said Sir Theobald. Election confirmed Liddington, Feb. 14, 1299.

GREAT GLEN. V. John of Oundle (Undel) pr. nominated by the bishop to the A. and C. of Alcester for presentation to the vicarage of Great Glen, after his first nominee, William of Swineshead (Swynesheved') had withdrawn. The vacancy was caused by the death of Robert of Edwinstone (Edenstowe), and the procedure followed was that laid down in the ordinance drawn up by Bishop Gravesend in 1266.[1] No inquiry was made, since the facts were well known to the bishop. Inst. Buckden, Mar. 10, 1299.

———

[f. 291v] QUARTODECIMO KALENDAS JUNII VIDELICET DIE SANCTI DUNSTANI ANNO DOMINI M.CC. NONAGESIMO NONO INCIPIT ANNUS PONTIFICATUS DOMINI OLIVERI EPISCOPI LINCOLN' VICESIMUS.

———

[1] L.R.S. 20, pp. 146–7.

SHOULDBY (Siwoldeby). R. John of Somerby, clerk in minor orders p. by the P. and C. of Launde to the church of Shouldby vacant because Robert Prudfot' had been inst. to Little Dalby. Ordained subd. Huntingdon June 13, 1299[1] and inst. Buckingham, June 14, 1299.

HARSTON (Hareston'). R. Thomas of Thorpe, clerk in minor orders, p. by the A. and C. of St. Mary de Pratis to the church of Harston vacant by the res. of Walter of Leicester. Ordained subd. Huntingdon, June 13, 1299 and inst. Buckingham June 14, 1299.

DISHLEY (Dixle). R. William de Werminitr' ch. p. by the A. and C. of St. Mary de Pratis to the church of Dishley vacant because William of Buxton had not been ordained pr. within a year of institution. Inst. Sleaford, July 20, 1299.

ASTON FLAMVILLE (Astonflamvyle). R. William of Stratford (Stretteford') ch. p. by Sir John of Hastings knight to the church of Aston Flamville vacant by the death of Geoffrey of Mountsorrel. Inst. Nettleham, Oct. 27, 1299.

ARCHDEACONRY OF HUNTINGDON 1290–99

[*f. 294*] INSTITUTIONES HUNTINGDON[2]

QUARTODECIMO KALENDAS JUNII DIE SANCTI DUNSTANI ANNO DOMINI M.CC. NONAGESIMO INCIPIT ANNUS PONTIFICATUS DOMINI OLIVERI EPISCOPI LYNC' UNDECIMUS.

WALKERN. R. Hervey de Launvaley subd. p. by the A. and C. of Colchester to the church of St Mary, Walkern, vacant by the death of William of Walkern & the res. of Hamo le

---

[1] Date wrongly given as July 15.
[2] This archdeaconry included the four northern rural deaneries of Hertfordshire, viz. Berkhampstead, Hertford, Hitchin and Baldock.

Parker, first presented. Presentation opposed by Sir Walter FitzWalter and Lady Avis de Grelle, who subsequently withdrew their objection. Inst. London, Old Temple, June 20, 1290.

STONELY (Stonle). John of Ripton, canon of St. Mary's, Huntingdon, appointed by the bishop, with licence from the patron of the house, Humphrey de Bohun Earl of Essex and Hereford, to the office of prior of Stonely, vacant by the death of Simon. Unsuccessful attempts had already been made to elect Walter of Gidding and Simon of Wool. Sleaford, July 19, 1290. Humphrey de Bohun's letter of assent received Sleaford, July 18. Letters announcing John's appointment sent to the Archdeacon of Huntingdon or his official and to Humphrey de Bohun, July 19.

Vacante prioratu de Stonle per mortem fratris Simonis ultimi prioris ejusdem, petita a domino Umfrido comite Essex' et Hereford' patrono domus eligendi licencia et optenta, fratres ejusdem loci concanonicum suum fratrem Walterum de Gidding ut dicebatur elegerunt. Cumque orta esset[1] inter ipsum fratrem Walterum et electores suos discordia, ita quod non habuit facultatem exeundi domum suam pro prosecutione negotii electionis ejusdem, ad instanciam cujusdam pro- curatoris sui, episcopus Magistro Henrico de Nassington' officiali suo in loco vicino dicto prioratui existente ad examinandum processum electionis facte de eodem fratre Waltero et ad pronunciandum et faciendum uno modo vel alio in ipso negotio quod secundum Deum et justiciam expedire videret vices suos commisit. Unde examinato negotio et admissis testibus, facta etiam relatione per eundem officialem de facto suo in hac parte, memoratus frater Walterus consensum patroni predicti impetrare non valens, cessit juri suo immo potius desistit a juris sui prosecutione. Quo facto, frater Simon de Wulle concanonicus dicte domus assistens dicto fratri Waltero prosequenti erga patronum pro consensu suo habendo, optinuit consensum ejusdem patroni per litteram patentem directam episcopo ut episcopus circa eundem[2] fratrem Simonem tanquam electum ut in ipsa littera dicebatur cum tamen nullimoda precessisset electio de eodem benignius exequi dignaretur. Quo comperto, episcopus eundem[2] fratrem Simonem, tum pro eo quod non fuerat electus a fratribus suis tum pro eo quod ad officium prioris minus ydoneus videbatur sicut constitit per visitationes episcopi prius factas in domo predicta, prorsus rejecit, dictis

[1] Interlined.
[2...2] Inserted in the margin.

canonicis contemplatione domini comitis predicti potetatem eligendi sibi personam ydoneam graciose concedens. Deinde memorati canonici fratrem Johannem de Ripton' canonicum domus beate Marie Huntingdon' sibi ut dicebatur elegerunt seu postularunt in priorem, cui dictus dominus comes per litteram patentem episcopo apud Lafford' XV kalendas Augusti anno domini M.CC. nonagesimo exhibitam et ostensam ad instanciam dictorum canonicorum de Stonle suum prestitit assensum prout in ipsa littera dicebatur. Set[1] quia non apparebat aliquis processus electionis facte de dicto fratre Johanne nec probatio electionis offerebatur licet requitetur cum effectu, episcopus constante sibi de consensu canonicorum de Stonle predictorum in dictum fratrem Johannem necnon de dimissione prioris de Huntingdon dicto fratri Johanni ad suasionem episcopi per litteram suam exhortatoriam dicto priori de Huntingdon' directam facta, die sequente loco predicto memoratum fratrem Johannem admisit, ipsumque instituendo in dicti prioratus de Stonle priorem prefecit. Unde prestito ab eo juramento de obediendo episcopo et suis officialibus in canonicis mandatis, scriptum fuit archidiacono Hunt' vel ejus officiali prout sequitur: ... O. etc. archidiacono Huntingdon vel ejus officiali salutem etc. Quia fratrem Johannem de Ripton canonicum monasterii beate Marie Hunt' in quem canonici prioratus de Stonle vacantis ad presens consenserunt ut eisdem preficeretur in priorem, patrono etiam ejusdem domus persone dicti fratris Johannis suum in hoc prebente assensum, admisimus, ipsumque dicti prioratus de Stonle instituendo prefecimus in priorem, vobis mandamus quatinus eundem fratrem Johannem in coporalem possessionem dicti prioratus inducatis, canonicis, fratribus conversis et ceteris dicte domus ministris injungentes vice nostra quod dicto fratri Johanni tanquam priori suo decetero plenius obediant et intendant. Valete. Datum apud Lafford' XIII kalendas Augusti pontificatus nostri anno XI. ... Item scriptum fuit dicto domino comiti ad instanciam dicti fratris Johannis sub forma infrascripta: Nobili viro domino Umfrido de Boun comiti Essex' et Hereford', Oliverus permissione divina Lincoln' episcopus salutem, graciam et benedictionem. Fratrem Johannem de Ripton' canonicum [f. 294v] monasterii de Huntingdon' cui vestrum per litteram vestram prebuistis assensum in priorem domus de Stonle juxta juris exigenciam auctoritate pontificali prefecimus hiis diebus, quod ad instanciam dicti fratris Johannis discretioni vestre significandum duximus per presentes. Valete. Datum apud Lafford' XIIII kalendas Augusti anno domini M.CC. nonagesimo.

[1] Sic, recte 'Sed'.

ST. MARY, HERTFORD (Sancte Marie Parve Hertford'). R. Henry of Sandridge (Sanrugge) ch. p. by the A. and C. of Waltham Holy Cross to the church of St. Mary, Hertford, vacant by the death of William. Inst. Louth, Aug. 28, 1290.

CHESTERTON. R. Henry of Mordon, ch. p. by the P. and C. of Royston to the church of Chesterton vacant by the death of Richard of Stamford. Inst. Buckden, Oct. 31, 1290.

WHEATHAMPSTEAD. R. William of Stockton pr. collated by the bishop to the church of Wheathampstead vacant by the death of Master John of Leicester. Inst., after a period when he held the church *in commendam*, Biggleswade, Nov. 23, 1290.

WYMONDLEY (Wylmundele). John of Wymondley, canon of the house, elected *per viam scrutinii* to the office of prior in succession to John of Mordon, deceased. Election confirmed Hitchin, Nov. 27, 1290.

CALDECOTE. R. Adam de la Mare, clerk in minor orders, p. by William of Hurst to the church of Caldecote vacant by the death of Simon of Bassingham. Had custody for a period. Ordained subd. and inst. Wycombe, Dec. 23, 1290.

WOOD WALTON. R. Hugh of Nottingham, clerk in minor orders, p. by the A. and C. of Ramsey to the church of Wood Walton vacant by the death of Richard of Stamford. Ordained subd. and inst. Wycombe, Dec. 23, 1290.

GLATTON. R. Robert of Swillington (Swylington') d. re-presented by the A. and C. of Missenden to the church of Glatton vacant because the said Robert had not been ordained priest within a year of institution. Fingest, Jan. 2, 1291.

GREAT GADDESDEN (Magna Gatesden'). R. Peter Martin subd. re-presented by Alan de la Zouche to the church of Great Gaddesden vacant because the said Peter had not been ordained priest within a year of institution. Eynsham, Feb. 25, 1291.

BROUGHTON (Brocton'). R. John of Sutton, clerk in minor orders p. by the A. and C. of Ramsey to the church of Broughton vacant by the death of Ivo. Had custody for a period. Ordained subd. and inst. Northampton, March 17, 1291.

[*f. 295*] ASPENDEN (Aspeden). V. John of Fincham, clerk in minor orders p. by Peter of Hagham acting as Provincial

Prior of the Hospitallers to the vicarage of Aspenden vacant because Master William had been inst. to the vicarage of Stratford. Ordained subd. and inst. Northampton, March 17, 1291.

GODMANCHESTER (Gumcestr'). V. Master John called Heare subd. p. by the P. and C. of Merton to the vicarage of Godmanchester vacant by the death of Reyner. Ordained d. and inst. Northampton, March 17, 1291.

ARDELEY[1] (Erdele). V. Edmund of Clavering ch. p. by Master Robert Archdeacon of Essex, representing the dean and the chapter of St. Paul's Cathedral to the vicarage newly set up in the church of Ardeley. Inst. Daventry, March 16, 1291. Sutton's ordinance establishing the vicarage is given in full. Same place and date.

Edmundo de Clavering capellano ad vicariam ecclesie de Erdele ordinandam per Magistrum Robertum Archidiaconum Essex', gerentem vices Decani sancti Pauli London', et ejusdem loci capitulum presentato sub hac forma: Venerabili in Christo patri domino O. dei gracia Lincoln' episcopo sui humiles et devoti R. Archidiaconus gerens vices Decani sancti Pauli London' et capitulum loci ejusdem salutem, reverenciam et honorem. Ut in ecclesia nostra de Erdele vestre diocesis, comune nostre usibus deputata, perpetuus instituatur vicarius penes quem ejusdem ecclesie cura resideat, et qui onera ordinaria ejusdem ecclesie excepta refectione cancelli sustineat in futurum, omnes oblationes et minutas decimas ipsius parochie quas presbiter parochialis ejusdem percipere hactenus consuevit, una cum dimidia marca de nobis annuatim percipienda ad sustentationem vicarii in eadem ecclesia, una cum manso in quo dictus presbiter inhabitare solebat tenore presentium assignamus, ad quam vicariam in hujusmodi videlicet portionibus consistentem, seu ad portiones ipsas nomine vicarie, Edmundum de Clavering capellanum vobis presentamus, humiliter supplicantes ut ipsum juxta formam hujus presentationis admittere et vicarium in eadem instituere volitis,[2] salvis nobis et successoribus nostris omnibus que extra portiones premissas ad nos spectare solebant. In cujus rei testimonium sigillum capituli nostri apponi fecimus. Datum in capitulo nostro die circumcisionis domini anno ejusdem

[1] The words 'ordinatio vicarie' have been added in the margin in a fourteenth century hand.
[2] Sic.

M.CC. nonagesimo.[1] ... factaque inquisitione per officialem R. Archidiaconi Huntingdon' per quam acceptum extitit, quod omnes oblationes et obventiones debite et consuete minute decime, saltem in aucis, porcellis, vitulis, pullis equorum, lana, agnis, lacte, lino, gardinis, mercatoribus, columbariis et aliis minutis quas presbiter parochialis consuevit percipere existentes et ad dictam ecclesiam pertinentes valent per annum octo marcas, mansus autem ad dictam vicariam deputatus est infra cimiterium et non est satis competens. Onera autem ecclesie predicte incumbentia sunt hec, sustentatio vicarii et unius clerici, procuratio archidiaconi, sinodalia et *Letare* quibus modo onerandus est vicarius per formam presentationis. Oblationes, obventiones et minute decime supradicte ad congruam sustentationem vicarii non sufficiunt. Competenter tamen posset sustentari habito respectu ad facultates ejusdem si viginti acre terre, de terra ad dictam ecclesiam spectante, dicte vicarie essent assignate, in quibus convenientius dicta vicaria poteret ordinari, suggesto dictis decano et capitulo quod adjectioni viginti acrarum predictarum suum preberent assensum, ipsisque suasioni hujusmodi quiescentibus suum adjectioni predicte consensum prebendo, episcopus XVII kalendas Aprilis anno domini M.CC. non-agesimo apud Daventr' vicariam predictam prout sequitur ordinavit. ... In Dei nomine amen. Nos Oliverus permissione divina Lincoln' episcopus, visa inquisitione facta ad presen-tationem discreti viri Magistri [*f. 295v*] Roberti Archidiaconi Essex' vices Decani ecclesie sancti Pauli London' in ejus absencia gerentis et capituli ejusdem loci factam de Edmundo de Clavering capellano ad vicariam in parochiale ecclesia de Erdele nostre diocesis usibus eorundem decani et capituli appropriata per nos ordinandum, et ejusmodi inquisitione et ipsius ecclesie facultatibus exquisitius ponderatis, habita etiam prout honeste potuimus consideratione ad formam littere presentationis predicte et alia in hac parte pensanda, statuimus et ordinamus quod vicaria in dicta ecclesia perpetuis temporibus maneat in futurum, cujus vicarius inibi instituendus habeat omnes obventiones altaragii, utputa decima lane, agnorum, lactis, lini, canabi, aucarum, gallinorum, porcellorum, vitulorum, pullorum equinorum, gardinorum, negotiationum, columbariorum et aliorum minutorum quocumque nomine censeantur, una cum omnimodis oblationibus et mortuariis, necnon viginti acris terre propinquioris illo loco, in quo rector dicte ecclesie antiquitus degere consuevit, ad eandem ecclesiam pertinentis. Qui quidem vicarius solvet sinodalia, *Letare Jerusalem*, libros, vestimenta et alia ornamenta, luminare

[1] Jan. 1, 1291.

competens in cancello, vinum, oblatas, ac clerum ydoneum et hiis similia inveniet et exhibebit. Dicti vero decanus et capitulum cancellum reficient et reparabunt quotiens res exegerit illum refici vel reparari debere. Extraordinaria etiam onera veluti decimam, quintamdecimam[1] et consimiliam prestationem cum contigerit plenius agnoscent. Ceterum quantum ad procurationem archidiaconi quam dicti decani et capitulum de jure invenire tenentur nisi aliter specialius ordinetur, volumus et ordinamus quod ipsi vicario pro tempore existenti annuatim in festo nativitatis sancti Johannis Baptiste solvant dimidiam marcam ita quod ipse vicarius onus hujusmodi procurationis supportet. Quod si iidem decanus et capitulum in prestatione dicte dimidie marce cessarint, ex tunc teneantur loci archidiaconum procurare. Incompetenciam mansi quem ad vicarium dicti decanus et capitulum assignari petebant emendari facient prout decet. Hanc autem ordin-ationem volumus firmiter observari, ipsam tamen mutandi, corrigendi, augmentandi ac interpretandi et declarandi si quid in ea ambiguum fuerit vel obscurum nobis et successoribus nostris cum visa fuerit opportunum potestate specialiter reservata. ... Quibus peractis dictus Edmundus ad prefatam vicariam est admissus XVII kalendas Aprilis anno X1 apud Daventr' et vicarius perpetuus cum onere personaliter ministrandi et continue residendi canonice institutus in eadem, jurataque episcopo canonica obediencia, etc. scriptum est, etc.

ST. GILES' NEAR BERKHAMPSTEAD. Joan of Wheathampstead, nun of St. Giles', elected *per viam inspirationis* to the office of prioress in succession to Lora who had died. Licence to elect given by Sir Ralph de Thony the patron. Election confirmed by Master Walter of Wootton, canon of Lincoln, to whom the bishop had deputed the task 'because of the poverty of the said nuns', St. Giles' near Berkhampstead, Mar. 25, 1291.

ROWNER (Rouney).[2] Alice of Chingford, sub-prioress of Rowner, elected *per viam inspirationis* to the office of prioress in succession to Agnes of London who had resigned. Licence to elect given by Sir William of Kirkby the patron. Election confirmed Lutterworth, Sept. 19, 1291.

---

[1] Interlined.
[2] This entry, in John de Scalleby's hand, is at the foot of the page and seems to have been misplaced from the following year of Sutton's episcopate.

[*f. 296*] QUARTODECIMO KALENDAS JUNII VIDELICET DIE SANCTI DUNSTANI ANNO DOMINI M.CC. NONAGESIMO PRIMO INCIPIT ANNUS PONTIFICATUS DOMINI OLIVERI EPISCOPI LINCOLN' DUODECIMUS.

––––––––

KING'S RIPTON. R. Roger of Ashridge (Asserigge) subd. p. by the King to the church of King's Ripton vacant by the death of Henry of Westminster (Westmonasterio). Inst. Sleaford, June 23, 1291.

BRINGTON (Brincton'). R. John Maunsel pr. p. by the A. and C. of Ramsey to the church of Brington vacant by the lapse of two years since the grant of a papal indulgence to Master William of Clifford, Bishop of Emly, to hold in plurality with his see the church of Brington with its dependent chapels of Old Weston and Bythorn, and of a further two years during which Master William claimed to be seeking a renewal of his indulgence. Sir William of Hamilton, first presented, had not wished to be instituted. Inst. Spaldwick, July 7, 1291.

ABBOT'S RIPTON (Ripton' Abbatis). R. John of Gateford (Geytford') d. p. by the A. and C. of Ramsey to the church of Abbot's Ripton vacant because John Maunsel had been inst. to Brington. Inst. Spaldwick, July 14, 1291.

BENNINGTON. R. Henry of Edstone (Edriston'), clerk in minor orders p. by Sir Alexander de Balliol (Balliolo) to the church of Bennington vacant by the death of Henry de Balliol. Ordained subd. and inst. Wycombe, Dec. 22, 1291.

SOMERSHAM. R. Master John d'Osevile pr. by W. bishop of Ely[1] to the church of Somersham vacant by the res. of Master Guy de Tilbrok'. Inst. in the person of Master Walter of Wootton, canon of Lincoln, his proctor, Canterbury, Mar. 15, 1292.

BROUGHTON (Brocton'). R. John of Sutton, clerk in minor orders re-presented by the A. and C. of Ramsey to the church of Broughton vacant because the said John had not been ordained pr. within a year of institution. Inst. Wheathampstead, Mar. 26, 1292.

ABBOT'S RIPTON (Ripton' Abbatis). R. Master Reginald of St. Alban's pr. by the A. and C. of Ramsey to the church of

––––––––

[1] William of Louth, bishop from 1290–1298.

Abbot's Ripton vacant by the res. of John of Gateford. Inst. in the person of Master Gerard of Stondon (Staundon') his proctor London, Old Temple, Apr. 17, 1292.

DIE SANCTI DUNSTANI VIDELICET QUARTODECIMO KALENDAS JUNII ANNO DOMINI M.CC. NONAGESIMO SECUNDO INCIPIT ANNUS PONTIFICATUS DOMINI OLIVERI DEI GRACIA EPISCOPI LINCOLNIEN' TERTIUS-DECIMUS.

SHENLEY (Schenle). R. Richard of Barford (Bereford') subd. p. by the King to the church of Shenley vacant because John of Wyddial (Wydihill') had been deprived[1] after an inquiry carried out by Bishop Sutton's official, acting as his special commissary. Inst. in the person of Philip of Hardwick (Herdewyk') clerk, his proctor, Leicester, May 26, 1292.

WOODSTONE (Wudestone'). R. William of Spanby (Spannesby) ch. p. by the A. and C. of Thorney to the church of St. Augustine at Woodstone vacant by the res. of Nicholas of Sparkford. Inst. in the person of Robert of Spanby clerk, his proctor, Stow Park, June 8, 1292.

GREAT STAUGHTON (Stokton'). R. Richard Delisle (de Insula) d. p. by Sir Adam of Creeting (Cretting) knight to the church of Great Staughton vacant by the res. of John Dupont (de Ponte). Inst. Stow Park, June 13, 1292.

ALCONBURY (Alkemundbir'). V. Richard Louve of St. Edmund's ch. p. by the P. and C. of Merton to the vicarage of Alconbury vacant by the death of John of Appletree (Appeltre). Inst Stow Park, June 17, 1292.

HADDON. R. John of Nassington ch. p. by the A. and C. of Thorney to the church vacant by the res. of Master Alan of Frieston (Freston'). Inst. Banbury, Oct. 6, 1292.

DATCHWORTH (Dachewrth'). R. Thomas of Ayot (Ayete) pr. p. by Sir Robert FitzWalter knight to the church of Datchworth vacant because Walter de Gyse had been inst. to the church of Cosgrave. Inst. Spaldwick, Nov. 21, 1292.

---

[1] 'privato et sentencialiter amoto'.

[*f. 297*] WELWYN (Weluwes). R. John of Paxton pr. p. by Christina prioress of Haliwell and the convent thereof to the church of Welwyn vacant by the death of Master Merlo. Presentation disputed by Adam de Maundevile. Case settled in favour of Haliwell, writ dated Westminster Dec. 2, 1292, witnessed by J. of Mettingham. Inst. Dorchester-on-Thames, Dec. 9, 1292.[1]

ST. ANDREW, HUNTINGDON. R. Ascelin of Bury (Biry), clerk in minor orders p. by the A. and C. of Ramsey to the church of St. Andrew, Huntingdon vacant by the death of John of St. Ives (de sancto Ivone). Ordained subd. and inst. Dorchester-on-Thames, Dec. 20, 1292.

ST. MARY, HERTFORD. R. Henry of Swavesey ch. p. by the A. and C. of Waltham Holy Cross to the church of St. Mary, Hertford, vacant by the death of Henry of Sandridge (Sanderigg'). Inst. Fingest Jan. 27, 1293.

ST. JAMES NEAR HUNTINGDON. Alice of Barwick subprioress elected 'after their fashion'[2] to the office of prioress of St. James's vacant by the death of Helen Welsh (la Waleys). Election confirmed, in consideration of the 'simplicity and inexperience'[3] of the electors, London, Old Temple, Mar. 15, 1293.

ST. NEOT'S. John de Sicca Valle, monk of Bec, p. by Ymer Abbot of Bec to the office of Prior of St. Neot's, vacant by the res. of John de Bois Reynaud. The abbot's letter of presentation, dated at Bec June 30, 1292, and given in full, was technically incorrect. John de Bois Reynaud's letter of resignation, given in full and dated Ogbourne, Aug. 31, 1292, was produced by the prior-elect on the bishop's demand. The Earl of Gloucester, patron, opposed the presentation unless his consent were obtained, and his argument was supported by evidence from the register of Hugh of Wells. He gave his consent in a letter, given in full and dated at Westminster, Apr. 22, 1293. John de Sicca Villa was admitted London, Old Temple, Apr. 23, 1293.

Memorandum quod nonis Augusti anno XIII apud Parcum Stowe venit frater Johannes de Sicca Valle monachus monasterii de Becco Heluini exhibens episcopo quamdam litteram

---

[1] The next entry, referring to Heyford, is cancelled.
[2] 'suo modo'.
[3] 'simplicitatem et imperitiam'.

patentem sigillo abbatis ejusdem monasterii ut prima facie videbatur signatam sub continentia infrascripta: Reverendo in Christo patri ac domino carissimo, domino O. Dei gracia Lincoln' episcopo, Ymerus permissione divina humilis abbas monasterii beate Marie de Becco Heluini salutem in domino sempiternam cum omni reverencia pariter et honore. Presentamus vobis dilectum filium in Christo [*f. 297v*] fratrem Johannem de Sicca Valle monachum nostrum cui commisimus curam et administrationem prioratus nostre de sancto Neoto, paternitati vestre humiliter supplicantes quatinus ipsum in priorem prioratus nostri predicti admittere benigne dignemini et velitis. Valeat et vigeat paternitas vestra reverenda bene et diu in domino Jesu Christo. Datum anno domini M.CC. nonagesimo secundo die lune proxima post festum apostolorum Petri et Pauli. ..8. Cumque super resignatione fratris Johannis de Bosco Reynaldi ultimi prioris ejusdem loci per Abbatem de Becco revocati et in priorem de Couwyk'¹ Exon' diocesis ut dicebatur prefati, quam episcopus necessariam asserebat ad hoc quod posset dicti vacans hujusmodi prioratus, et super formam littere predicte ac aliis esset aliquamdiu altercatum, prout in rotulo custodiarum² plenius continetur, demum dictus frater Johannes de Sicca Valle presentatus ad tunc recedens et post aliquod temporis spacium ad episcopum rediens litteram resignatoriam dicti fratris Johannis de Bosco Reynaldi episcopo exhibuit sub hac forma: Pateat universis quod nos frater Johannes de Bosco Reynaldi quondam prior de sancto Neoto quondam regimini nostre commissum pure, sponte et absolute tenore presentium resignamus, juri si quod nobis competere dicatur in eodem penitus renunciantes. In cujus rei testimonium, quia sigillum proprium non habeamus, sigillum officialis prebende de Okeburn' nobis procurantibus presentibus est appensum. Datum apud Okeburn' die dominica proxime post festum decollationis beate Johannis Baptiste anno gracie M.CC. nonagesimo secundo. ... Verum quia dominus comes Glovernie patronus domus de sancto Neoto medio tempore se opposuerat, provocando et appellando ne absque ipsius consensu admitteretur presentatus predictus, compertumque fuerat in registro quondam Hugonis de Welles episcopum Lincoln' consensum cujusdam progenitoris sui in casu hujusmodi adhibitum extitisse, dictus presentatus prefatum dominum comitem adiens post multum temporis ad episcopum rediit, exhibens sibi litteram dicti domini comitis sub hac forma: Reverendo patri in Christo

¹ Cowick Priory, in Devon.
² This roll is lost.

domino O. Dei gracia Lincoln' episcopo, G. de Clara comes Glouc' et Hereford' salutem, reverenciam et honorem. Presentavit nobis Ymerius[1] Dei gracia Abbas de Becco Heluini fratrem Johannem de Sicca Villa commonachum suum de Becco ad prioratum sancti Neoti vestre diocesis, quem ad presentationem predictam gratanter admisimus, paternitatem vestram rogantes quatinus ipsum ad curam et regimen dicti prioratus prout vestro incumbit officio admittere velitis. In cujus rei testimonium has litteras nostras vobis transmittimus patentes. Datum apud Westmonasterium XXII die Aprilis anno domini M.CC. nonagesimo tertio. ... Episcopus vero intellectis premissis licet littera presentationis predicta videretur calumpnie subjacere, in hiis verbis 'cui commisimus curam et administrationem prioratus nostri' etc. cum ad ipsum non pertineret curam committere set[1] solummodo presentare, volens tamen graciose agere cum predicto fratre Johanne presentato, ipsum ad dictum prioratum admisit et priorem IX Kalendas Maii anno XIII apud Vetus Templum London' canonice instituit in eodem, curam et administrationem dicte domus in spiritualibus et temporalibus sibi plenius committendo. Jurataque etc., scriptum fuit, etc.

———

DIE SANCTI DUNSTANI VIDELICET QUARTODECIMO KALENDAS JUNII ANNO DOMINI M.CC. NONAGESIMO TERTIO INCIPIT ANNUS PONTIFI- CATUS DOMINI OLIVERI LINCOLNIEN' EPISCOPI QUARTUSDECIMUS.

———

ST. ANDREW, HERTFORD. R. Philip of Hardwick, clerk in minor orders p. by the King to the church of St. Andrew, Hertford, vacant because Richard of Barford (Berford') had been inst. to Shenley. Ordained subd. (by licence of the Bishop of London) and inst. London, Old Temple, May 23, 1293.

HINXWORTH (Hengstewrth'). R. Peter of Leicester d. p. by Lady Millicent de Montalt to the church of Hinxworth vacant by the death of Master Thomas of Sechefeld'. Inst. in the person of Alan of Barkby his proctor, Banbury, July 21, 1293. Note that though no other presentation reached the bishop, the right of Lady Millicent and John of Hastings[2] was contested by Isobel widow of Ralph de Scopham and settled in favour of the former. Writ dated at Westminster June 30, 1293, and witnessed by J. of Mettingham.

———

[1] Sic.
[2] Who is not mentioned previously in this entry.

[*f. 298*] LITTLE GADDESDEN. V. Richard of Heyford ch. p. by the A. and C. of St. James outside Northampton to the vicarage of Little Gaddesden vacant by the death of Robert. Inst. Theydon Mount, Oct. 15, 1293.

WYMONDLEY. V. William of Bedford ch. p. by the P. and C. of Wymondley to the vicarage thereof vacant by the death of John. Inst. London, Old Temple, Dec. 6, 1293.

WARBOYS. R. Master Nicholas of Elton (Aylington') clerk in minor orders p. by the A. and C. of Ramsey to the church of Warboys vacant by the death of Walter. Had custody for a period. Ordained subd. and inst. Wycombe, Dec. 9, 1293.

GLATTON. R. Sir Robert of Swillington d. re-presented by the A. and C. of Missenden to the church of Glatton vacant because the said Robert had not been ordained pr. within a year of institution. Inst., in the person of John de Scalleby his proctor, Cheshunt, Apr. 20, 1294.

CONINGTON. R. Gilbert of Shengay ch. p. by Sir Robert de Bayus knight to the church of Conington vacant by the death of Richard. Inst Spaldwick, Apr. 30, 1294.

BRADFIELD. R. William of Dunham ch. p. by Master John de Wengham, precentor of St. Paul's Cathedral, to the church of Bradfield vacant by the death of Simon. Inst. Watton near Ware, May 9, 1294.

———

[*f. 298v*] DIE SANCTI DUNSTANI EPISCOPI VIDELICET QUARTODECIMO KALENDAS JUNII ANNO DOMINI MILLESIMO DUCENTESIMO NONAGESIMO QUARTO INCIPIT ANNUS PONTIFICATUS DOMINI OLIVERI DEI GRACIA LINCOLN' EPISCOPI QUINTUSDECIMUS.

———

WOOD WALTON. R. Roger de Castr', clerk in minor orders p. by the A. and C. of Ramsey to the church of Wood Walton vacant by the res. of Sir Hugh of Nottingham. Ordained subd. and inst. London, Old Temple, June 12, 1294.

ORTON LONGUEVILLE. R. Philip of Faversham ch. p. by Sir Henry de Longueville knight to the church of Orton Longueville vacant by the death of William. Inst. Basingstoke, July 18, 1294.

KNEBWORTH. R. William of Offley ch. p. by Sir Robert of Hoo knight to the church of Knebworth vacant by the death of Richard d'Audavilla. Inst. Dunstable, Sept. 18, 1294.

WATER NEWTON. R. Thomas of Burgh, clerk in minor orders[1] p. by the A. and C. of Thorney to the church of All Saints Water Newton vacant by the death of Gumbald Market (de Mercato). Had custody for a period. Ordained subd. and inst. Dunstable, Sept. 18, 1294.

FOLKSWORTH. R. Master Nicholas of Calton (Calveton') subd. p. by the A. and C. of Crowland to the church of Folksworth vacant because Master Thomas of Freston had been inst. to the church of Paston.[2] Inst. Nettleham, Nov. 12, 1294.

BERKHAMSTEAD. R. Roger de Castr' subd. p. by Brother William called Le Clerk, proctor of the A. and C. of Grestein, to the church of Berkhamstead vacant by the res. of Hugh of Nottingham (Notingham). Nettleham, Feb. 10, 1295.

STIBBINGTON. R. Institutio Willelmi de Spanneby in ecclesia de Stibington' que hic deberet inseri inseritur in archidiaconatu Lincoln'.[3]

[f. 299] DATCHWORTH. R. Ralph of Higham, clerk in minor orders p. by Sir Robert FitzWalter to the church of Datchworth vacant by the res. of Thomas of Ayot (Ayete) the incumbent and of Roger of Foxley, clerk, first presented. Ordained subd. and inst. Lincoln, Feb 26, 1295.

SOUTHOE. R. Ralph of Cambridge ch. p. by the P. and C. of Huntingdon to the church of Southoe vacant by the res. of Master John of St. Leofard. Inst. Stixwould Mar. 4, 1295.

LETCHWORTH. R. John of Ulceby, clerk in minor orders provided by the Pope to the church of Letchworth in succession to Gregory of Staines who had died at Rome. Executors, the Bishop of Durham, the Dean of St. Paul's and Master Geoffrey of Piacenza canon of Tournai. Notary-public, William de Pisquerio. Inst. in the person of Richard of Ulceby clerk his proctor, Feb. 27, 1296.

[1] Wrongly called subd.
[2] See L.R.S. vol. 43, p. 117.
[3] William of Spanby ch. p. by the A. and C. of Thorney to the church of Stibbington vacant by the lapse of its commendation to William of Coppingford (Copmanford') pr. Inst. Louth Jan. 3, 1295. (register, f. 228) The entry was wrongly recorded in the archdeaconry of Lincoln. L.R.S. vol. 39, p. 196.

TRING (Treng'). R. Robert Inge ch. p. by the A. and C. of Faversham to the church of Tring vacant by the res. of Gilbert[1] f Ivinghoe. Inst. Nettleham, Mar. 18, 1295.

LITTLE GADDESDEN. V. Adam of Hanging Houghton (Hangendehouton'). Subd. p. by the A. and C. of St. James outside Northampton to the vicarage of Little Gaddesden vacant by the res. of Richard of Heyford. Ordained d. and inst. Stow in Lindsey, Mar. 19, 1295.

———

DIE SANCTI DUNSTANI EPISCOPI VIDELICET QUARTODECIMO KALENDAS JUNII ANNO DOMINI M.CC. NONAGESIMO QUINTO INCIPIT ANNUS PONTIFICATUS DOMINI OLIVERI LINCOLN' EPISCOPI SEXTUSDECIMUS.

———

WOODSTONE. R. Institutio Johannis Derling in ecclesia de Wudeston' que deberet hic inseri inseritur inter institutiones archidiaconatus Buck' de anno suprascripto.

WOOD WALTON. R. John of Ipswich, clerk in minor orders, p. by the A. and C. of Ramsey to the church of Wood Walton vacant because Roger de Castr' had been inst. to St. Peter's Berkhampstead. Had custody for a period. Then ordained subd. (by licence of the Bishop of London) and inst. London, Old Temple, May 28, 1295.

HEMINGFORD ABBOTS. R. Robert of Sawtry, clerk in minor orders, p. by the A. and C. of Ramsey to the church of Hemmingford Abbots vacant by the death of John Clarel. Ordained subd. (by licence of the Bishop of London) and inst. London, Old Temple, May 28, 1295.

[f. 300] LILLEY. R. William Abel, clerk in minor orders, p. by John Peyure knight to the church of Lilley vacant by the death of John de Castello. Ordained subd. and inst. (by licence of the Bishop of London), London, Old Temple, May 28, 1295.

ELLINGTON. R. Robert of Barford (Bereford) ch. p. by the A. and C. of Ramsey to the church of Ellington vacant by the death of Master John de Ravenghom. Inst. Spaldwick, Nov. 2, 1295.

---

[1] Almost illegible.

PAXTON. V. William of Hampton ch. p. by the Dean and Chapter of Lincoln to the vicarage of Paxton vacant by the death of Thomas of Banbury. Inst. Biggleswade, Dec. 20, 1295.

KEYSTON (Kestan'). R. Hugh of Birdsall (Brideshale), clerk in minor orders p. by the Lady Eleanor Ferrars, Countess of Derby, to the church of Keyston vacant by the death of Robert of Higham. Ordained subd. and inst. Huntingdon, Dec. 17, 1295.

THURNING (Thirning).[1] R. Ralph de Culverdon', clerk in minor orders p. by Gilbert de Clare, Earl of Gloucester and Hereford, to the church of Thurning vacant by the res. of Sir Simon of Elsworth (Ellesworth'). Had custody for a period. Then ordained subd. and inst. Huntingdon, Dec. 17, 1295.

NORTH MIMMS. R. John of Kirkby, clerk in minor orders p. by Peter Pygot *alias* Pykot to the church of North Mimms vacant by the death of Hugh Birne. The presentation was opposed by Ranulf de Montchesney who himself presented the said John of Kirkby, and by Walter Castle (de Castello) and Sara his wife who presented John de Roubir'. Writ in favour of Peter Pygot against Walter and Sara, Westminster, July 4, 1295, and against Ranulf de Montchesney, Westminster, July 10, 1295. Writ in favour of Ranulf against Walter and Sara, Westminster, July 4, 1295. All witnessed by J. of Mettingham. John of Kirkby, having been previously ordained subd., was inst. on the presentation of Peter Pykot, Fingest, Jan. 7, 1296.

[*f. 300v*] OFFLEY. V. Richard of Eycote ch. p. by Master Thomas of Siddington (Sudington') rector of Offley to the vicarage thereof vacant by the res. of William. The P. and C. of Bradstone, patrons of the church, signified consent by letters patent. Banbury, Feb. 14, 1296.

HINXWORTH (Henxstewurth'). R. Hugh of Leicester (Leyc') ch. p. by Lady Millicent de Montalt to the church of Hinxworth vacant by the res. of Peter of Leicester. Inst. Banbury, Feb. 8, 1296.

ORTON WATERVILLE. R. William of Carleton, clerk in minor orders, p. by Robert de Waterville to the church of Orton Waterville, vacant by the death of Roger of Witham (Wyma) and the res. of John of Husthwaite first presented. Ordained subd. and inst. Rothwell, Feb. 18, 1296.

---

[1] This entry really belongs to the Archdeaconry of Northampton.

FENSTANTON. R. Master Gilbert of Seagrave (Segrave) ch. p. by Sir Nicholas of Seagrave to the church of Fen Stanton vacant by the res. of the said Master Gilbert on being inst. to the church of Aylestone near Leicester. Held *in commendam* for a time. Meanwhile Sir Nicholas died, and his son and heir Sir John of Seagrave re-presented Gilbert, who was inst. Lidding-ton, Mar. 2, 1296. No mention of an indulgence to hold in plurality.

ST. JOHN, HUNTINGDON. R. Roger of Kimbolton (Kynebauton') ch. p. by the P. and C. of Huntingdon to the church of St John, vacant by the death of John of Lindsey. Inst. Nettleham, Apr. 11, 1296.

———

DIE SANCTI DUNSTANI EPISCOPI VIDELICET QUARTODECIMO KALENDAS JUNII ANNO DOMINI M.CC. NONAGESIMO SEXTO INCIPIT ANNUS PONTIFICATUS DOMINI OLIVERI LINCOLNIEN' EPISCOPI SEXTUS-DECIMUS.

———

LITTLE BERKHAMSTEAD (Parva Berkhamsted'). R. Michael Crok', clerk in minor orders p. by the P. and C. of Lewes to the church of Little Berkhamstead vacant by the death of Simon. Ordained subd. and inst. Lincoln, May 19, 1296.

WASHINGLEY (Wassingle). R. Alan of Bullington (Boliton'), clerk in minor orders p. by Humphrey of Walden (Waleden'), by reason of his custody of the lands and heir of Ralph of Washingley, to the church of Washingley vacant by the death of Hugh. Ordained subd. and inst. Lincoln, May 19, 1296.

[*f. 301*] MORBORNE (Morburn'). R. John of March, clerk in minor orders p. by the A. and C. of Crowland to the church of Morborne vacant by the res. of Robert de Greneburn'. Ordained subd. and inst. Lincoln, May 19, 1296.

EYNESBURY. R. Hugh of Enfield, clerk in minor orders, p. by Lady Eleanor Ferrars Countess of Derby and John Ferrars to the church of Eynesbury vacant by the death of Master Richard of Clifford. Presentation opposed in the King's Courts by Sir Thomas de Berkele and Joan his wife and by Sir John Comyn Earl of Buchan (Boghan) who presented other clerks. Writ in favour of John Ferrars against John Comyn and Elizabeth his mother, St. Ives, Mar. 29, 1296, witnessed by

Robert of Retford (Henry Spigurnel also being present). Writ in favour Eleanor Ferrars against Thomas and Joan of Berkeley and John Ferrars Westminster Nov.[1] 29, 1296. Witnessed by J. of Mettingham. Eleanor and John Ferrars thereafter seem to have agreed on the presentation. Ordained subd. and inst. Lincoln, May 19, 1296.

STAPLEFORD. R. Hugh of Noseley (Novesle) ch. p. by Godfrey of Acre (Acr') clerk, proctor of Sir Hugh of Bardolf who was abroad, to the church of Stapleford vacant by the death of Roger of Rattlesden. Inst. Sleaford, July 8, 1296.

ASTON. R. Robert of Guildford, clerk in minor orders p. by the A. and C. of Reading to the church of Aston vacant by the death of Walter of Graveley. Ordained subd. and inst. Lincoln, Sept. 22, 1296.

HARTFORD (Hereford') V. John of Hargrave d. p. by the P. and C. of St. Mary's Huntingdon to the vicarage of Hartford near Huntingdon vacant by the death of Elias. Inst. Sutton-on-Trent, Oct. 8, 1296.

[f. 301v] STANGROUND. R. William of Spanby ch. p. by the A. and C. of Thorney to the church of Stanground vacant by the death of William. Inst. Huntingdon, Dec. 22, 1296.

FLAMSTEAD. R. Andrew of Lincoln re-presented by the King as guardian of the lands and heir of Sir Ralph de Thony (Tony) to the church of Flamstead vacant because the said Andrew had not been ordained priest within a year of institution. Ordained pr. and inst. Huntingdon, Dec. 22, 1296.

ROYSTON (Cruce Roys). John of Litlington ch. p. by Sir Reginald d'Argentein knight to the office of custodian of the hospital of St. John and St. James, Royston, vacant by the death of William of Meldreth. Inst. after a detailed inquiry, Buckden, Dec. 26, 1296.

Johannes de Litlington' capellanus presentatus per dominum Reginaldum de Argentein militem ad custodiam hospitalis sanctorum Johannis et Jacobi de Cruce Roys vacantem per mortem Willelmi de Melreth ultimi custodis ejusdem, facta prius inquisitione per officialem W. Archidiaconi Hunt' per

---

[1] The date is wrongly given, since the institution was performed on May 19, 1296.

quam acceptum extitit inter cetera dictum hospitale fundatum fuisse per antecessores domini Reginaldi predicti ad recipiendum hospitiendo pauperes transeuntes, et ad sepulturam morientium in eodem absque prejudicio parochialium ecclesiarum, quodque capella in eodem hospitali facta non habet curam animarum annexam, quodque custos ejusdem hospitalis et alii secum commorantes ibidem de elemosinis fidelium patrie adjacentis et de quadam portione terre continente circiter quadraginta acras vivunt, ad hujusmodi custodiam est admissus XII kalendas Januarii anno XVII apud Bukkeden' et canonice institutus. Jurataque etc., scriptum est etc.

STIBBINGTON. R. Alexander of Higham (Hecham) d. p. by the A. and C. of Thorney to the church of Stibbington vacant because William of Spanby had been inst. to the church of Stanground. Inst. Buckden, Jan. 11, 1297.

GODMANCHESTER. V. Roger of Drayton ch. p. by the King by reason of his custody of Merton priory during vacancy to the vicarage of Godmanchester vacant because Master John Here had been inst. to a living in the diocese of Canterbury. Presentation opposed by Robert de Brok' d. who had been p. by the P. and C. of Merton before the vacancy. Robert afterwards resigned by letters patent sealed with the common seal of Merton. Roger was inst. Ware, Jan. 13, 1297.

ALL SAINTS, HUNTINGDON. R. William of Peterborough ch. p. by the A. and C. of Thorney to the church of All Saints, Huntingdon, vacant because Roger of Drayton had been inst. to the vicarage of Godmanchester (Gomecestr'). Inst. Buckden, Feb. 9, 1297.

LILLEY (Lynle, Lynlegh). R. William Abel subd. re-presented by Sir John Peyvre knight to the church of Lilley vacant because the said William had not been ordained pr. within a year of his institution. Inst. (in the person of Hugh Cook (Cok') of Bedford (Bedeford') his proctor, Wooburn near Wycombe, Apr. 10, 1297.

[f. 302] WESTMILL. R. Thomas Cosyn pr. by Lady Lucy, widow of Sir Thomas of Lewknor (Leukenovere) knight, as guardian of the lands and heir of the said Thomas, to the church of Westmill vacant by the death of Master Stephen of Tathwell. Inst. Hatfield, May 14, 1297.

QUARTODECIMO KALENDAS JUNII VIDELICET DIE SANCTI DUNSTANI ANNO DOMINI M.CC. NONAGESIMO SEPTIMO INCIPIT ANNUS PONTIFI-CATUS DOMINI OLIVERI DEI GRACIA LINCOLN' EPISCOPI OCTAVUS-DECIMUS.

———

WOODSTONE. R. Robert of Walmesford ch. p. by the A. and C. of Thorney to the church of Woodstone vacant by the death of John Derling. Inst. Nun Coton, Jan. 20, 1297.

HATFIELD. R. Master Guy of Tilbrook ch. p. by the Bishop of Ely to the church of Hatfield vacant by the death of Sir Hugh of Cressingham.[1] Inst. in the person of Master Hugh of Wansford (Walmesford') his proctor, Thornholm, Jan. 25, 1298.

LITTLE BERKHAMSTEAD. R. John Herberd of Banstead (Bensted') subd. p. by the sub-prior and C. of Lewes (the prior being abroad) to the church of Little Berkhamstead vacant by the res. of Michael Crok'. Inst. Empingham, Apr. 29, 1298. 'Et est sciendum quod dicta presentatio facta fuit priore dicti loci in tranmarinis agente, et sic fieri consuevit ut dicebatur pro certo'.

———

QUARTODECIMO KALENDAS JUNII VIDELICET DIE SANCTI DUNSTANI ANNO DOMINI M.CC. NONAGESIMO OCTAVO INCIPIT ANNUS PONTIFI-CATUS DOMINI OLIVERI EPISCOPI LINCOLN NONUSDECIMUS.

———

OFFORD DARCY. R. John of Offord, clerk in minor orders p. by Sir John of Offord knight and Isobel his wife to the church of Offord Darcy vacant by the death of William of Tadcaster. Ordained subd. and inst. (after he had taken an oath that he was of lawful age) Brampton near Huntingdon, May 31, 1298.

GLATTON. Institutio domini Walter de Agmundesham in ecclesia de Glatton' que hic inseri deberet inseritur in archi-diaconatu Buck' per errorem. Folio CXXII.[2]

---

[1] Treasurer of Scotland, killed at Stirling Bridge, August 1297.
[2] See p. 169 below.

[*f. 302v*] BRADFIELD (Bradefeld). R. Thomas de Ressenden', ch. p. by Master John de Wengham, precentor of St, Paul's Cathedral, to the church of Bradfield vacant by the death of William of Dunham. Inst. Buckden, Sept. 4, 1298.

ST. MARY, HERTFORD. R. William of Stow ch. p. by the A. and C. of Waltham Holy Cross to the church of St. Mary, vacant because Henry had been inst. to the church of Wormley (Wurmele).[1] Inst. Liddington, Dec. 19, 1298.

HERTFORD. William of Romsey, p. by J. Abbot of St. Alban's to the cell of Hertford, in a letter dated at St. Alban's, Feb. 10, 1299. Admitted, after an examination of the register of admissions, 'according to the form of the agreement entered into by the church of Lincoln and the monastery of St. Alban's,' Liddington, Feb. 14, 1299.

STILTON. R. William of Swayfield pr. collated by Bishop Sutton to the church of Stilton, vacant by the collation of Richard of Toynton (Tynton') to the church of Greetham Biggleswade, Mar. 16, 1299, in the presence of Jocelyn Archdeacon of Stow, Nicholas of Whitchurch official-principal, and Robert of Kilworth canon of Lincoln.

ORTON WATERVILLE. R. John of Husthwaite, from York, clerk in minor orders p. by Sir Robert de Waterville knight to the church of Orton Waterville vacant by the death of William of Carleton, who was reported by witnesses to have died at Viterbo. Ordained subd., by letters dimissory, by the Archbishop of Canterbury. Inst. Buckden, Apr. 13, 1299.

HOLY TRINITY, HUNTINGDON. R. John of Walcot(e) ch. p. by the P. and C. of St. Neot's to the church of Holy Trinity vacant by the res. of Robert of Boxworth. Inst. Buckden, May 5, 1299.

WAKELEY.[2] R. Stephen de Wyckale, clerk in minor orders p. by Walter Gacelin of Sheldon (Scheldon'), in right of custody of the daughter and heiress of Richard son of Ralph Mouchet, to the church of Wakeley vacant because Ralph of Hackthorn had been inst. to the church of Raithby-by-Louth (Ratyeby). Ordained subd. Huntingdon, June 5, 1299. Inst. Buckden June 14, 1299.

---

[1] In Hertfordshire, but in the diocese of London.
[2] This entry is in B's hand.

QUARTODECIMO KALENDAS JUNII VIDELICET DIE SANCTI DUNSTANI ANNO DOMINI M.CC. NONAGESIMO NONO INCIPIT ANNUS PONTIFICATUS DOMINI OLIVERI EPISCOPI LINCOLN' VICESIMUS.

———

BUCKDEN. V. Richard of Fingest ('Tyngehirst') ch. p. by Master Walter of Wootton prebendary of Buckden to the prebendal vicarage thereof vacant because John of Oundle (Undel) had been inst. to the church of Great Glen. Inst. in the person of Geoffrey le Parker clerk, his proctor, Spaldwick, June 27, 1299.

OFFLEY.[1] R. Master John de Grundewell' ch. p. by the P. and C. of Bradstone to the church of Offley vacant by the death of Master Thomas of Siddington (Sudington'). Inst. Liddington, July 3, 1299.

OFFORD DARCY. R. John of Offord d. p. by Sir John of Offord knight to the church of Offord Darcy vacant by the res. of Robert de Laffenham who held it *in commendam*. Inst. Sleaford, July 20, 1299.[2]

ST. MARY, HUNTINGDON.[3] V. Geoffrey of Barking ch. p. by the P. and C. of Huntingdon to the church of St. Mary vacant by the res. of Ralph of Islip. Inst. Stow Park, Sept. 2, 1299.

ST. ANDREW, HERTFORD. R. William of Leicester (Leyc'), clerk in minor orders p. by the King to the church of St. Andrew vacant by the res. of Philip of Hardwick. Ordained subd. (no date). Inst. Nettleham, Sept. 20, 1299.

ARCHDEACONRY OF BEDFORD 1280–99

———

[*Roll. Membrane 1.*] INSTITUTIONES ET CARTE FACTE PER OFFICIALEM LINCOLN' SEDE LINCOLN VACANTE PER MORTEM DOMINI RICARDI LINCOLN' EPISCOPI ET PER DOMINUM OLIVERUM LINCOLN' ELECTUM, A DIE CONFIRMATIONIS SUE VIDELICET A V KALENDAS MARTII ANNO DOMINI MCCLXXIX, IN ARCHIDIACONATU BEDEFORD'.

———

[1] This entry and the next are in the hand of a clerk, not B.
[2] Compare the entry on p. 90 above. I cannot explain the discrepancy.
[3] In John de Scalleby's hand.

POTTON. R. John of Kent (status not given) p. by the P. and C. of St. Andrew's Northampton to the church of Potton, vacant by the death of ...[1] Richard of Carlton ch. who had opposed the institution on the grounds of papal provision withdrew his objection. Inst. Apr. 8, 1280.

EATON SOCON. V. Roger de Blaysworth' ch. p. by the Prior of the Hospitallers in England to the vicarage of Eaton Socon, vacant by the death of Roger of Bedford. Inst. by the Archdeacon of Bedford (commissioned by the bishop-elect), Mar. 28, 1280. (Place not given).

INCIPIT ANNUS PRIMUS CONSECRATIONIS DOMINI OLIVERI EPISCOPI LINCOLN' XIIII KALENDAS JUNII ANNO DOMINI MCC OCTOGESIMO.

HARROLD (Harewold'). V. Adam of Perry (Pirie) ch. p. by the Prioress and C. of Harrold to the vicarage thereof, vacant by the death of Robert. Inst. Stretton-on-Dunsmore, Aug. 12, 1280.

COCKAYNE HATLEY (Biri Hattele). R. Master John of Bushmead (Bissemed') subd. p. by the P. and C. of Newnham to the church of Cockayne Hatley, vacant by the res. of Master Robert of Nassington. Inst. Nettleham, Sept. 10, 1280, and had letters patent.

CRANFIELD (Craunfeld'). R. Robert of Hale (Hal') subd. represented by the A. and C. of Ramsey to the church of Cranfield, vacant by the res. of the said Robert. Inst. Spaldwick, Oct. 16, 1280.

HARLINGTON (Herlingdon'). R. Master John of Radnor (Radenor') subd. p. by the P. and C. of Dunstable to the church of Harlington, vacant by the death of Master W. de la Mare. Inst. Theydon Mount, Nov. 12, 1280.

PODINGTON. V. Adam of Banbury ch. p. by the P. and C. of Canons' Ashby to the vicarage of Podington, vacant by the death of William. Inst. Ivinghoe, Nov. 30, 1280.

HARLINGTON. R. Master Walter de Lodeford subd. p. by the P. and C. of Dunstable to the church of Harlington, vacant by

[1] Blank in MS.

the res. of Master John of Radnor. Inst. Ivinghoe, Nov. 30, 1280.

SALFORD. V. John of Barton ch. p. by the P. and C. of Newnham to the vicarage of Salford vacant by the res. of Robert of Stapleford. Inst. Upton, Dec. 16, 1280.

DUNSTABLE. William de Wederover' elected as prior of Dunstable in succession to ...[1] who had resigned. Election reported to the bishop by Richard of Mentmore, proctor of the community, with five witnesses, and quashed for incorrect procedure. William was then appointed by the bishop. Milton, prebendal church, Jan. 25, 1281.

MARSTON MORTAYNE. R. Master Walter of Wootton subd. p. by Robert of Wootton and Constance his wife to the church of Marston Mortayne vacant by the death of Sir William de Mortayne (Morteyn). Inst. London O.T., May 8, 1281, saving the rights of Sir Richard d'Argentein patron of the dependent chapel of Roxhill (Wroxhille) and of Master Giles de Filliol its incumbent.

Later a dispute was held in the King's Court between Richard d'Argentein and Robert and Constance of Wootton, concerning the right of presentation to Roxhill. Walter appealed to the Court of Arches, but the bishop was told to accept the judgement of the King's Court in favour of Robert and Constance. (Letter from the Official of Canterbury dated Feb. 7, 1282.) Walter was re-instituted to the church of Marston Mortayne, this time with the addition of the chapel of Roxhill, and had letters patent under the great seal. Buckden, May 8, 1282.

MARKYATE. Alice Baswill', sub-prioress of Markyate, elected *per viam inspirationis* as prioress in succession to Isabel Gobuin who had resigned. Licence given by the dean and chapter of St. Paul's, London, patrons. Election confirmed by the bishop London, O.T., May 13, 1281.

ANNUS PONTIFICATUS DOMINI OLIVERI SECUNDUS[2] ET INCAR-NATIONIS M.CC. OCTOGESIMO PRIMUS.

---

[1] Blank in MS.
[2] The account of the dispute was endorsed upon the roll about a year after the date of the original entry.

POTTESGROVE. V. Baldwin Peleyn ch. p. by the A. and C. of St. Alban's to the vicarage of Pottesgrave vacant by the death of Henry. Lincoln, June 1,[1] 1281.

BEADLOW (Bellus Locus). Roger de Thebregg' monk of St. Alban's, p. by the abbot thereof to the dependent priory of Beadlow, in virtue of an agreement made between the bishop and the abbot. The execution of the first letter of presentation (dated St. Alban's, Mar. 15, 1280), received by the bishop at Stillington, Mar. 28, was delayed until the terms of the agreement could be investigated. Second letter of presentation (dated St. Alban's Oct. 16) accepted after some dispute. Inst. Caldwell. Oct. 30, 1281.

ELSTOW (Elnestowe). Beatrix de Scotney, appointed by the bishop as abbess of Elstow in succession to Anora who had died after he had quashed an attempt by the nuns to elect her on Aug. 15, 1281, on account of incorrect procedure. This election had been opposed on behalf of Agatha Gifford, prioress. Licence obtained from the King as patron. Elstow, Nov. 4, 1281.

Vacante monasterio de Elnestowe per mortem Anore ultime abbatisse ejusdem petita prius a domino Rege prout moris est licencia eligendi et optenta, convenit conventus ejusdem loci in capitulo suo tractans de die electionis faciende, statutus fuit dies mercurii post festum Assumptionis Beate Marie anno domini M.CC. octogesimo primo, quo die convenerunt in capitulo omnes qui[2] debuerunt, voluerunt et potuerunt interesse, invocata spiritus Sancti gracia, lecta etiam et exposita constitutione generali, quapropter placuit omnibus et singulis de eodem conventu per formam scrutinii ecclesie sue de abbatissa ydonea providere, que tres sibi auditrices et scrutatrices de senioribus et fidedignioribus gremii sui concorditer elegerunt, scilicet dominas Ceciliam de Chiselhampton', Mabilliam de Wermunscastr', Philippam de Maryny commoniales suas, que in negotio scrutinii qualequaliter procedentes, dominam Beatricem de Scotenay monialem dicte domus elegerunt vice sua et in ipsam consentientium in abbatissam habentem numerum in duplo fere majorem, domina Agatha Gifford' priorissa ejusdem loci ab aliis de eodem conventu viginti tamen numero ex adverso ut dicebatur in discordia electa, tandem utraque electa predicta electionem de se factam ab episcopo petente confirmari, et alterutra

---

[1] Probably a mistake for July 1. Sutton was at Buckden on June 1.
[2] Sic, recte 'que'.

alterutrius electionem tanquam contra formam juris celebratam irritari, ordinatoque inter partes judicio, demum placuit utrique parti predicte hinc inde quod episcopus omissa judiciali indagine de plano et absque ullo strepitu in negotio procederet memorato, qui in hac parte juxta formam consensus partium earundem procedens et merita utriusque electionis predicte examinans utramque electionem predictam tanquam contra formam concilii generalis improvide attemptatam et non vitio personarum electarum cassavit justicia exigente, dictas moniales propter culpam suam potestate eligendi illa [*Membrane 2.*] vice privantes, quo peracto, episcopus de diutina vacatione ejusdem monasterii paterna pietate motus in provisione et perfectione abbatisse processit. Singulas de conventu predicto singillatim examinans et merita personarum et vota omnium singulariter percunctans, invenit quod domina Beatrix de Scotenaya predicta consensibus plurium de eodem conventu munita fuit, cui et religionis honestas, mundicia vite et aliarum virtutum prerogative inter alias consortes suas et laudabile testimonium tam intra quam extra extendenter perhibebant et suffragabantur, ipsam jure ad eum ratione previa legitime devoluto, dicto monasterio vacanti canonice prefecit in abbatissam, curam ejusdem monasterii cum omnibus suis juribus et pertinenciis quantum ad ipsam pertinebat plenius committendo. Acta in capitulo de Eln' die martis proxima post festum Omnium Sanctorum II nonas Novembris anno domini M.CC. octogesimo primo et pontificatus domini Oliveri secundo. Tenores cassationis utriusque electionis et prefectionis predictarum, sunt in rotulo memorandorum ejusdem anni.[1] Et habuit dicta domina Beatrix prefecta in abbatissam litteram domini Regis patenter directa, cujus tenor similiter est in rotulo.

LITTLE STAUGHTON (Parva Stocton'). William de la Rivere ch. p. by the Master of the Templars in England to the church of Little Staughton vacant by the death of Sir Philip. Inst. Chelsing near Ware, Apr. 28, 1282.

———

TERTIUS. XIIII KALENDAS JUNII SANCTI DUNSTANI ANNUS PONTIFICATUS DOMINI OLIVERI TERTIUS ET INCARNATIONIS DOMINI M.CC. OCTOGESIMUS SECUNDUS.

———

[1] Now lost.

STEPPINGLEY. R. Robert of Lincoln' subd. p. by the P. and C. of Dunstable to the church of Steppingley vacant by the res. of Master John Shorne[1] (Schorn). Inst. Stamford, May 24, 1282.

WYMINGTON. R. Thomas of Sherwood (Schirewode), status not given, re-presented by the Bishop of Bath and Wells to the church of Wymington, in order to clear the conscience of the said Thomas, incumbent. Inst. Louth, Sept. 4, 1282.

SHARNBROOK. V. Roger of Belgrave ch. p. by the A. and C. of St. Mary de Pratis, Leicester, to the vicarage of Sharnbrook vacant by the death of Henry. Inst. Nocton, Sept. 6, 1282.

SUNDON (Soningdon'). V. Robert of Sundon, p. by the Prioress and C. of Markyate to the vicarage of Sundon, vacant by the death of Robert. Inst. Missenden, Dec. 21, 1282.

ASPLEY GUISE. R. Thomas of Bradwell, clerk in minor orders p. by the A. and C. of Newnham to the church of Apsley Guise vacant by the death of Anselm. Ordained subd. and inst. Wycombe, Dec. 19, 1282, and had letters patent under the small seal.

EDWORTH. R. Hugh de Valle ch. p. by the P. and C. of St. Neot's to the church of Edworth vacant by the death of John of Daventry (Davintre). Inst. Northampton, Feb. 15, 1283. Note that a pension of two shillings was due from the church to the said P. and C.

ARLESEY (Alrichseya). V. Robert of Wellington ch. p. by the A. and C. of Waltham to the vicarage of Arlesey vacant by the death of Robert. Inst. Northampton, Feb. 20, 1283.

STEVINGTON. V. John son of Roger of Wootton ch. p. by the Prioress and C. of Harrold to the vicarage of Stevington vacant by the death of Nicholas of Bristol. Inst. Northampton, Feb. 20, 1283.

LIDLINGTON. R. Master John of Dover subd. p. by the Abbess and C. of Barking to the church of Lidlington vacant by the death of Master Pagan Alienigena. (He died away from his parish and the bishop was duly notified). Inst. Milton, Mar. 28, 1283.

------

[1] Who, according to a popular legend, acquired fame by conjuring the devil into a boot.

XIII KALENDAS JUNII DIE SANCTI DUNSTANI ANNUS INCARNATIONIS M.CC. OCTOGESIMUS III ET PONTIFICATUS DOMINI OLIVERI QUARTUS.

PERTENHALL. R. Robert of Holcot, clerk in minor orders p. by Roger Peywere to the church of Pertenhall vacant by the death of Master William of Keysoe (Kayso). Ordained subd. and inst. Stamford, June 12, 1283, and had letters patent.

NEWNHAM. John of Bedford appointed by the bishop as prior in succession to Michael who had died. An attempted election of the said John was quashed for incorrect procedure. Licence to elect was obtained from Sir Roger Le Straunge, patron. Leicester, July 1, 1283.

TILSWORTH (Tullesworth'). V. Thomas of Dagnall (Dagenhale) ch. p. by the Prioress and nuns[1] of St. Giles-in-the-Wood of Flamstead to the vicarage of Tilsworth vacant by the death of ...[2] Inst. Louth Aug. 19, 1283.

CHICKSANDS. V. Simon of Bedford ch. p. by the P. and C. of Chicksands to the vicarage thereof vacant by the death of Geoffrey of Langford. Inst. Buckingham, Nov. 25, 1283.

ODELL (Wahull') R. Thomas of Pattishall (Patishull) ch. p. by Sir John of Odell knight to the church of Odell vacant by the death of William of Odell. Inst. Stow Park, Jan. 25, 1284.

XIII KALENDAS JUNII DIE SANCTI DUNSTANI ANNUS DOMINI M.CC.LXXX QUARTUS ET PONTIFICATUS DOMINI OLIVERI QUINTUS.

MARKYATE (Markeyate). Lora of Kent (Kantia) appointed by the bishop as Prioress of Holy-Trinity-in-the-Wood of Markyate in succession to Alice de Basevile who had resigned. An attempt to elect her was quashed on account of incorrect procedure. Licence to elect had been obtained from the D. and C. of St. Paul's, London, patrons. Sleaford, Sept. 11, 1284.

[1] Sic.
[2] Blank in MS.

ELSTOW. R. Robert of Willey (Welye), clerk in minor orders p. by the Abbess and C. of Elstow to the mediety of the church thereof, vacant by the death of John of Barton. Ordained subd. and inst. Torksey, Sept. 23, 1284.

CARDINGTON. V. Nicholas of Pennington subd. by the P. and C. of Newnham to the vicarage of Cardington vacant by the death of Fulk. Ordained subd. Torksey, Sept. 23, 1284, and inst. Nettleham, Sept. 29.

HOLCOT. R. John son of Walter of Leighton (Leycton') status not given, p. by Lady Amabel de Passelewe to the church of Holcot, vacant because Nicholas Frombold', to whom the bishop had granted custody until he should be ordained subd., had changed his mind. Inst. Milton, Nov. 5, 1284.

[*Membrane 3*] CHELLINGTON (Chelvington'). R. Hugh de Givelden' subd. re-presented by Sir Walter Trayli knight to the church of Chellington vacant becase the said Hugh had not been ordained within a year of institution. Inst. Milton, Nov. 24, 1284, and had letters patent.

BEDFORD, ST. PETER'S. R. Peter of Haverhill subd. p. by the P. and C. of Dunstable to the church of St. Peter of Dunstable in Bedford, vacant because the last rector (un-named) had not been ordained priest within a year of institution. Inst. Dec. 15, 1284 (place not given).

CARLTON.[1] R. Richard of Southill (Suthgivel) subd. p. by Sir Ralph Pyrot knight to the church of Carlton vacant by the res. of Thomas Pyrot. Inst. Buckden, Dec. 16, 1284. Appended to this is a copy of an agreement made before the bishop by which Richard of Southill promised that he and his successors would pay to Thomas Pyrot an annual pension of five marks, payable in two parts at Michaelmas and Easter. Sealed with seals of the bishop and the two contracting parties. Buckden, Dec. 16, 1284.

SHELTON. R. Thomas called Le Engleys, clerk in minor orders p. by Sir Robert of Sulby knight to the church of Shelton vacant because Sewal the last rector had married.[2] Inquiry into Thomas's character from the official of the Bishop of Carlisle in whose diocese he was born. Custody committed

---

[1] This entry is endorsed.
[2] Matrimonium carnale solempnizavit in facie ecclesie.

first to the Archdeacon of Bedford and then to Master William de Bosco the bishop's sequestrator. Ordained subd. and inst. Brampton near Huntingdon Mar. 10, 1285, and had letters patent.

BEADLOW (Bello Loco). John of Stopsley, monk of St. Alban's, p. by the Abbot of St. Alban's to the priory of Beadlow. The bishop took exception to the words 'saving our privileges' in the abbot's letter (dated St. Alban's, Apr. 4, 1285) and, with the consent of John and another monk, the bishop's clerk cut them out with a knife borrowed from Master Durand of Lincoln. Inst. Biggleswade Apr. 9, 1285, in presence of Masters Durand of Lincoln, John le Fleming, William of Langworth and Jocelyn of Kirmington, canons of Lincoln, and John of Beverley, a Franciscan.

V idus Aprilis anno quinto apud Bikkelswad' venit frater Johannes de Stoppesle monachus monasterii de Sancto Albano ad prioratum celle de Bello Loco vacantis per ...¹ Abbatem de Sancto Albano presentatus, litteram procuratoriam exhibens sub hac forma: Reverendo etc. O. etc. R. etc. abbas monasterii Sancti Albani salutem, reverenciam et honorem. Dilectum nobis in Christo fratrem Johannem de Stoppesle commonachum nostrum presentium portitorem quem in priorem in cella nostra de Bello Loco providimus vestre sanctitati presentamus, administrationem spiritualium, ecclesiarum videlicet parochialium et decimarum, salvis privilegiis nostris et vestris suscepturum et pro hiis vobis canonicam obedienciam prestiturum, humiliter rogantes quatinus juxta formam compositionis inter vos et nos inite ipsum sine difficultate admittere eundemque in suis negotiis habere dignemini recommendatum. Conservet vos Deus ecclesie sue sancte per tempora diuterna. Datum apud Sanctum Albanum die Sancti Ambrosii anno domini M.CC. octogesimo quinto. Deinde deliberato aliquantulum juxta tenore littere prenotate et habita collatione ad formam litterarum qua dictus abbas in consimilibus retropresentationibus prius usus fuerat necnon et compositionis serie inter ecclesiam Lincoln' et ecclesiam de Sancto Albano dudum inite recitata, compertum fuit quod in littera suprascripta illa verba 'salvis privilegiis nostris' aliter quam solebat vel dicta compositio requirebat inserta fuere, que quidam clericus dicto presentato et cuidam alio monacho de Sancto Albano tunc assistens de concensu eorundem monachorum cultello Magistri Durandi de Lincoln' sibi commodato totaliter

¹ Blank in MS.

interlevit. At episcopus prefatum presentatum post dictam interlectionem eo quod forme prius usitate a[1] compositioni[1] supradicte[1] intendebat inherere, ad privilegia dictorum religiosorum que non apparebant nullatenus respiciendo, dictum fratrem Johannem[2] ad cellam prescriptam nulla inquisitione premissa admisit et administrationem in spiritualibus et temporalibus ad ipsam pertinentibus sibi secundum formam compositionis prenotate et secundum quod prius fieri consuevit committendo. Demum dictus frater Johannes juravit episcopo et suis officialibus canonica obediencia, nec habuit aliam litteram archidiacono loci de sua inductione quia non fuerat ita prius factum ut dicebat. Hiis autem interfuerunt dictus Magister Durandus, Magister J. Le Flemeng', W. de Langewath', Gocelinus de Kirmington' canonici Lincoln', et quidam frater minor Johannes de Beverlaco.

WYMINGTON. R. William of Holcot ch. p. by John de Exemue as guardian of the lands and heir of William de Montfort (Monteforti) to the church of Wymington vacant by the death of Sir Thomas of Sherwood. Presentation disputed by the Bishop of Bath and Wells, who presented the said William of Holcot while John de Exemue presented Henry Tilley. Case settled in the King's Court, Westminster, May 4, 1285, (witnessed by T. de Weyland) in favour of John de Exemue who thereupon dropped his own candidate and presented the bishop's. Inst. London, Old Temple, May 8, 1285.

XIIII KALENDAS JUNII DIE SANCTI DUNSTANI ANNUS DOMINI M.CC. LXXX QUINTUS ET PONTIFICATUS DOMINI OLIVERI SEXTUS.

HOCKLIFFE. R. Master William Durand, subd. and under age, p. by the Master and brethren of Hockliffe Hospital, in the time of Bishop Gravesend, to the church of Hockliffe vacant by the death of Martin. Custody given to Master John Le Fleming until Durand reached canonical age. Inst. Dunstable, May 26, 1285.

HOCKLIFFE. Alan of Frieston, *conversus* of the Hospital of St. John at Brackley (Brakkele), appointed by the bishop (saving the rights of Hockliffe Hospital) as master of the said hospital

---

[1] Sic.
[2] Interlined.

in succession to Thomas who had resigned. Aspley Guise, June 9, 1285.

BEDFORD, ST. JOHN'S HOSPITAL. Care of the Hospital of St. John committed by the bishop to Baldwin, a brother of the house. Nettleham, Sept. 23, 1285.

CRANFIELD. R. Master Thomas of Potterspury subd. p. by the A. and C. of Ramsey to the church of Cranfield vacant by the res. of Sir Robert of Hale. Inst. Buckden, Dec. 13, 1285, and had letters patent.

HOUGHTON CONQUEST (Hocton'). Master Geoffrey Conquest p. when under age, in the time of Bishop Gravesend, to the mediety of the church of Houghton Conquest. Name of presenter unknown. Custody given to Master Walter of Stow. Ordained subd. and inst. Brampton near Huntingdon, Dec. 22, 1285.

Et est sciendum quod nescitur ubi presentatio et inquisitio sunt nisi sint inter matriculas prefati episcopi Ricardi.[1]

BEDFORD, ST. PETER'S. R. Robert of Ambewyk' ch. p. by the P. and C. of Dunstable to the church of St. Peter, vacant because Peter of Haverhill had failed to be ordained pr. within a year of institution and had resigned. Inst. Leicester, Mar. 31, 1286.

———

XIIII KALENDAS JUNII DIE SANCTI DUNSTANI ANNO DOMINI M.CC. OCTOGESIMO SEXTO INCIPIT ANNUS PONTIFICATUS DOMINI OLIVERI EPISCOPI LINCOLN' SEPTIMUS.

———

ROXTON (Rokesden'). V. Robert Blauncfrunt' ch. p. by the P. and C. of Caldwell to the vicarage of Roxton vacant because Augustine the last vicar had joined the Franciscans. Lidding-ton, Aug. 19, 1286

BLUNHAM. R. John of St. Valery (de Sancto Walerico), clerk in minor orders and under age p. by Edmund Earl of Cornwall to the church of Blunham vacant by the lapse of six months since its commendation to Master Nicholas of Marlborough. Custody given to Master Philip of Waltham. Ordained subd. and inst. Thame, Dec. 21, 1286.

[1] If so it has not survived.

POTTON. R. Master John of Siddington (Sudington'), clerk in minor orders p. by the monks[1] of St. Andrew's, Northampton, to the church of Potton vacant by the death of John of Kent (Kancia). Given custody Dec. 15, and ordained subd. and inst. Thame, Dec. 21, 1286.

RISELY (Risle). V. Philip of Faversham ch. p. by the Prior of the Hospitallers in England to the vicarage of Riseley vacant by the death of Salomon and the res. of Adam of Odell (Wodehull) who was first presented. Inst. Fingest, Feb. 24, 1287, and had letters patent.

GRAVENHURST. R. Nicholas called Scort, ch. p. by the P. and C. of Newnham to the church of Gravenhurst vacant by the death of Master Robert Coreye. Inst. Fingest, Feb. 24, 1287, and had letters patent.

———

XIIII KALENDAS JUNII DIE SANCTI DUNSTANI ANNO DOMINI M.CC. OCTOGESIMO SEPTIMO INCIPIT ANNUS PONTIFICATUS DOMINI OLIVERI EPISCOPI LINCOLN' OCTAVUS.

———

MAULDEN. R. Master Ralph of Luffenham ch. p. by the Abbess and C. of Elstow to the church of Maulden vacant by the death of Simon Abel. Inst. Leicester, July 7, 1287, and had letters patent.

BEDFORD, ST. CUTHBERT'S. R. Richard Troue, clerk in minor orders and under age p. by the P. and C. of Dunstable to the church of St. Cuthbert vacant by the death of ...[1] Custody given to Master Walter of Wootton. Ordained subd. and inst. Huntingdon, Dec. 20, 1287.

EASTWICK[2] (Estewyk') R. John de Barmington' ch. p. by the P. and C. of Chicksands to the chapel of Eastwick vacant by the death of Laurence. Inst. Eltisley, Feb. 10, 1298.

[Membrane 4] DUNTON. V. Richard of Stratton ch. p. by the Prioress and C. of Halliwell to the vicarage of Dunton vacant by the death of Robert of Stanste[a]d. (Stanstede). Inst. Biggleswade, Feb. 12, 1288.

[1] Sic.
[2] In Hertfordshire.

HOLCOT. R. John of Leighton (Leycton') subd. re-presented by Nicholas Ferinbaud and Annabel his wife to the church of Holcot vacant because the said John had not been ordained pr. within a year of institution. Inst. Newnham, Feb. 28, 1288, and had letters patent.

CALDWELL (Caldewell'). John of Ypres (Ipre) canonically elected as Prior of Caldwell in succession to Matthew, who had resigned, no licence having been sought since this was not the custom. Election approved Caldwell, Feb. 21, 1288.

AMPTHILL. V. Eudo of Papworth ch. p. by the P. and C. of Beadlow to the vicarage of Ampthill vacant because Simon had been deprived for non-residence. Inst. Caldwell, Mar. 9, 1288, and had letters patent.

———

XIIII KALENDAS JUNII DIE SANCTI DUNSTANI ANNO DOMINI M.CC. OCTOGESIMO OCTAVO INCIPIT ANNUS PONTIFICATUS DOMINI OLIVERI EPISCOPI LINCOLN' NONUS.

———

TEMSPFORD. R. Hugh de Roubir', clerk in minor orders p. by ...[1] P. and C. of St. Neot's to the church of Tempsford vacant by the death of Hugh d'Oyly. Nicholas de Cernes and Henry de la Leye disputed the right to present, but a royal writ (dated Westminster May 18, 1287 witnessed by T. de Weland' and given in full) ordered the bishop to accept the candidate of the P. and C. of St. Neot's. After being ordained subd. Hugh was inst. Stainfield July 22, 1288, in the person of William of Thorntoft his proctor.

TOTTERNHOE. V. William of Shortwood d. p. by the P. and C. of Dunstable to the vicarage of Totternhoe vacant by the death of William. Inst. Stow Park, Aug. 2, 1288.

BROMHAM. V. Roger of Granby ch. p. by the P. and C. of Caldwell to the vicarage of Bromham vacant by the death of Sir Ralph of Bedford. Inst. Buckden, Sept. 12, 1288.

ASPLEY GUISE. R. John of Hardmead (Haremeade) subd. p. by the P. and C. of Newnham to the church of Aspley Guise vacant by the death of Master Thomas. Inst. London O.T., Oct. 14, 1288 and had letters patent.

[1] Blank in MS.

HOCKLIFFE (Hocclive). Thomas of Battlesden (Badelesdon') brother of Hockliffe Hospital, appointed by the bishop to the office of master thereof in succession to Alan of Frieston (Freston) who had resigned. Buckden, Aug. 25, 1288.

BEDFORD, ST. LEONARD'S HOSPITAL. Walter, rector of the chapel of St. Mary, Bedford, apppointed by the bishop to the office of Master of St. Leonard's Hospital in succession to William who had resigned, on the presentation of the mayor and four burgesses of Bedford, who had been summoned to Buckden to choose a candidate. Buckden, Dec. 11, 1288.

TODDINGTON. R. William of Caddington (Cadingdon') ch. p. by Sir John Peyure knight to the portion which Nicholas of Harrowden (Harwdon') ch. held in the church of Toddington, vacant by the death of the said Nicholas. Inst. Banbury, May 17, 1289.

———

XIIII KALENDAS JUNII DIE SANCTI DUNSTANI ANNO DOMINI M.CC. OCTOGESIMO NONO INCIPIT ANNUS PONTIFICATUS DOMINI OLIVERI EPISCOPI LINCOLN' DECIMUS.

———

STREATLEY (Strale). V. Alexander of Coleshill (Coleshull') ch. p. by the Prioress and C. of Markyate to the vicarage of Streatley vacant because William of Caddington had been inst. to a portion in the church of Toddington. Inst. London, O.T., May 25, 1289.

HOCKLIFFE. Ralph of Easton pr. appointed by the bishop to the office of Master of Hockliffe Hospital in succession to Walter of Houghton who had resigned. Note that induction of the said Walter of Houghton was not enrolled, because the Prior of Dunstable who had acted as the bishop's commissary had not certified the fact, though he had repeatedly been asked to do so. Greens Norton, June 8, 1289.

BARFORD (Berkeford'). Fulk of Norton pr. p. by Cecily La Bretun, widow of William de la Mare, to the church of Barford vacant by the res. of John of Hatfield in a letter given in full and dated at London, June 10, 1289, and sealed with John's seal and that of Master Robert of Winchelsea (Wynchelse), Archdeacon of Essex and Canon of Lincoln. The presentation was disputed in the King's Court by

Benedict of Cockfield (Cokefeld') and Margery his wife, John and Olivia of Layham (Leyham, Leyam) and Sir Ralph de Beauchamp who was guardian of Isabel's daughter and heiress of William son of Ida de la Mare. A royal writ, given in full, witnessed by T. de Weylaund' and dated at Westminster, May 7, 1289, established Cecily's right against Ralph, Benedict and Margery, and another, given in full, witnessed by T. de Weylaund and dated at Westminster June 23, 1289, established it against John and Olivia. Fulk was therefore inst. Liddington, June 26, 1289.

HOUGHTON CONQUEST. R. Master Geoffrey Conquest subd. re-presented by Sir John Conquest knight to the mediety of the church of Houghton Conquest vacant because the said Geoffrey had not been ordained pr. within a year of institution. Inst. Lincoln, Aug. 15, 1289, and had letters patent.

EYWORTH (Eywrth). R. Richard de Purle ch. p. by the Prioress and C. of St. Helen's London to the church of Eyworth vacant by the death of Robert de Aspehale. Inst. Haverhill, Sept. 16, 1289.

HOLWELL.[1] R. Robert le Baud clerk in minor orders p. by John Mellore to the church of Holwell vacant by the res. of Richard de Bray. Made proof of age and received custody June 16, and ordained subd. and inst. Lincoln, Sept. 24, 1289. Had letters patent.

MILLBROOK (Melebrok') V. John of Papworth ch. p. by the P. and C. of Beadlow to the vicarage of Millbrook vacant by the res. of Gilbert. Inst. Norton, Oct. 6, 1289.

HAYNES (Hawenes). V. Simon of Bedford ch. p. by the P. and C. of Chicksands to the vicarage of Haynes vacant by the death of Godeman. Inst. London O.T., Jan. 20, 1290.

CHICKSANDS. V. Nicholas of Campton (Camelton') ch. p. by the P. and C. of Chicksands to the vicarage thereof vacant because Simon of Bedford had been inst. to the vicarage of Haynes. Inst. Biggleswade, Jan. 26, 1290.

WYMINGTON. R. Master Richard called Inge subd. by the Bishop of Bath and Wells to the church of Wymington vacant because William of Holcot had been inst. to the church of

---

[1] In Hertfordshire.

Catworth. Given custody for a period, then inst. Northampton, Feb. 26, 1290, and had letters patent.

[*Register, f. 304*] BEDEFORD'. QUARTODECIMO KALENDAS JUNII DIE SANCTI DUNSTANI M.CC. NONAGESIMO INCIPIT ANNUS PONTIFICATUS DOMINI OLIVERI EPISCOPI LINCOLN' UNDECIMUS.

TEMPSFORD. R. Master Adam of Newcastle, clerk in minor orders p. by the P. and C. of St. Neot's to the church of Tempsford vacant because Hugh de Roubir' had been inst. to the church of Holywell. Given custody for a period, then ordained subd. and inst. Hertford, May 28, 1290.

GRAVENHURST. R. Master Hugh of Swaffham, clerk in minor orders p. by the P. and C. of Newnham to the church of Gravenhurst vacant by the death of Nicholas. Given custody for a period, then ordained subd, and inst. Hertford, May 28, 1290.

ASPLEY GUISE. R. John of Hardmead d. re-presented by the P. and C. of Newnham to the church of Aspley Guise, vacant because the said John had not been ordained within a year of institution. Inst. Peterborough, June 22, 1290, and had letters patent.

STAGSDEN (Stacheden'). V. John Germeyn ch. p. by the P. and C. of Newnham to the vicarage of Stagsden vacant by the death of Ralph, Inst. Kirton in Holland, June 30, 1290.

HIGHAM GOBION. R. Gilbert of Kingsbury (Kynesbir') ch. p. by the Prioress and C. of Markyate to the church of Higham Gobion vacant by the death of Master Robert of Berkhamstead. Inst. Ely, Oct. 1, 1290.

STREATLEY. V. Robert de Craumfeud' ch. p. by the Prioress and C. of Markyate to the vicarage of Streatley vacant because Alexander had been inst. to the church of Eversden in the diocese of Ely. Inst. Buckden, Nov. 16, 1290.

EVERSHOLT. R. Master Stephen of Weston (status not given) p. by Peter de Hagham, proxy of the Prior of the Hospitallers in England, to the church of Eversholt vacant by the death of Robert de la Mare. Presentation disputed by Cecily, daughter of John, son of Miles of Eversholt, who presented Henry of Sewell but later withdrew her claim. Inst. Glatton, Oct. 26, 1290.

[*f. 304v*] SOULDROP (Suldrop'). R. Master Adam Hook, clerk in minor orders p. by Peter de Hagham, proxy of the Prior of the Hospitallers in England, to the church of Souldrop vacant by the death of John Chauncy. Given custody for a period, then ordained subd. and inst. Wycombe, Dec. 23, 1290.

COLMWORTH. R. Thomas of Braybrooke, clerk in minor orders and under age, p. by Sir John of Braybrooke to the church of Colmworth vacant because Master John of Compton (Cumpton') had been inst. to the church of Kibworth. Custody for a period given to Master William Meynil. Ordained subd. and inst. Wycombe, Dec. 23, 1290.

CADDINGTON. V. Thomas of Laxton ch. p. by the D. and C. of St. Paul's, London, to the vicarage of Caddington vacant by the res. of John of Stokes. Inst. Banbury, Mar. 6, 1291.

FLITWICK. V. Geoffrey of Marston, canon of Dunstable, p. by the P. and C. thereof, in virtue of a papal privilege granted to them, to serve the vicarage of Flitwick by one of their own canons. Inst. Sleaford, Apr. 6, 1291.

———

QUARTODECIMO KALENDAS JUNII VIDELICET DIE SANCTI DUNSTANI ANNO DOMINI M.CC. NONAGESIMO PRIMO INCIPIT ANNUS PONTIFI-CATUS DOMINI OLIVERI EPISCOPI LINCOLN' DUODECIMUS.

———

THURLEIGH (Lega). R. Elias of Ashby, clerk in minor orders p. by the P. and C. of Canons' Ashby to the church of Thurleigh vacant because Sir William of Windsor had been inst. to St. Peter's, Northampton. Given custody for a period, then ordained subd. and inst. Boston, June 16, 1291.

[*f. 305*] HOUGHTON REGIS. V. Simon of Wendover (Wendovere) ch. p. by the P. and C. of St. Alban's (the abbot-elect having gone to Rome for confirmation of his election) to the vicarage of Houghton Regis vacant by the death of Walter de Kemesey. Inst. Boston, June 16, 1291.

MARKYATE. Matilda of Luton appointed by the bishop as Prioress of Markyate in succession to Loretta who had died.

Licence obtained from the D. and C. of St. Paul's, patrons. An attempt to elect the said Matilda *per viam scrutinii* was quashed for extremely incorrect procedure. Spaldwick, Aug. 24, 1291.

BIRCHMORE. R. Philip ...[1] p. by the A. and C. of Woburn to the church of Birchmore vacant by the death of William of Houghton (Hocton'). Inst. Stow Park, Oct. 7, 1291.

COCKAYNE HATLEY (Hattelporte). R. Master Richard of Southill (Suthgivele) ch. p. by the P. and C. of Newnham to the church of Hatley vacant by the death of Master John of Bushmead (Bissemed'). Granted the church *in commendam* for a period, then inst. London O.T., Dec. 3, 1291, and had letters patent.

CARLTON. R. Thomas Pyrot ch. p. by Sir Ralph Pyrot knight to the church of Carlton vacant because Master Richard of Southill had been inst. to Cockayne Hatley. Inst. London, O.T., Dec. 3, 1291, and had letters patent.

CARDINGTON. V. John of Barton ch. p. by the P. and C. of Newnham to the vicarage of Cardington vacant by the death of Nicholas. Inst. Wooburn near Wycombe, Jan 14, 1292.

[*f. 305v*] SALFORD V. Simon of Leighton ch. p. by the P. and C. of Newnham to the vicarage of Salford vacant by the res. of John of Barton. Inst. London, O.T., Feb. 10, 1292.

BARTON-IN-THE-CLAY. R. Henry de Lascy, clerk in minor orders and under age, p. by the A. and C. of Ramsey to the church of Barton-in-the-Clay vacant by the res. of Sir W. of Brompton (Brumpton'). Given custody for a period, then ordained subd. and inst. Wycombe, Mar. 1, 1292.

TODDINGTON[2] (Tudington). R. Nicholas of Oakham (Ockham) clerk in minor orders p. by Sir John Peyure knight to the portion in the church of Toddington vacant by the death of Peter de Gorgivoco.[3] Given custody for a period, then ordained subd. and inst. Lincoln, May 31, 1292.

QUARTODECIMO KALENDAS JUNII VIDELICET DIE SANCTI DUNSTANI EPISCOPI ANNO DOMINI MILLESIMO DUCENTESIMO NONAGESIMO

---

[1] Blank in MS.
[2] This entry should appear among those of the following year.
[3] Curginoto in L.R.S. vol. 20, p. 200.

SECUNDO INCIPIT ANNUS PONTIFICATUS DOMINI OLIVERI EPISCOPI LINCOLN' TERTIUSDECIMUS.

———

GOLDINGTON. V. Thomas of Walkern ch. p. by the P. and C. of Newnham to the vicarage of Goldington vacant by the death of Stephen. Inst. Louth, July 10, 1292.

ODELL (Wahull'). R. Master Richard of Southill (Suthgivel) pr. p. by Sir John of Odell knight to the church thereof, vacant by the death of Thomas of Fritwell (Frettewell'). Inst. Liddington, Sept. 9, 1292.

SUTTON. R. Richard of Thorpe ch. p. by Sir William Le Latimer to the church of Sutton vacant by the death of Master Solomon de Burn'. Presentation at first disputed by Lady Christina widow of Sir John Le Latimer, who later withdrew her candidate and agreed to support Sir William's. Inst. Northampton Sept. 22, 1292, and had letters patent.

BATTLESDEN (Baddelesdon'). R. John of Leighton (Leycton') ch. p. by Nicholas Ferinbaud[1] to the church of Battlesden vacant because Master Peter Passelewe who held it had no canonical title to it. Granted the church *in commendam* for a period, then inst. Banbury Oct. 10, 1292.

[*f. 306*] LEIGHTON BUZZARD. V. James of Frieston (Freston') ch. p. by Master Thomas of Sutton prebendary of Leighton Buzzard to the vicarage thereof vacant by the death of Thomas of Kirtling (Kirlington'). Inst. Spaldwick, Nov. 22, 1292, and had letters patent.

COCKAYNE HATLEY (Hattlele). R. John of Hardmead d. p. by the P. and C. of Newnham to the church of Cockayne Hatley vacant by the death of Master John of Bushmead (Bissemed'). Inst. Dorchester-on-Thames, Dec. 20, 1292.

LANGFORD. V. John of Scratby (Scrouteby) ch. p. by Brother Guy Forest (de Foresta) Master of the Templars in England to the vicarage of Langford vacant by the death of John of Linley. Inst. Fingest, Jan. 29, 1293.

EATON SOCON. V. John of Wendy ch. p. by the Prior of the Hospitallers in England to the vicarage of Eaton Socon vacant

[1] This appears to be the name, but MS. is torn.

by the death of Robert of Yaxley. Inst. London, O.T., Feb. 21, 1293.

CAMPTON. R. John of Higham (Hecham) subd. p. by the P. and C. of Beadlow to the church of Campton vacant by the death of Sir Simon of Flegg. Inst. Biggleswade, Apr. 6, 1293. (Note that presentation was first made to a vicarage, but that by investigation it was found that the church was really a rectory and had been incorrectly described in the time of Bishop Gravesend[1]). Had letters patent.

[*f. 306v*] DIE SANCTI DUNSTANI EPISCOPI VIDELICET QUARTODECIMO KALENDAS JUNII ANNO DOMINI MILLESIMO DUCENTESIMO NONAGESIMO TERTIO INCIPIT ANNUS PONTIFICATUS DOMINI OLIVERI DEI GRACIA LINCOLNIEN' EPISCOPI QUARTUSDECIMUS.

ASPLEY GUISE. R. John of Ferriby, clerk in minor orders p. by the P. and C. of Newnham to the church of Aspley Guise vacant because John of Hardmead had been inst. to the church of Cockayne Hatley. Given custody for a period, then ordained subd. and inst. at the O.T. London, May 23, 1293, by licence of the Bishop of London. Had letters patent.

HOLCOT. R. Adam Gerlaund' of Blythe, clerk in minor orders p. by Sir Nicholas Ferinbaud' and Amabel his wife to the church of Holcot vacant because John of Leighton had been inst. to the church of Battlesden. Given custody for a period, then ordained subd. and inst. at the O.T., London, May 23, 1293, by licence of the Bishop of London. Had letters patent.

LEIGHTON BUZZARD. V. John of Hampton ch. p. by Master John Le Fleming prebendary of Leighton Buzzard vacant because James of Frieston had been inst. to the prebendal vicarage of Thame. Inst. Waltham near Croxton, Aug. 7, 1293.

BATTLESDEN. R. Adam of Leighton, clerk in minor orders p. by Sir Nicholas Ferinbaud' knight to the church of Battlesden vacant because John of Leighton had received other preferment. Ordained subd. and inst. Banbury Mar. 13, 1294.

---

[1] L.R.S. vol. 20, p. 199.

EVERSHOLT. R. Richard de Hauterive, clerk in minor orders p. by the Prior of the Hospitallers in England to the church of Eversholt vacant by the res. of Master Stephen of Weston on receiving preferment in the diocese of Rochester. Presentation opposed by the A. and C. of Woburn and by Cecily daughter of John Le Heyr of Eversholt, who presented Master Peter Passelewe, but all these later withdrew their claims. Richard was ordained subd. and inst. Banbury, Mar. 13, 1294.

[f. 307] BIDDENHAM. R. Gilbert of Foulmere, clerk in minor orders p. by Sir William of Kirby knight to the church of Biddenham vacant by the death of Master Richard. Presentation disputed by Sir Nicholas Ferinbaud and Amabel his wife, the Master and brethren of St. John's Hospital, Bedford, and Simon of Braham and Sara his wife, in the King's court. Judgement was given in favour of Sir William, and three royal writs, given in full and dated respectively Westminster Dec. 3, 1293, (witnessed by J. de Metingham) and Westminster Jan. 28, 1294 (witnessed by J. de Metingham) and Westminster, Feb. 2, 1294 (witnessed by J. de Metingham) ordered the bishop to accept his candidate. Gilbert was therefore ordained subd. and inst. Banbury, Mar. 13, 1294, and had letters patent.

BROMHAM. V. Hugh of Linford ch. p. by the P. and C. of Caldwell to the vicarage of Bromham vacant because Roger had been inst. to the living of Clifton, Bicester, Mar. 23, 1294.

COCKAYNE HATLEY. R. John of Hardmead d. re-presented by the P. and C. of Newnham to the church of Cockayne Hatley vacant because the said John had not been ordained pr. within a year of institution. Inst. Spaldwick, Apr. 3, 1294.

––––––

[f. 307v] DIE SANCTI DUNSTANI EPISCOPI VIDELICET QUARTODECIMO KALENDAS JUNII ANNO DOMINI MILLESIMO DUCENTESIMO NONAGESIMO QUARTO INCIPIT ANNUS PONTIFICATUS DOMINI OLIVERI DEI GRACIA LINCOLNIEN' EPISCOPI QUINTUSDECIMUS.

––––––

ASPLEY GUISE. R. John of Ferriby d. p. by the P. and C. of Newnham. No reason given for vacancy.[1] No inquisition

[1] Presumably a re-presentation, since John, p. on May 23, 1293 had not yet been ordained pr.

because the facts were well known. Inst. London O.T., May 31, 1294, and had letters patent.

KEMPSTON. John of Barnwell ch. p. by John Balliol King of Scotland to the chapel of Kempston vacant because Guy had received preferment in Barnard Castle. Inst. Spaldwick, July 6, 1294. An inquisition by the archdeacon found that this was a free chapel dating back to the foundation of the manor of Kempston, and that its endowments consisted of forty acres of arable land and six acres of meadow, with a tenement.[1]

RISELY. V. William of Louth p. by the Prior of the Hospitallers in England to the vicarage of Risely vacant because Philip of Faversham had been inst. to the church of Orton Longueville. Inst. Woburn near Wycombe, Aug. 25, 1294.

COPLE (Coupol). V. Nicholas of Campton ch. p. by the P. and C. of Chicksands to the vicarage of Cople vacant by the death of Thomas. Inst. Edlesborough, Sept. 16, 1294.

ELSTOW.[2] Clemency de Balliol, precentrix of Elstow elected *per viam scrutinii* to be abbess thereof in succession to Beatrix who had died. Licence to elect obtained from the King as patron. Process of the election, under the seal of the abbey, submitted to the bishop for his approval, Dunstable, Sept. 18, 1294. Election confirmed Edlesborough Sept. 19, and notification to the king from Watford, same day. Solemn benediction of Clemency as abbess, London O.T., Sept. 26, 1294.

[*f. 308*] GRAVENHURST. R. Richard of Bottisham (Bodekesham), clerk in minor orders p. by the P. and C. of Newnham to the church of Gravenhurst because Henry of Swaffham had been inst. to the vicarage of Ryhall. Given custody for a period then ordained subd. and inst. Dunstable, Sept. 18, 1294, and had letters patent.

CHICKSANDS. V. John of Campton ch. p. by the P. and C. of Chicksands to the vicarage thereof vacant because Nicholas of Chicksands had received other preferment. Inst. Thame, Oct. 18, 1294.

BLETSOE (Blechesho). Richard of Bagthorpe ch. p. by John de Pabenham to the chapel of Bletsoe vacant by the death of Nicholas of Sharnbrook. Inst. Courteenhall Oct. 25, 1294.

---

[1] The following entry concerning Orton Longueville (Co. Hunt.) is marked 'vacat'.
[2] In B's hand.

BEDFORD, ST. LEONARD'S. Robert of Bedford (alias Copee), brother of St. Leonard's Hospital, nominated by the brethren as master thereof in succession to Walter of Torksey who had resigned. (Their letter, under their common seal, is given in full and dated Bedford, Nov. 1, 1294.) A letter from Richard Dieudonné of Bedford, patron, is also given in full and dated the same place and date. The bishop looked up the register and found that Walter had been nominated by the brethren with no mention of Richard Dieudonné, and therefore ordered an enquiry to be made by the official of the archdeacon. This showed that Richard held the patronage in right of Agnes his wife, daughter and heiress of Simon Basset, and that the right of nomination belonged to the brethren. The bishop therefore wrote to the Prior of Newnham and Master Ralph, rector of Maulden ordering them to grant custody of the hospital to the said Robert until he could conveniently come to the bishop for institution. (Letter given in full and dated Sleaford, Nov. 8, 1294.) They certified by letters patent that this had been done Nov. 10, 1294.[1]

CHALGRAVE. V. Richard of Northwood (Northwode) subd. p. by the P. and C. of Dunstable to the vicarage of Chalgrave vacant by the death of Walter de la March. Ordained d. and inst. Stow in Lindsey, Dec. 18, 1294.

SOUTHILL. V. John of Norton subd. p. by the P. and C. of Newnham to the vicarage of Southill vacant by the death of Richard. Ordained d. and inst. Lincoln, Feb. 26, 1295.

EDWORTH. R. Master Geoffrey de Brunne, clerk in minor orders p. by the P. and C. of St. Neot's to the church of Edworth vacant because Hugh de Valle had received other preferment. Presentation disputed in the King's Court by Laurence de St. Maur and Sybil his wife. A royal writ (given in full, witnessed by J. de Metingham and dated Westminster, Feb. 10, 1295) directed the bishop to accept the prior's candidate. Geoffrey was therefore given custody for a period and then ordained subd. and inst. Lincoln, Feb. 26, 1295, and had letters patent.

HOLWELL.[2] R. Adam of Everdon, clerk in minor orders p. by Joan widow of John Malure, formerly lord of Great Holwwell, to the church thereof vacant by the death of Robert Bland. Ordained subd and inst. Stow in Lindsey, Mar. 19, 1295, and had letters patent.

[1] Date wrongly given as Nov. 2.
[2] In Hertfordshire.

MILTON BRYANT. R. John le Bretoun ch. p. by the P. and C. of Merton to the church of Milton vacant by the res. of Master Peter de Gauth'. Inst. Tinwell, Mar. 30, 1295, and had letters patent.

[*f. 309*] HOLCOT. R. Adam called Garland (Gerlaund') of Blyth subd. re-presented by Sir Nicholas Ferinbaud' knight to the church of Holcot vacant because the said Adam had not been ordained pr. within a year of institution. Inst. Spaldwick, May 5, 1295, and had letters patent.

BEDFORD, ST. LEONARD'S HOSPITAL.[1] Note that after the burgesses of Bedford had recognised Richard Dieudonné as patron, in right of his wife, of St. Leonard's Hospital Robert Coupe[2] was instituted as master thereof, Biggleswade, May 8, 1295, and had letters patent (given in full).

DIE SANCTI DUNSTANI EPISCOPI VIDELICET QUARTODECIMO KALENDAS JUNII DOMINI M.CC. NONAGESIMO QUINTO INCIPIT ANNUS PONTIFICATUS DOMINI OLIVERI EPISCOPI SEXTUSDECIMUS.

COCKAYNE HATLEY. R. John of Hardmead d. re-presented by the P. and C. of Newnham to the church of Cockayne Hatley vacant because the said John had not been ordained pr. within a year of institution. Inst. London, O.T., May 28, 1295 and had letters patent.

CARLTON. R. Thomas Pirot, clerk in minor orders p. by Sir Ralph Pirot knight vacant by the death of ...[3] Pirot. Beatrix de la Leye, who disputed the presentation, subsequently resigned her claim by letters patent. Thomas was given custody for a time, then ordained subd. and inst. Berkhamstead, Sept. 24, 1295, and had letters patent.

ASPLEY GUISE. R. Stephen Duket subd. p. by the P. and C. of Newnham to the church of Aspley Guise vacant because John of Ferriby had received other preferment. Inst. London, O.T., Sept. 28, 1295, and had letters patent.

---

[1] Repetition of the marginal sign given as above, p. 21.
[2] Otherwise called Robert of Bedford or Robert Copee.
[3] No Christian name is given.

CRANFIELD. R. John of Wistow (Wystowe), clerk in minor orders p. by the A. and C. of Ramsey to the church of Cranfield vacant by the death of Master Thomas de Pontesbir'. Given custody for a period, then ordained subd. and inst. Huntingdon, Dec. 17, 1295.

[*f. 309v*] BIGGLESWADE. V. Master William de Braundeston' d. p. by Master Thomas of Northfleet, prebendary of Biggleswade, to the vicarage thereof vacant by the death of Walter. Inst. Fingest, Jan. 21, 1296, and had letters patent.

———

DIE SANCTI DUNSTANI EPISCOPI VIDELICET QUARTODECIMO KALENDAS JUNII ANNO DOMINI MILLESIMO DUCENTESIMO NONAGESIMO SEXTO INCIPIT ANNUS PONTIFICATUS DOMINI OLIVERI LINCOLN' EPISCOPI SEPTIMUSDECIMUS.

———

SHELTON. R. Richard Malure, clerk in minor orders p. by Edmund Earl of Cornwall, as guardian of the lands and heir of Richard of Croxton, to the church of Shelton vacant by the death of Thomas English (Le Engeleys). Presentation disputed by Sir John Wake, knight, who likewise claimed custody of the said lands and heir, and p. John of Arden (Adern') pr., but afterwards withdrew his claim. Richard was ordained subd. and inst. Lincoln, May 19, 1296, and had letters patent.

OAKLEY with CLAPHAM. Appropriation to the P. and C. of Caldwell of the church of Oakley with the chapel of Clapham, saving a competent vicarage and an annual payment to the archdeacon of half a mark. (This appropriation had first been granted by St. Hugh, but Bishop Hugh of Wells had divided the church and compelled the P. and C. to present secular clergy, while retaining half the tithes). On Aug. 11, 1296 at the New Temple, London, Geoffrey de Vezano, canon of Cambrai and papal nuncio issued under his seal a letter of resignation containing a notarial instrument drawn up by John son of Master Peter de Unzela, notary-public, dated Feb. 26, 1296. In this he quotes in full a letter by which Schiatta, Bishop-elect of Bologna and rector of the mediety of Oakley, appoints the said Geoffrey together with Guido de Vichio rector of St. Mary's, Hayes, as his proctors to resign the said mediety, given under Schiatta's seal, Bologna, Feb. 26, 1296, and witnessed by Hugolino de Monte Acenico, Giovannino and Manfredino de Regio. Bishop Sutton's letter, under his seal, authorising the appropriation, is dated at Lincoln, Aug. 18, 1296, and witnessed by Masters Richard of Horton, Treasurer, Walter of Wootton and Roger of Rothwell, Archdeacons oi Huntingdon and Bedford, Henry of Benniworth subdean, Jocelyn of Kirmington Archdeacon of Stow, Thomas de Perariis, William of Thornton, William of Langworth, and Simon of Worth, Richard of Rothwell, Richard of Winchcomb, William of Heanor and Hugh of Normanton, canons of Lincoln. Appropriation to the P. and C. of Caldwell completed Mar. 18, 1297.

GRAVENHURST (Gravenhirst). R. William de Culleswrth' d. p. by the P. and C. of Newnham to the church of Gravenhurst vacant because Richard of Bottisham had been inst. to the church of Fillingham (Filingham).[1] Inst. Bury St. Edmund's, Nov. 13, 1296, and had letters patent.

MILTON ERNEST. V. Robert of Conington ch. p. by the P. and C. of Beadlow to the vicarage of Milton Ernest vacant by the death of Matthew. Inst. Buckden, Dec. 3, 1296.

OAKLEY. V. Richard of Bromham pr. p. by the P. and C. of Caldwell to the newly-ordained vicarage of Oakley with the chapel of Clapham. Inst. Buckden, Dec. 4, 1296. At the same time, in the presence of the said Richard and of Thomas de Bowels canon of Caldwell, the bishop ordained the said vicarage, after an inquiry had been made by the official of the archdeacon into the revenues and obligations of the said church and chapel. He assigned to the vicar the lesser tithes, the oblations, the tithes of hay from certain fields, and a manse free from all secular service to be built by the P. and C. of Caldwell, who were also to keep the chancel and furnishings of the church in repair and pay the procurations. The vicar was to be responsible for serving the church and chapel, providing lights and paying the synodalia.

Memorandum quod ...[2] priore et conventu de Caldewell' domino episcopo Ricardo de Bruham presbitero ad vicariam ecclesie de Acle eisdem religiosis per eundem episcopum appropriate seu ad statum appropriationis dudum facte iterato reducte noviter ordinandum presentibus, factaque ad mandatum dicti episcopi per ...[2] officialem Archidiaconi Bedeford', vocatis vocandis, inquisitione diligenti, tam per obedienciarios totius capituli de Clopham quam per viros

---

[1] The institution is not recorded in archdeaconry of Lincoln.
[2] Blank in MS.

alios fidedignos et juratos super vero valore omnium proventuum ad dictam ecclesiam pertinentium ac omnibus eidem
incumbentibus, necnon in quibus portionibus predicta vicaria
posset competentius ordinari, per quam quidem inquisitionem
acceptum fuit quod proventus[1] dicte[1] ecclesie[1] in portionibus
infrascriptis consistebant prout sequitur estimatis, videlicet in
dominica terra ecclesie sive redditu tenentium eandem ad
XVI solidos in decima garbarum ad XIIII marcas, in decima
feni ad unam marcam, decima lane ad XXX solidos, decima
agnorum ad XV solidos, decima lactis ad II marcas, decima
molendinorum ad X solidos, decima pullorum et vitulorum
ad XII denarios, decima curtilagiorum et gardinorum ad III
solidos, decima columbariorum ad X denarios, decima lini et
canabi ad III solidos, quatuor oblationibus principalibus cum
aliis oblationibus, purificationibus, anniversariis et sponsalibus
ad XLVIII solidos, cera die purificationis ad dimidiam
marcam, caruagium[2] ad VII solidos et principale ad XXVII
solidos estimatis, et in manso rectorie necnon dictam ecclesiam
esse oneratam in dimidia marca ...[3] Archidiacono Bed'
annuatim solvenda, et ipsius archidiaconi procuratione
annuatim invenienda, et in tribus solidos pro sinodo annuatim
solvendis, ac insuper in sustentatione unius capellani in
ecclesia de Acle et alterius in capella de Clopham, episcopus II
nonas Novembris[4] anno domini M.CC. nonagesimo sexto
apud Bukkeden' presente dicto presentato et fratre Thoma
de Bowels canonico de Caldewell' vicariam predictam
ordinavit sub hac forma: ORDINATIO VICARIE DE ACLE[5]
In Dei nomine amen. Nos Oliverus permissione divina
Lincoln' Episcopus vicariam perpetuam in ecclesia de Acle
ordinantes ipsam consistere debere decrevimus in portionibus
infrascriptis, videlicet in decimus agnorum, lane, lactis,
porcellorum, aucarum, vitulorum, pullanorum, pullorum,
columbariorum, lini, canabi, molendinorum, omnimodarum
oblationum in quibuscumque rebus fiant, carucagiorum,
curtilagiorum, gardinorum, mortuariorum et omnium
aliorum si que sint que nomine alteragii valeant comprehendi,
necnon in decima feni in pratis de Clopham et prato expectante
ad dictam ecclesiam quod dicitur Castelmade, et etiam in
manso competenti ab omni servicio seculari prorsus immuni
sumptibus religiosorum virorum ...[3] prioris et conventus de
Caldewell' dictam ecclesiam in usus proprios habentium

---

[1] Interlined.
[2] The carucage: plough alms.
[3] Blank in MS.
[4] Recte 'Decembris'.
[5] This heading is written in the margin.

edificando, manso principali una cum dominica terra ecclesie sive redditu tenentium eandem, decima feni residua a feno predicto vicario assignato et decimis garbarum quas dicti prior et conventus in proprios usus habebunt dumtaxat exceptis. Preterea ordinamus quod iidem prior et conventus libros et ornamenta inveniant, cancellum reficiant et emendent, et loci archidiaconum procurare similiter teneatur. Volumus insuper quod vicarius ecclesie de Acle et capelle de Clopham per ministros idoneos faciat deserviri, et luminaria competentia inveniat, ac sinodalia juxta morem loci consueta persolvat. Demum si quid in dicta ordinatione diminute aut insufficienter factum dubium [*f. 311*] ve aut obscurum appareat in futurum, illud emendandi et vicariam ipsam augendi si oportuerit, interpretandi etiam et declarandi quotiens res exigerit, nobis et successoribus nostris potestatem specialiter reservamus. Datum apud Buggeden' II nonas Decembris anno domini M.CC. nonagesimo sexto ... Dictum insuper Ricardum ad dictam vicariam admisit eisdem die, anno et loco, et vicarium perpetuum cum onere personaliter ministrandi et continue residendi canonice instituit in eadem. Jurataque episcopo canonica obediencia in forma consueta, prestitoque ab eo ad sancta Dei ewangelia juramento de residendo in dicta vicaria secundum formam constitutionis edite super vicarios admittendum, scriptum fuit dicto archidiacono vel ejus officiali quod ipsum R. in possessionem dicte vicarie et mansi induceret corporalem ipsumque extunc proventus habere faceret supradictos.

CARLTON. R. Thomas Pyrot subd. re-presented by Sir Ralph Pyrot knight to the church of Carlton vacant because the said Thomas had not been ordained pr. within a year of institution. Inst. Buckden, Dec. 12, 1296, and had letters patent.

RENHOLD. V. William of Renhold ch. p. by the P. and C. of Newnham to the vicarage of Renhold vacant by the death of John of March. Inst. Buckden, Jan. 2, 1297.

POTSGROVE. V. Simon of Leighton ch. p. by the Abbot of St. Alban's to the vicarage of Potsgrove vacant by the res. of Baldwin. Inst. London, Apr. 3, 1297.

———

QUARTODECIMO KALENDAS JUNII DIE VIDELICET SANCTI DUNSTANI ANNO DOMINI M.CC. NONAGESIMO SEPTIMO INCIPIT ANNUS PONTIFICATUS DOMINI OLIVERI DEI GRACIA LINCOLN, EPISCOPI OCTAVUSDECIMUS.

———

EATON BRAY. V. Adam Cross (de Cruce) ch. p. by the P. and
C. of Merton to the vicarage of Eaton Bray vacant by the res.
of Walter. Inst. London, O.T., July 11, 1297.

BEADLOW. William of Paris, monk of St. Alban's p. by the
Abbot thereof, in a letter dated at St. Alban's June 24, 1297,
to the office of prior of Beadlow, vacant by the translation of
John of Stathern to the priory of Belvoir. The bishop
received satisfaction from William concerning his attempts to
interfere in the secular administration of the said priory
before appointment, on account of which a sequestration had
been imposed. William was admitted, and the sequestration
raised, at Biggleswade, Aug. 20, 1297, in the presence of
Masters Jocelyn of Kirmington and Henry of Nassington,
canons of Lincoln, John of Fotheringhay clerk and John of
Clipston notary-public, according to the form of the agreement
made between the said bishop and abbot.

Vacante prioratu de Bello Loco per translationem fratris
Johannis de Stakedorn' ultimi prioris ejusdem ad prioratum
de Belvero XIII Kalendas Septembris anno domini M.CC.
nonagesimo septimo apud Bikk' venit frater Willelmus de
Parys monachus monasterii Sancti Albani litteras presen-
tatorias abbatis monasterii de Sancto Albano episcopo
exhibens sub hac forma: Reverendo etc. O. etc., suus J. etc.
salutem, reverenciam et honorem. Dilectum nobis in Christo
fratrem Willelmum de Parys commonachum nostrum
presentium portitorem, quem in priorem in cella nostra de
Bello Loco providimus, vestre sanctitati presentamus,
administrationem spiritualium ecclesiarum videlicet parochialium et decimarum salvis privilegiis nostris et vobis[1]
suscepturus et pro hiis canonicam obedienciam juxta formam
compositionis inter vos et nos inite prestiturus, humiliter
rogantes quatinus eundem sine difficultate admittere et in suis
negotiis habere [f. 311v] dignemini recommendatum. Conservet vos Deus ecclesie sue sancte per tempora diuterna.
Datum apud Sanctum Albanum die Nativitatis Sancti Johannis
Baptiste anno domini M.CC. nonagesimo septimo. ...
Cumque quereretur ab eodem fratre Willelmo utrum
administrationi bonorum ad dictum prioratum de Bello Loco
pertinentium se aliqualiter immiscuerat sicut prior, respondit
quod in bonis spiritualibus nullatenus administraverat nisi
colligi faciendo decimas ecclesiarum ad dictum prioratum
pertinentium ne perirent, super quo gracie episcopi totaliter
se submisit, petens sepius et instanter ut secum graciose ageret

---

[1] Sic, for 'vestris'.

in hac parte. Episcopus vero amotis dicto fratre Willelmo et[1] quibusdam aliis commonachis suis qui venerant cum eodem super premissis aliquamdiu deliberans, tandem cum eodem fratre Willelmo volens graciose agere ut dicebat ipsum ad dictum prioratum admisit per librum, et administrationem ipsius prioratus quantum ad eum spectabat juxta morem preteriti temporis et formam compositionis inite inter ecclesiam Lincoln' et monasterium de Sancto Albano predictum eidem commisit, pena pro commisso predicto dicto fratri Willelmo infligenda donec episcopus expedire videret reservata. Dictus autem frater Willelmus canonicam obedienciam episcopo et officialibus suis tactis sacrosanctis ewangeliis incontinenti juravit. Acta sunt hec presentibus Magistris G. Archidiacono Stowe, Henrico de Nassington' canonicis Lincoln', Johanne de Foderingeye clerico et Johanne de Clipston' publico notario. Subsequenter vero dictus prior ad instanciam suam et dictorum commonachorum suorum habuit quamdam litteram officiali ...[2] Archidiaconi Bed' directam sub hac forma: O. etc. officiali etc. salutem. Sequestrum in ecclesiis spectantibus ad prioratum de Bello Loco ad mandatum nostrum per vos interpositum pro eo quod quidam monachus administrationi in eodem prioratu antequam per nos admittebatur ut dicebatur se immiscuerat sicut prior, ad instanciam fratris Willelmi de Parys prioris dicti loci per nos admissi de novo duximus relaxandum. Quocirca vobis mandamus quatinus dictum sequestrum habeatis taliter relaxatum. Valete. Datum apud Bikkeleswad' XIII Kalendas Septembris anno domini M.CC. nonagesimo septimo.[3]

CLIFTON. R. Robert Spigurnel,, clerk in minor orders, p. by Henry Spigurnel and Sara his wife to the church of Clifton vacant because John Pikard had been inst. to a church in the diocese of Norwich. Presentation disputed in the King's court by Sir Roger Peyure of Pertenhall, and decided in favour of Henry and Sara Spigurnel. A royal writ in their favour is given in full, dated Westminster June 19, 1297, witnessed by J. de Metingham. Robert was ordained subd. and inst. Leicester, Sept. 21, 1297.

MELCHBOURNE. R. Richard de Hauterive ch. p. by the Prior of the Hospitallers in England to the church of Melchbourne vacant by the death of Master William of Manby. Inst. Nettleham, Oct. 17, 1297.

[1] Interlined.
[2] Blank in MS.
[3] The next entry, unfinished is marked 'vacat'.

RISELEY. V. Walter of Odell (Wahull') ch. p. by the Prior of the Hospitallers in England to the vicarage of Riseley vacant by the res. of William of Louth. Inst. Stow Park, Oct. 31, 1297.

EVERSHOLT. R. John of Stamfordham, clerk in minor orders p. by the Prior of the Hospitallers in England to the church of Eversholt vacant by the res. of Richard de Hauterive. Ordained subd. and inst. Louth, Dec. 21, 1297.

[f. 312] GOLDINGTON. V. John of Irthlingborough, clerk in minor orders p. by the P. and C. of Newnham to the vicarage of Goldington vacant by the death of Thomas. Ordained subd. and d. (date not mentioned). Inst. Louth, Dec. 21, 1297.

HOLCOT. R. Adam Gerlond' of Blyth (status not given) re-presented by Sir Nicholas Ferinbaud knight to the church of Holcot vacant because the said Adam had not been ordained pr. within a year of institution. Inst. in the person of Richard of Blyth his proctor, Nettleham, Feb. 22, 1298.

TODDINGTON. R. Richard of Caddington ch. p. by Sir John Peyure knight to the portion which Peter the chaplain held in the church of Toddington, vacant by the death of the said Peter. Inst. Nettleham, Feb. 27, 1298.

MARSTON MORETAINE. R. John of Hardmead (Hardemede) ch. p. by Master Walter of Wootton Archdeacon of Hunting-don, by reason of his holding in farm the lands of the late Sir John de Morteyn, knight, patron of the said church, to the church of Marston Mortaine vacant by the res. of the said Master Walter. Inst. in the person of Walter of South Witham clerk his proctor by Master John le Fleming, canon of Lincoln, acting as the bishop's commissary. Lincoln, Feb. 9, 1298.

COCKAYNE HATLEY. R. Master Ralph of Luffenham ch. p. by the P. and C. of Newnham to the church of Cockayne Hatley vacant by the res. of John of Hardmead. Held the church *in commendam* for six months. Inst. Stow Park, Mar. 9, 1298.

SHILLINGTON (Schyttelingdon'). R. Sir Gilbert de Roubir' pr. p. by the A. and C. of Ramsey to the church of Shillington vacant because Sir Ralph of Higham had never been inst. but had held custody only. Inst. after his proctor John de Roubir' had resigned in his name the living of Carleton, Nettleham, Mar. 20, 1298. He was allowed to retain in plurality the church of ?Staindrop, and to hold custody of the sequestrations of Christleton and Laxfield. Witnessed by Masters Jocelyn of Kirmington and Walter of Wootton.

BOLNHURST. R. John of Langtoft, clerk in minor orders p. by the A. and C. of Thorney to the church of Bolnhurst vacant because Robert of Wansford (Walmesford') had received other preferment. Ordained subd. and inst. Nettleham, Mar. 22, 1298.

[*f. 312v*] FELMERSHAM. R. Master Antony de Niviano ch. p. by King Edward to the church of Felmersham vacant by the death of Master Campanus de Novaria. Inst. in the person of Master James de Briga his proctor, Nettleham, Mar. 23, 1298, and had letters patent.

TINGRITH. R. John Maleherbe pr. p. by Peter of Tingrith to the church of Tingrith vacant by the death of Master Thomas of Tingrith. Inst. Nettleham Mar. 27, 1298.

STEPPINGLEY. R. John of Rothwell pr. p. by the P. and C. of Dunstable to the church of Steppingley vacant by the death of Master Robert of Lincoln. Inst. Sleaford, Apr. 9, 1298.

SILSOE (Sivelsho). Hugh of Blunham ch. p. by Thomas of Bray to the chantry in the chapel of Silsoe vacant by the death of Richard the chaplain. Inst. Liddington, May 2, 1298.

TILSWORTH (Tuleswrth'). V. John of Stoke ch. p. by the Prioress and C. of St. Giles-in-the-Wood, Flamstead, to the vicarage of Tilsworth vacant by the res. of Thomas of Dagnall. Inst. Liddington, May 3, 1298

QUARTODECIMO KALENDAS JUNII VIDELICET DIE SANCTI DUNSTANI ANNO DOMINI M.CC. NONAGESIMO OCTAVO INCIPIT ANNUS PONTIFI-CATUS DOMINI OLIVERI EPISCOPI LINCOLN' NONUSDECIMUS.

WILDEN. R. Simon of Pavenham (Pabe(n)ham), clerk in minor orders p. by Sir John Ridel knight to the church of Wilden vacant by the death of Malcolm of Harley (Harle). Presentation opposed by Ralph Tirel of Wilden who p. Thomas Haliday of Bedford, but later revoked this presentation by letters patent. Simon made proof of age, and was ordained subd. and inst. at Brampton near Huntingdon, May 31, 1298.

SILSOE (Sivelsho). John of Hythe (Huthe) ch. p. by Sir Thomas of Bray knight to the chantry in the chapel of Silsoe vacant by the res. of Hugh of Blunham. Inst. Wooburn, July 6, 1298, and swore on the Gospels that he would observe all the ordinances concerning the said chantry.

BEDFORD, ST. PETER'S. R. Master John of Tixover (Tykes-hovere), clerk in minor orders, p. by the P. and C. of Merton to the church of St. Peter of Merton in Bedford, vacant by the death of William. Ordained subd. and inst. Brampton near Huntingdon, Sept. 20, 1298.

[f. 313] MAULDEN. R. Hugh son of Ralph of South Luffenham, clerk in minor orders p. by the Abbess and C. of Elstow to the church of Maulden vacant because Master Ralph of Luffenham had been inst. to Cockayne Hatley. Ordained subd. and inst. Brampton near Huntingdon, Sept. 20, 1298.

CAMPTON. R. Peter of Cosgrove subd. p. by the P. and C. of Beadlow to the church of Campton vacant by the res. of John of Higham. Inst. Nettleham, Nov. 19, 1298, and had letters patent.

BUSHMEAD (Bissemed'). Simon of Redbourn, cellarer of Bushmead, appointed by the bishop as prior of Bushmead in succession to Richard Foliot who had died. The canons, having obtained licence from Sir William Le Latimer the patron, had first elected Jocelyn of Stockton, but the bishop quashed the election for incorrect procedure and other unspecified reasons. No date, ?Nov. 1298–Feb. 1299.

GOLDINGTON. V. William of Lubbenham (Lobenham) ch. p. by the P. and C. of Newnham to the vicarage of Goldington vacant by the death of John of Irthlingborough (Erthling-bury). Inst. Nassington, Feb 25, 1299.[2]

BEADLOW. Peter of Maidford, monk of St. Alban's p. by the Abbot thereof, in a letter dated at St. Alban's May 6, 1299, to the office of prior of Beadlow. Reason for vacancy not given. The bishop complained that the letters of presentation were issued close and not patent, according to custom, and sent Peter back to St. Alban's for fresh ones. He returned bearing letters patent issued on the same date as the letters close.[3]

---

[1] This word had been added in a later hand.
[2] The remainder of f. 313 is left blank.
[3] Unless John de Scalleby copied it incorrectly.

Peter was admitted at Buckden, May 25, 1299, in the presence of Masters Jocelyn of Kirmington, Nicholas of Whitchurch the official-principal, and Richard of Toynton and John de Scalleby, with others of the bishop's household, according to the form of the agreement made between the said bishop and abbot. The admission was by book (*per librum*).

PODINGTON. V. Roger of Stevington (Stivington') ch. p. by the P. and C. of Canons' Ashby to the vicarage of Podington vacant by the res. of Adam of Banbury. Inst. Stow Park, Aug. 31, 1299.

ARCHDEACONRY OF BUCKINGHAM 1290–99

[*f. 316*] INSTITUTIONES BUCK' ANNO XI

———

QUARTODECIMO KALENDAS JUNII DIE SANCTI DUNSTANI ANNO DOMINI M.CC. NONAGESIMO INCIPIT ANNUS PONTIFICATUS DOMINI OLIVERI EPISCOPI LINCOLN' UNDECIMUS.

———

MARLOW. R. Master Walter of Bath subd. p. by Lady Matilda de Clare, Countess of Gloucester, to the church of Marlow vacant by the death of Master Geoffrey de Apphale. No letter of induction since Walter already had custody. Inst. London, Old Temple, May 26, 1290.

DINTON (Dunington'). V. Alan of Kilworth (Kyvelingwrth') ch. p. by the Abbess and C. of Godstow to the vicarage of Dinton vacant by the res. of Roger. Inst. Notley, June 4, 1290.

EDGCOTT (Achecote). R. Andrew of Englefield ch. p. by John of Cole to the church of Edgcott vacant by the death of Robert le Butiler. Held the church *in commendam* for a period. Inst Buckden, Oct. 16, 1290.

RADNAGE (Radenach). R. William of Bosworth (Boreswrth') ch. p. by Geoffrey de Vicher', visitor-general of the Templars in England, to the church of Radnage vacant by the res. of Geoffrey. Inst. Buckden, Oct. 19, 1290.

STEEPLE CLAYDON. V. Robert of Tilton ch. p. by the A. and C. of Osney to the church of Steeple Claydon vacant by the res. of Adam. Inst. Buckden, Nov. 10, 1290.

SAUNDERTON (Sauntresdon). R. William of Swayfield clerk of the bishop, collated to the church of St. Nicholas, Saunderton, vacant by the death of Reginald and the lapse of six months while the patronage was disputed in the King's court between Henry Dayrel of the one part and Ralph Brown (Brun) and Agnes La Mire his wife of the other. Inst. Buckden, Nov. 18, 1290.

WADDESDON. Ralph FitzBernard, clerk in minor orders p. by Sir Hugh of Courtenay knight to the portion which Richard of Stamford held in the church of Waddesdon, vacant by the death of the said Richard. Ordained subd. and inst. Wycombe, Dec. 23, 1290. William of Street d. re-presented by Sir Hugh of Courtenay to the portion in the church of Waddesdon from which the said William had res. because he had not been ordained priest within a year of institution. Ordained pr. and inst. Wycombe, Dec. 23, 1290.

[f. 316v] MARLOW. Agnes of Cliveden, subprioress of Marlow, elected *per viam scrutinii* to the office of prioress in succession to Agnes of London who had resigned. Licence to elect obtained from Gilbert Earl of Gloucester, patron. The bishop, in consideration of the poverty of the house, committed the examination to Masters Richard of St. Frideswide Archdeacon of Buckingham and Jocelyn of Kirmington. Election quashed because the prioress-elect had performed duties before confirmation (but through simplicity not malice), but a second election allowed. Agnes of Clivedon was confirmed in office, Fingest, Dec. 4, 1290. A letter on her behalf was sent to the Earl of Gloucester, Jan. 1, 1291.

BARTON HARTSHORN (Barton juxta Chetewud'). V. Brother William of Brixworth (Brikeleswrth') canon of Chetwode p. by the P. and C. thereof to the vicarage of Barton Hartshorn, according to the form of appropriation between Bishop Gravesend and the said P. and C. No reason given for vacancy. Inst. Banbury, Mar. 8, 1291.

LECKHAMPSTEAD. R. Robert FitzBernard subd. p. by Hugh de Chastiloun' to the church of Leckhampstead vacant by the death of William de Wauton'. Inst. Daventry Mar. 14, 1290.

[f. 317] MAIDS MORETON. R. Robert Inge, clerk in minor orders p. by Sir John Peyvre knight to the church of Maids

Moreton vacant by the res. of Richard of Osgodby. Ordained subd. and inst. Northampton, Mar. 17, 1291.

BEACHAMPTON. R. Mediety. Master James of Buckingham subd. p. by the P. and C. of Luffield to the church of Beachampton vacant by the res. of Richard on his being inst. to the church of Dodford. Inst. in the person of Master Ralph of Buckingham his proctor, Northampton, Mar. 18, 1291.

NEWTON BLOSSOMVILLE. R. Robert of Richmond ch. p. by Sir John Dynel knight to the church of Newton Blossomville vacant by the death of William. Inst. Northampton, Mar. 20, 1291.

———

QUARTODECIMUS KALENDAS JUNII VIDELICET DIE SANCTI DUNSTANI ANNO DOMINI M.CC. NONAGESIMO PRIMO INCIPIT ANNUS PONTIFI-CATUS DOMINI OLIVERI EPISCOPI LINCOLN' UNDECIMUS.

———

HULCOTT (Huccote). R. Simon of Wigginton (Wyginton') ch. p. by William Le Graunt lord of Hulcott to the church thereof because (another) William Le Graunt, rector, had not been ordained pr. within a year of being inst. Inst. Louth, June 6, 1291.

HAVERSHAM. R. William of Letcombe (Ledecumb'), clerk in minor orders p. by James de La Plaunch' to the church of Haversham vacant by the death of Master Angelus. Ordained subd. Boston, June 16, 1291, and inst. Kirton-in-Holland, June 17.

LATHBURY. R. Master John de Lacy subd. p. by the A. and C. of Lavendon to the church of Lathbury vacant by the res. of Robert of Harley the last rector and of Sir Malcolm of Harley first presented. Inst. Sempringham, June 17, 1291.

[f. 317v] ST. JOHN'S HOSPITAL, NEWPORT PAGNELL. Brother Gilbert of Louth p. by Sir Roger de Sumery knight to the mastership of St. John's Hospital, vacant by the res. of Adam Russel. Inst. Spaldwick, July 11, 1291.

AMERSHAM (Agmundesham). R. William of March subd. p. by Humphrey de Bohun Earl of Hereford and Essex to the church of Amersham vacant by the death, of Master William of Bridlington. Inst. in virtue of a papal dispensation (no reason given) London, Old Temple, Oct. 21, 1291.

CHALFONT ST. GILES. R. Robert de Pratellis pr. collated by the bishop to the church of Chalfont St. Giles which he had held *in commendam* for six months. No reason given for vacancy. Inst. (in the person of John de Scalleby his proctor and in the presence of Master John Le Fleming, canon of Lincoln), London, Old Temple, Nov. 28, 1291.

FILGRAVE. R. John of Bray, clerk in minor orders p. by the Abbess and C. of Delapré to the church of Filgrave vacant by the death of .... Presentation disputed by John son of John of Tyringham who p. Walter de la Stave, but afterwards withdrew his claim by letters patent. John of Bray ordained subd. and inst. Wycombe, Dec. 22, 1291.

LITTLE KIMBLE (Parva Kenebelle). R. John de Bavak', clerk in minor orders p. by the Abbot of St. Alban's to the church of Little Kimble vacant by the res. of Thomas de la Le. Had custody for a period. Ordained subd. and inst. Wycombe, Dec. 22, 1291.

SIMPSON (Seweneston'). R. Hugh de la Leye, clerk in minor orders p. by Sir John de Grey knight to the church of Simpson vacant by the death of Master John of Morden. Ordained subd. (by licence of the Bishop of London) and inst. London, Old Temple, Mar. 22, 1292.

TICKFORD. Vacancy caused by the deposition of Simon of Reed, prior, by the bishop's commissaries during a visitation for crimes of dilapidation, incontinence and homicide, Sept. 27, 1291. On Feb. 5, 1292, Robert, Abbot of St. Martin's, Tours (the mother-house of Tickford) met Bishop Sutton at London, Old Temple, and claimed exemption for Tickford. Sutton claimed authority over Tickford as a result of a papal ruling in a dispute between Bishop Grosseteste and the A. and C. of St. Martin's, and subsequently produced a privilege of Innocent IV (Lyons, June 22, 1249) in support. The A. and C. produced two privileges of Alexander IV (Lateran, Dec. 17, 1256 and Viterbo, Nov. 8, 1257) which they claimed to supersede Innocent's. An agreement defining the rights of the parties was concluded 'in the month of February' 1292. Thereafter Geoffrey called Vig', monk of St. Martin's, p. by the A. and C. of St. Martin's, was admitted as prior, in the presence of Masters Henry of Nassington, John le Fleming,

Jocelyn of Kirmington and Walter of Wootton, canons of Lincoln, London, Old Temple, Feb. 20, 1292.

Vacante prioratu de Tykeford' per hoc quod frater Simon de Reda ultimus ejusdem loci in visitatione auctoritate episcopi per certos commissarios suos ad hoc specialiter deputatos IIII idus Julii anno domini M.CC. nonagesimo primo facta, super dilapidatione bonorum domus tam immobilium quam mobilium et etiam incontinencia ac crimine homicidii inventus enormiter diffamatus, et super hujusmodi dilapidatione et incontinencia per confessionem propriam et super alio enormi crimine pretacto per defectum purgationis legitime convictus, ab officio et regimine prioratus VI kalendas Septembris anno prefato per dictos commissarios extitit judicialiter amotus. Labente insuper tempore frater Robertus Abbas majoris monasterii Turon' dictum prioratum ad prefatum monasterium specialiter pertinere pretendens ad episcopum apud Vetus Templum, London' die mercurii proxima post festum purificationis beate Marie anno prescripto personaliter accessit una cum ...[1] tunc priore sancte Trinitatis Ebor' et priore de Maunteny et domus beate Marie extra Parisiis ac pluribus aliis monachis monasterii prefati, dicens memoratum prioratum de Tykeford' memorato monasterio Turon' esse subjectum et ab omni jurisdictione episcopali et ordinaria auctoritate sedis apostolice prorsus exemptum, [f. 318] et rogans episcopum quod ipse ob reverenciam sedis predicte a mo/lestatione dicto prioratui de Tykeford' imposterum facienda desistere dignaretur. Cui episcopus econtra respondit quod idem prioratus de Tykeford' tanquam in dicto episcopatu notorie situs fuerat et erat predecessoribus suis et sibi ut in visitationibus et correctionibus inibi faciendis et procurationibus recipiendis ac aliis jure communi longissima possessione pacifica notorie munito subjectus, cujusmodi subjectio per processum inter Abbatem et conventum monasterii Turon' predicti, actores, et felicis recordationis Robertum Grosetest' Episcopum Lincoln', reum, in curia Romana ratione dicti prioratus habitum, et sentenciam in hac parte ibidem latam et auctoritate apostolica confirmatam fuit clarius declarata. Super quibus altercato plurimum utrobique, tandem fuit hinc inde amicabiliter consensum quod dictus abbas et commonachi sui una cum prioribus predictis tunc presentes id quod pro se habebant super exemptione per ipsos allegata episcopo ostendent bona fide, et ipse vice versa sentenciam pro predecessore suo ut premittitur latam similiter in medio exhiberet, et sic deinceps fieret de bono et

[1] Blank in MS.

equo concorditer inter partes si in unum possent forsitan convenire quod viderent amicabiliter faciendum, alioquin utraque pars per viam litis vel alio modo jus suum prosequeretur prout melius crederet expedire. Deinde ex parte dictorum abbatis et monachorum exhibita fuerunt coram dicto episcopo privilegia Alexandri pape quarti sub continentiis infrascriptis: ... Alexander episcopus servus servorum Dei dilectis filiis ...[1] abbati majoris monasterii Turon' ejusque fratribus tam presentibus quam futuris regularem vitam professis imperpetuum. Apostolici moderaminis clemencie convenit religiosas personas eligere et eorum loca apostolice protectionis munimine defensare. Eapropter dilecti in domino filii vestris justis postulationibus annuimus et beati Martini confessoris monasterium quod majus dicitur, cui disponente divina providencia presidetis, ab eodem beato Martino quondam edificatum, ad instar felicis recordationis Innocentii pape secundi, predecessoris nostri in sancte Romane sedis tutelam protectionemque suscipimus, et cum omnibus rebus ad ipsum pertinentibus presentis scripti pagina communimus. Statuimus enim ut quascumque possessiones, quascumque bona, idem cenobium impresentiarum juste et legitime possidet, aut in futurum concessione pontificum, largitione regum vel principum, oblatione fidelium seu aliis modis rationabiliter poterit adipisci, firma vobis vestrique successoribus et illabata permaneant, in quibus hec propriis vocabulis duximus annotanda in pago Turonico, etc. Electus autem ad Romanum pontificem consecrandus accedat et cui voluerit catholico episcopo pro ejusdem consecrationis susceptione se offerat, qui nimirum nostra fultus auctoritate quod postulatur indulgeat. Idem autem de crismate, de oleo sancto, de consecrationibus altarum seu basilicarum, de ordinationibus monachorum qui ad sacros ordines fuerint promovendi presentis pagine auctoritate sanccimus, quatinus hoc monasterium vestrum soli Romane ecclesie subditum de tanta libertate atque auctoritate imperpetuum gaudeat. Interdicimus autem ne quis cujusdam loci monachos in aliquam ecclesiam ad stationem aut exequias celebrandas preter suam et abbatis voluntatem compellat, adicientes et precipientes ne quisquam deinceps archiepiscopus aut episcopus beati Martini majus monasterium aut ipsius majoris monasterii monachos pro ulla causa ullo in loco excommunicare presumat. Sub dato Lateran' per manum Rolandi sancte Romane ecclesie vicecancellarii XVI kalendas Januarii indictione XV incarnationis dominice anno M.CC. LVI, pontificatus vero domini Alexandri pape quarti anno secundo.

[1] Blank in MS.

... Item: ... Alexander episcopus servus servorum Dei dilectis filiis ...[1] abbati et conventui majoris monasterii Turon' ad Romanam ecclesiam nullo medio pertinentes, ordinis sancti Benedicti, salutem et apostolicam benedictionem. Laudabilis religio que in monasterio vestro colitur sic ab eo mundane dissolutionis relegavit illecebras ut inter alia claustralis obstinencie nexibus religatum observancie puritate fulgeat regularis et voluntatis libitum coarcans omnino sub obediencie debito dignam et sedulam exhibeat domino servitutem. Unde tanquam potentiori devotione premuniens attolli jamdudum exemptionis privilegio meruit et velit sanctitatis eminencia presignitum nonnullis diversarum graciarum titulis honorari. Cum itaque in privilegiis ipsius monasterii contineatur expresse, sicut nosipsi ex inspectione ipsorum privilegiorum collegimus, ne quisquam archiepiscopus aut episcopus beati Martini majus monasterium aut ipsius majoris monasterii monachos pro ulla causa in loco excommunicare presumat, ac universi priores et monachi vestri sive in ipso monasterio sive in ipsius prioratibus commorentur et membris, in eodem monasterio prout asseritis professionem emittant, et ad voluntatem abbatis ipsius monasterii qui est pro tempore mittantur ad prioratus et membra eadem moraturi in eis ac ab ipso abbate cum ei placuerit ad idem monasterium revocentur cum conveniens sit ut qui eidem monasterio pari se in illo professione alligant, eandem gaudere debeant libertatem, nos vestris devotis supplicationibus inclinati, ut universi priores et monachi predicti ubicumque fuerint, et utantur libere privilegiis [f. 318v], indulgenciis, libertatibus, immunitatibus et graciis quibus gaudent ac utuntur monachi in ipso monasterio commorantes, constitutione seu declaratione felicis recordationis Innocentii pape predecessoris nostri circa exemptos edita vel quibuslibet aliis statutis seu declarationibus factis et promulgatis ab apostolica sede ad instanciam quorumcumque et quibuscumque, litteris apostolicis per quoscumque obtentis nequaquam obstantibus, auctoritate vobis de speciali gracia indulgemus. Nos enim interdicti, excommunicationis et suspensionis sentencias et processus si quos in vos et monasterium vestrum vel prioratus aut monachos predictos seu prioratus et membra vestra contra presentis indulti tenorem per quoscumque ferri vel haberi contingerit, irritos decernimus et inanes. Nulli ergo, etc. Si quis, etc. Datum Viterbii sexto[2] idus Novembris pontificatus nostri anno tertio. ... Super quibus et eorum effectu per plures dies subsequentes continuatos altercato plurimum, episcopus asseruit inter cetera

---

[1] Blank in MS.
[2] Interlined.

dictum prioratum de Tykeford' per primum privilegium predictum quoad exceptionem pretactam non posse juvari, et hoc propter sentenciam de qua superius mentio fit expressa, quam sub vera bulla domini Innocentii quarti protulit in hec verba: Innocentius episcopus servus servorum Dei venerabili fratri episcopo Lincoln' salutem et apostolicam benedictionem. Ea que vel judicio vel concordia terminantur firma debent et illibata persistere, et ne in recidive contentionis scrupulum relabantur apostolico convenit presidio conveniri. Eapropter, venerabilis in Christo frater, tuis justis precibus inclinati, diffinitivam sentenciam quam pro te contra abbatem et conventum majoris monasterii Turon' ad Romanam ecclesiam nullo medio pertinentis dilectus filius noster G. Sancta Eustachii diaconus cardinalis quem concessimus partibus auditorem de mandato nostro protulit prout in ejus litteras quarum tenores de verbo ad verbum presentibus inseri fecimus plenius continetur, auctoritate apostolica confirmamus et presentis scripti patrocinio communimus, cujus tenor talis est: ... Universis presentes litteras inspecturis Guillelmus miseratione divina sancti Eustachii diaconus cardinalis salutem in domino. Noverit universitas vestra quod dudum inter abbatem et conventum majoris monasterii Turon' ex parte una et venerabilem patrem episcopum Lincoln' ex altera super diversis articulis contingentibus prioratum de Neuport-paynel Lincoln' diocesis questione suborta, pars dicti monasterii coram Magistro Johanne Asten' domini pape capellano ab eodem domino partibus auditore concesso libellum obtulit in hunc modum: Coram vobis domino Johanne Asten' domini pape capellano ac ejusdem palacii causarum generali auditore proponit frater Gaufridus procurator abbatis et conventus majoris monasterii Turon' contra dominum episcopum Lincoln' quod cum ipse ex liberalitate sedis apostolice eis indulta obtinerent quod nullus in ipsos seu in monachos ipsorum in quibuslibet locis commorantes excommunicationis sentencias debeat promulgare, dictus episcopus in monachos suos in prioratu de Neuportpaynel Lincoln' diocesis existentes excommunicationis sentencias temere fulminavit, in apostolice sedis et ejusdem monasterii injuriam et contemptum, quare petit ipsas excommunicationis sentencias denunciari irritas et inanas, ac ipsi sentencialiter inhiberi ne decetero talia attemptare presumat, cum idem jus non habeat talia faciendi. Petit etiam ipsum condempnari ad injurias, quas estimat ad mille marcas. Item proponit contra eundem quod cum abbas ejusdem monasterii et antecessores sui sint fuerint in possessione vel quasi instituendi vel destituendi priores pro sue voluntatis arbitrio in prioratibus predicto monasterio subjectis, ita quod institui per eosdem abbates in ipsis prioratibus sine contradictione episcoporum in quorum sunt diocesibus libere administrarunt et administrant, dominus Lincoln' priorem in prefato prioratu ab abbate ipsius monasterii institutum quominus in temporalibus et spiritualibus ad institutionem ipsius abbatis administret impedit minus juste. Unde petit ipsum episcopum per sentenciam vestram ab hujusmodi impedimentum compesci et inhiberi sibi quod decetero non attemptet. Item dicit quod idem episcopus impedit quominus prior ibidem institutus ab abbate eidem abbati obediat ut tenetur, unde petit dictum episcopum per vestram sentenciam a predicto impedimento compesci et eidem inhiberi ne decetero talia attemptare presumat. Anno domini M.CC. XLV mense Augusto die sexto exeunte Dominicus procurator domini episcopi Lincoln' litem contestando respondens negat narrata vera esse ut narrantur et dicit petita fieri non debere cum fratre Gaufrido procuratore abbatis et conventus predictorum. Eodem die a prefato Dominico procuratore domini Lincoln' ex parte una et a fratre Gaufrido procuratore abbatis et conventus predictorum juratum est super predicto libello de veritate dicenda. Lite vero coram predicto Magistro Johanne legitime contestata, jurato a partibus de veritate dicenda, factis positionibus hinc ac responsionibus ad easdem, productis testibus ab utraque parte et attestationibus pupplicatis, dominus papa negotium ipsum nobis audiendum commisit. Partibus igitur competentibus coram nobis de jure utriusque partis fuit diutius disceptatum et demum in causa conclusum. Unde nos visis et intellectis rationibus utriusque partis et domino pape et fratribus suis plenius recitatis, et super premissis deliberatione habita diligenti, de speciali mandato ejusdem domini pape Robertum de Wroxton' procuratorem constitutum a predicto Dominico qui litem fuerat contestatus, ab impetitione [f. 319] predictorum abbatis et conventus super omnibus articulis contentis in premisso libello nomine sepedicti episcopi Lincoln' finaliter duximus absolvendum. In cujus rei testimonium presentes litteras fieri fecimus sigilli nostri munimine roborari. Actum Lugdun' presentibus dominis electo Taurinen', Magistro Berardo de Neapoli domini pape capellano, domino Philippo Archidiacono Bonon', Magistro Manducatare Archidiacono Lucan', Magistro Roberto de Argentio advocato, domino Manfredo vicario venerabilis patris Archiepiscopi Mediolan', Magistro Johanne de Ros capellano nostro et aliis pluribus, anno domini M.CC.XLVIII, IIII nonas Junii pontificatus domini Innocenti pape quarti anno sexto. ... Nulli ergo omnino hominum liceat hanc paginam nostre confirmationis infringere vel ei ausu temerario contraire. Si quis, etc. Datum Lugdun' X kalendas Julii pontificatus nostri anno sexto. ... Prefati vero abbas et conventus asserebant dictam sentenciam eis obstare non[1] debere propter secundum privilegium suprascriptum quod est posterioris date. Habita ibidem disputatione utriumque solempne super premissis, et specialiter super hoc utrum privilegium Alexandri predictum quoad dictum prioratum de Tykeford' possit habere locum non obstante sentencia suprafata prius lata et auctoritate papali specialiter et ex certa sciencia confirmata, de qua in eodem privilegio nullimoda mentio fit tacite vel expresse, demum gravibus personis etiam canonicis Lincoln' assistentibus tunc episcopo in civitate London' et aliis amicis dictorum abbatis et monachorum intervenientibus, post multa et varia utrobique pensata fuit compositum, et ipsa compositio in scriptis redacta, signisque mutuo ad tunc signata et processum temporis realiter componenda et consummanda, prout ex tenore scripti subsequenter annotati colligi poterit evidenter, et scripti tenor est talis: ... Universis sancte matris ecclesie filiis pateat per presentes quod cum inter nos Oliverum permissione divina Lincoln' episcopum ac decanum et capitulum Lincoln' ex parte una, et nos fratrem Robertum ejusdem permissione abbatem et conventum majoris monasterii Turon' et priorem et monachos prioratus de Tykeford' juxta Newportpaynel Lincoln' diocesis ad dictum monasterium spectantis ex altera, super eo quod nos episcopus predictus prioratum predictum et ipsius priorem et monachos in visitatione, institutione et destitutione ac ceteris omnibus juribus episcopalibus de jure communi dicebamus nobis pleno jure subjectos, ac nos religiosi predicti pretendemus ipsos prioratum, priorem et monachos ab omni episcopali subjectione auctoritate sedis apostolice totaliter exemptos, suborta fuisset materia questionis, tandem considerantes quod lites non solum corporis inquietudinem set (sic) et mentium distractiones ac rerum consumptionem inducunt, et sic eas juxta consilium canonicarum et civilium sanctionum non immerito execrantes et pacis pulcritudinem affectantes, prefatam questionem per amicabilem compositionem duximus terminandum, a litis strepitu tunc inter nos protinus inchoande nisi sic inter nos fuisset amicabiliter compositum recedentes penitus sub hac forma: ... videlicet quod cum dominus Lincoln' episcopus qui pro tempore fuerit ad Tykeford' declinaverit, cum solempni processione prioris vel ejus locum tenentis ipso absente vel canonice impedito et monachorum in albis prima vice solummodo post ejus consecrationem sine procuratione, et aliis vicibus sine processione et procuratione reverenter tamen alias admittatur, et si voluerit clero aut populo ibidem pro

[1] Interlined.

voto suo convocando aut invento verbum Dei proponere, hoc faciendi in navi ecclesie vel in cimiterio ejusdem extra claustrum et capitulum prout elegerit liberam habeat facultatem, et in eodem prioratu cum transitum per partes illas fecerit suis libere valeat sumptibus hospitari, et tunc ut dictum est recipiatur sine processione, alias tamen reverenter. In vacatione siquidem dicti prioratus imposterum quotienscumque vacaverit prior illuc destinandus episcopo Lincoln' pro tempore existente litteratorie presentabitur per abbatem majoris monasterii qui ipsum episcopum per litteram suam presentatoriam et patentem rogabit quod eundem presentatum ad dictum prioratum admittat, et sic presentatus per episcopum sine examinatione et difficultate ac dilatione qualibet admittetur, et super hujusmodi admissione episcopi litteram sine difficultate ac dilatione qualibet admittetur, et super hujuscemodi admissione episcopi litteram sine difficultate et qualibet optinebit, ac canonicam sibi obedienciam ratione ecclesiarum dicto prioratui in Lincoln' diocese appropriatarum, salvis privilegiis prefati monasterii, in festo Omnium Sanctorum[1] proxime futuro jurabit nisi dictus abbas citra festum predictum coram prefato episcopo sufficienter docuerit ipsum priorem ad hujusmodi obedienciam prestandam non teneri ita quod per privilegia usque ad dictum festum impetranda in hoc casu non volerant se juvare. Licebitque dicto abbati priorem dicti loci quandocumque voluerit revocare. A visitatione autem et correctione de personis prioris et monachorum ac procuratione et jurisdictione episcopali infra dictum locum sint dicti prior et monachi ex nunc liberi et exempti. Ut autem honor debitus prefate Lincoln' ecclesie impendatur [*f. 319v*] ac ipsius et episcoporum ejusdem qui pro tempore fuerint indempnitati in hoc facto uberius prospiciatur, prefati abbas et conventus, prior et monachi, advocationem sive jus patronatus ecclesie de Schirinton que ad dictum prioratum spectabat in recompensationem procurationis et aliorum, que dictus episcopus et predecessores sui[1] in dicto prioratu percipere consueverant prefato episcopo et ipsius successoribus imperpetuum, contulerunt et assignarunt cum omni jure et possessione sibi competentibus in eadem, nichil juris omnino sibi retinentes, salvis in aliis privilegiis eorundem quatenus de jure sunt salvanda. In cujus rei testimonium, quia sigilla capitulorum hinc inde impresenciarum ad manus haberi non possunt, nos episcopus et abbas predicti presentibus apponi sigilla nostra fecimus alternatim, promittentes alter alteri quod citra festum Natalis Domini proxime futurum consimiles litteras sigillis nostris et capitulorum hinc inde et dictorum prioris et

---

[1] Interlined.

monachorum in testimonium hujusmodi compositionis realis faciemus communiri et alternatim tradi ac in ipsius traditionis eventu presentes litteras sursum reddi. Datum mense Februarii, anno domini M.CC. nonagesimo primo: ... Quibus sic peractis, dictus abbas fratrem Gaufridum dictum Vig' commonachum suum ad dictum prioratum de Tykeford' per litteram suam patentem presentavit sub hac forma: ... Venerabili in Christo patri domino Olivero Dei gracia Lincoln' episcopo, frater Robertus permissione divina majoris monasterii Turon' minister humilis salutem cum reverencia et honore. Ad prioratum nostrum de Tykeford' vestre diocesis nunc vacantem et ad nos ac monasterium nostrum spectantem, dilectum nostrum in Christo filium fratrem Gaufridum dictum Vig' nostri monasteri monachum exhibitorem presentium vobis presentamus, paternitatem vestram rogantes quatinus ipsum admittatis ad eundem. Valeat vestra paternitas in domino veneranda. Datum apud London' anno domini M.CC. nonagesimo primo undecimo kalendas Martii. ... Unde episcopus eisdem die et[1] anno, scilicet XI kalendas Martii anno domini M.CC. nonagesimo primo in camera sua apud Vetus Templum London', hora vesperarum, presentibus Magistris Henrico de Nassington', Johanne le Fleming', Gocelino de Kirnington' et Waltero de Wutton' canonicis Lincoln', aliquantula cum suis premissa, dictum presentatum genua flectentem cum libro admisit sub hiis verbis 'Admitto te ad prioratum de Tykeford' et eodem investio te per librum', exactione juramenti obediencie sub forma compositionis prescripti usque ad suum tempus dilata. Et post hec omnia habuit dictus frater Gaufridus de admissione sua litteram sub hac forma, sigillo dorso littere patenter impresso. ... Unversis pateat per presentes quod nos Oliverus permissione divina Lincoln' episcopus fratrem Gaufridum dictum Vig' monachum majoris monasterii Turon' per abbatem loci ejusdem ad prioratum de Tykeford' nostre diocesis prioris regimine vacantem, nobis canonice presentatum in priorem ipsius domus admisimus et ipsum per librum investivimus in eodem. Datum apud Vetus Templum London' XI kalendas Martii anno domini M.CC. nonagesimo primo. ... Et est sciendum pro memoria rei geste habenda quod dictus abbas promiserat ut dictum prioratum cum omnibus suis pertinenciis episcopo seu ecclesie Lincoln' concedi procurasset perpetuis temporibus optinendum pro certo annuo inde dicto monasterio Turon' reddendo, set[2] quia heres patroni ejusdem prioratus fuit tenellus et in

---

[1] Interlined.
[2] Sic.

custodia domini regis non fuit effectualiter tractatum, eo quod non videbatur tractatum posse sortiri effectum. Vide residuum in quarteno sequente ad hoc signum.[1]

WADDESDON ('Wuttesdon'). Thomas de Arches subd. p. by the King as guardian of the lands and heir of Sir Hugh de Courtenay to the portion which Anketil le Normaunt held in the church of Waddesden, vacant by the death of the said Auketil. Inst. Biggleswade, Apr. 27, 1292.

QUARTODECIMO KALENDAS JUNII VIDELICET DIE SANCTI ANNO DOMINI M.CC. NONAGESIMO SECUNDO INCIPIUNT INSTITUTIONES DE ANNO PONTIFICATUS DOMINI OLIVERI LINCOLNIEN' EPISCOPI TERTIODECIMO

CIPPENHAM (Cippeham). Licence to the Abbess and C. of Burnham to appropriate the chapel of Cippenham, the advowson of which had been given to them by Richard of Cornwall, King of the Romans, according to a grant made by Bishop Gravesend to come into effect on the death of the rector, Master Roger Geve. Licence granted by Bishop Sutton, Peatling Magna, May 23, 1292. Note that despite a search of the register the original grant could not be found.

WALTON.[2] R. Mediety. Master Richard of Ely, clerk in minor orders, p. by Margaret Rixbaud who had divorced her husband Nicholas of Hemington (*divorcio inter ipsam et dictum Nicholaum celebrato*) to the mediety of the church of Walton vacant by the death of Reginald. Presentation opposed by the said Nicholas who p. Robert de la Kervayle clerk, but later withdrew his claim by letters patent and agreed to allow Margaret to present. Had custody for a period. Then ordained subd. and inst. Lincoln Cathedral, May 31, 1292.

HARDWICK. R. Master Thomas Cantok' subd. p. by the King as guardian of the lands and heir of James Russel to the church of Hardwick, vacant by the death of Walter Russel and the fact that Master Edmund of London, clerk, who had been p. by Sir Richard de Moeles *alias* Moles (who had recovered his right of patronage in the King's court against Queen

---

[1] Marginal drawing of a man's head in profile.
[2] Near Newport Pagnell.

Eleanor) had not wished to be instituted. Presentation opposed by Sir Roger de Moeles who p. John of St. Amand. Writ in favour of the King, Westminster, Jan. 31, 1292, witnessed by J. de Mettingham. Thomas had custody for a period. Inst. Stow Park, June 7, 1292.

[*f. 320v*] EDLESBOROUGH. R. Oliver of Sutton, rector of the church of Churchill, ch. p. by the A. and C. of Bardney to the church of Edlesborough vacant because Master Thomas of Sutton had become Archdeacon of Northampton. held the church *in commendam* while he obtained a dispensation from Pope Nicholas IV (dated at Rome, Santa Maria Maggiore, Jan. 5, 1292) to hold in plurality. The bishop issued to or on behalf of Oliver Sutton four letters of testimonial, dated Stow Park, Aug. 9, 1292. Inst. same place and day.

TICKFORD.[1] Note that on Oct. 26, 1292, at Spaldwick the Priors of Rillé and Mantenay appeared as lawful proctors (appointed Paris, Oct. 2, 1292) of the Abbot of St. Martin's, Tours to pursue the final agreement between the bishop and the A. and C. of St. Martin's concerning the priory of Tickford. On Oct. 27 the said proctors put forward the A. and C.'s claim to exemption, supported by privileges of Innocent III (no date), Innocent IV (Lyons, Apr. 10, 1251) and Alexander IV.[2] Bishop Sutton replied that the proctors had made no case why the Prior of Tickford should not swear obedience on behalf of those churches in the diocese appropriated to the Tickford Priory. This was accordingly done, Spaldwicke, Nov. 1, 1292, by Geoffrey, Prior of Tickford, in the presence of Master Jocelyn of Kirmington, Roger of Sixhills, John de Scalleby, Hugh Duket, Hugh of Harewood and other clerks of the bishop's household.

... Deinde quasdam allegationes juris in scriptis redactas exhibuerunt que sunt tales: ... Reverende pater domino O. Dei gracia Lincoln' Episcope, vos asseritis quod Prior de Tykeford' juxta Neuportpaynel' teneatur vobis facere canonicam obedienciam ratione ecclesiarum quas dicitis ipsum habere in diocese Lincoln' sibi in proprios usus appropriatarum, et hoc triplici ratione, primo de jure commune, secundo de consuetudine terre sive regni Anglie, tertio quia alias fuit vobis facta a ... priore dicti loci, et ad informandum vos nomine ... Abbatis et conventus majoris monasterii Turon' ... Prioris et monachorum de Tykeford', predictorum, et pro

---

[1] Marginal drawing of a man's head in profile. See above, p. 137.
[2] For which see above, pp. 130–1.

ipsis, dicimus et proponimus quod ad ipsam obedienciam faciendam non tenetur iste ... prior, respondemus ad proposita, et imprimis quod ad ipsam obedienciam non tenetur [*f. 322*] ex eo, et pro eo quia, postquam eedem ecclesie ad dictum prioratum devenerunt, prioratus prior et monachi ejusdem loci fuerunt exempti, et concessum eis quod gauderent et uterentur eisdem privilegiis, libertatibus, immunitatibus et graciis quibus gaudebant et gaudent et utuntur monasterium, ... abbas et monachi majoris monasterii Turon', quibus monasterio et abbati subsunt dicti prioratus, prior et monachi predicti, quodque monasterium, abbas et monachi tunc temporis habebant et habent inter alia talem exemptionem, libertatem, immunitatem et privilegium quod soli Romane ecclesie erant et sunt subjecti et nullum habebant nec habent superiorem nisi Romanum pontificem, et quod non possunt nec possent ab aliquo archiepiscopo aut episcopo excommunicari, per quam exemptionem et concessionem factam dictis priori et prioratui tolluntur et sublata fuerunt et sunt omnia jura episcopalia cum nichil episcopo fuerit reservatum *articulo capitulo extra de prescripto venerabilis et de utili vel inutili cum dilecta*, et quia verbis exemptionis et privilegiorum generaliter loquentium standum est *extra de privilegiis porro* et c. *dilectis*. Unde cum dicta exemptio et privilegia loquantur generaliter constat quod dominus papa nichil voluit reservare domino episcopo supradicto. Item, exemptio est caute efficacie et fit cum tanta deliberatione quod papa presumitur scire jus cujuslibet et etiam possessionem alterius se[1] eximendo totum tollit, et hoc expresse terminatur per dominum Innocentium, *extra de privilegiis capitulum dudum*. Item, si ad obedienciam predictam que petitur teneretur, sequeretur quod dictus episcopus esset ejus superior, quod noluit summus pontifex et non patitur exemptio predicta, quia si eam prestaret idem prior non gauderet privilegiis exemptionis predicte, immo contra eam veniret expresse, quod non tenetur facere idem prior, immo si hoc faceret, posset et deberet a sua administratione ammoveri per abbatem, quia jura et privilegia dicti monasterii non servasset. Item, si dictam obedienciam prestaret idem prior, sequeretur quod si esset inobediens dicto episcopo quod dictus episcopus posset eum punire et excommunicare tanquam inobedientem, quod est contra formam exemptionis dicti prioris et privilegiorum eorundem, cum super hoc habeat exemptionem et privilegia ut superius est expressum. Item, si bene consideretur substancia obediencie, que sit obediencia et quis et cui eam prestare teneatur secundum quod dicit Hostiensis in *summa de majoritate et obediencia* apparebit

---

[1] Interlined.

et liquere poterit manifeste quod eam prestare non tenetur
idem prior, cum superiori tantum et in certis casibus a minore
sit prestanda, ut ibidem dicitur, et ideo cum dictus episcopus
non sit superior dicti prioris in aliquo, cum nullum habeat
superiorem preter Romanum pontificem ut suum abbatem
propter exemptionem et privilegia predicta, certum est quod
eam prestare non tenetur. Item, certum est quod obediencia
est de lege juridico, ut *extra de officiis ordinariis, capitulum con-
querente*, et determinatur eodem titulo *capitulo dilectis filiis*, et
ideo cum dictus prior sit exemptus et summo pontifici et suo
abbati solummodo subjectus ut dictum est, constat quod ad
dictam obedienciam que est de lege juridico non tenetur
eidem episcopo. Item et alia ratione quia certum est quod
quando ecclesia pertinet ad aliquos religiosos non pleno jure
sufficit quod religiosi presbiterum presentent episcopo qui
sibi de plebis cura respondeat et religiosis de temporalibus, ut
expresse dicit textus *extra, de privilegiis, capitulum cum et plantare*, et
ideo cum prior dicti prioratus vicarium presentaverit dicto
domino episcopo, cui episcopus curam commisit et qui fecit
sibi obedienciam et qui vadit ad sinodum et omnia fecit que
spectare et imminent facienda ratione dicte ecclesie et populi
ejusdem, certum est quod idem prior ad dictam obedienciam
non tenetur. Item, cum dictus prior curam et populum non
recipiat a dicto domino episcopo nec habeat curam, eo quod
ad dictam obedienciam non tenetur nec ad aliquid etiam de
lege diocesano, ut XVIII questio in fine, immo[1] plus et si
dicto priori exempto cura commiteretur et populus a dicto
domino episcopo, quod non est verum, non propter hoc
teneretur idem prior ad obedienciam que est de lege juridico,
sed solummodo ad ea que sunt de lege diocesano, ut expresse
terminatur et per Innocentium et alios *extra de majoritate et
obediencia capitulum quod superbiis*, et in multis aliis locis. Item, ad
dictam obedienciam que est de lege juridico ut dictum est non
tenetur ex alia ratione, videlicet propter compositionem
dictorum domini episcopi et abbatis, quia per ipsam [*f. 322v*]
compositionem constat quod episcopus in priorem et monachos
dicti prioratus non habeat aliquam jurisdictionem saltem in
ipso prioratu, et ideo cum obediencia sit de lege juridico
constat quod ad eam non tenetur, et si diceret dominus
episcopus quod ratione bonorum que percepit dictus prior
tenetur facere obedienciam certum est talem allegationem
non valere, nam nunquam invenietur quod ratione rei
solummodo teneatur exemptus ad obedienciam prestandam,
licet ratione rei fiat homagium quando tenetur in feodum
quod non est in casu presenti. Item, inhonestum esset dicere

---

[1] Illegible, apparently sic.

et contra exemptionem predictam quod ratione bonorum teneretur idem prior ad dictam obedienciam, cum papa sciret et presumatur scire quod tempore dicte exemptionis dictus prior habebat bona infra metas alicujus diocesis et[1] eximendo voluit prejudicare omnibus episcopis, ut superius est expressum, alias enim nulla esset exemptio si[1] pro bonis subessent exempti, cum papa et quilibet foret et sciat quod sine bonis non possent vivere, quod est absurdum, et sic per predicta constat quod ratione dictarum ecclesiarum ad obedienciam petitam non tenetur ratione prime allegationis dicti domini episcopi qua asserit sibi eam de jure communi deberi, cum est[1] predictum jus commune sic sublatum secundum jura. Item, id quod proponit dictus dominus episcopus quod[1] de consuetudine alii exempti dictam obedienciam faciunt, et quod propter hoc eam facere tenetur dictus prior, non valet, nam salva gracia proponentis, et si omnes alii exempti vellent renunciare exceptionibus suis et contra eas facerent, non propter hoc tenetur dictus prior sue exemptioni renunciare et contra eam facere, nam res inter alios acta aliis non prejudicat, nec debet alteri per alterum iniqua conditio afferri. Item, consuetudo ad prejudicandum juri alterius est stricti juris et ad alios non extenditur quam ad personas cum quibus ipsa consuetudo extitit observata. Item, salva gracia dicti domini episcopi si alii exempti eam faciunt, non faciunt virtute consuetudinis set[2] ratione certarum conventionum habitarum inter eos et dictum dominum episcopum. Item, si quod proponit dictus dominus episcopus quod alius prior dicti loci fecit sibi dictam obedienciam, non valet, quia salva gracia proponentis si hoc esset verum, non tamen propter hoc prior qui nunc est teneretur ad eam, tamen etsi facisset non propter hoc unico tali actu vel etiam pluribus non posset tolli jus ecclesie et successorum ejus qui eam fecisset et sedis apostolice in exemptione predicta, cum talis exemptio sit honorabilis et utilis ecclesie, et in talibus non potest quis vel etiam superior ecclesie prejudicare, *articulo legis C. de transactionibus, L. preses*, cum suis similibus, et hoc expresse terminatum est per dominum Innocentium, *extra, de privilegiis, C. accedentibus*, immo plus, etsi omnes de ecclesia uno excepto vellent renunciare et renunciarent juribus honorabilibus et utilibus ecclesie, unus solus posset contradicere ut ibidem terminatur. Secus tamen est in hiis que sint onerosa, ut in eodem *C accedentibus* per dictum dominum Innocentium terminatur, non obstat capitulum *cum capella* de quo consuevit dictus dominus episcopus quam plurimum revocare, non enim aliquid facit

[1] Interlined.
[2] Sic.

pro eodem quia illud capitulum loquitur in privilegiis in uno articulo vel pluribus, et hoc indicat littera ibi *ratione dicte ecclesie parochialis vel alie*, et loquitur etiam quando ipse privilegiatus tenebat ecclesiam ab episcopo et hoc expresse indicat littera ibi *ecclesias a te tenent*, secus vero est omnino in casu vestro presenti, quia loquimur de omnino exemptis, et quia non tenent ecclesias ab episcopo, nam dictus prior omnino est exemptus et non habet aliquem superiorem nisi Romanum pontificem, et ecclesiam, curam et populum non tenet, immo presbiter presentatus dicto domino episcopo quem idem dominus episcopus recipit ad ipsam ecclesiam, et curam et populum commisit eidem. Item, omnia alia jura que pro parte dicti domini possent allegari que superfinaliter videretur facere pro eodem non obstant nec valent quia semper invenietur si qua contigerit allegari que videantur facere pro ipso quod loquitur in non exemptis prout superius est expressum. Item, hoc videtur esse determinatum unico verbo posito in glosa ordinaria cujusdam decreti XVI questio II, scilicet *de appellationibus* in summa illius questionis in glosa ibi posita Papini [*f. 323*] ultra medium illius glose ubi dicitur *ea que dicta sunt intelligas de non exemptis. In exemptis autem quod principi placuit legis habet vigorem. Unde ipse prior*, etc. Et per predicta et alia que dictus reverendus pater cum suo circumspecto consilio sciet addere liquet et linquere poterit manifestissime dictum priorem ad dictam obedienciam prestandam non teneri. Petebant etiam quod quantum ad consummationem com-positionis predicte per consensum et appositionem sigillorum capitulorum hincinde habendam episcopus suam eis diceret voluntatem. Quibus auditis, et prefatis prioribus secedentibus, episcopus habito tractatu cum suis, ipsis, prioribus revocatis, hec vel consimilia verba dixit: ... Privilegia que nunc exhibitus, excepto privilegio Innocenti III per cujus clausulas aliquas intimini vos juvare, que nichil pro vobis operantur omnino, et rationes per vos nunc[1] allegate, exhibite et allegate fuerunt in tractatu London' habito inter abbatem majoris monasterii et quosdam priores et commonachos suos ex parte una et nos ex altera coram jurisperitis ibidem tunc presentibus in multi-tudine copiosa. Et videbatur tunc etiam abbati vestro et consilio suo quod hujusmodi privilegia et rationes vobis prodesse non poterant quin dictus prior de Tykeford' pro ecclesias prioratui suo appropriatis in diocese Lincoln' obedienciam canonicam nobis et successoribus nostris facere teneretur, ex quo non obstantibus tunc propositis et allegatis

[1] Interlined.
[2] Sic.
[3] Sic, a double negative.

cepit diem alia exhibenda. Vobis ergo dicimus pro responso quod veniat dictus prior de Tyk' ad nos in festo Omnium Sanctorum vel citra, facturus nobis obedienciam pro appropriatis ecclesiis antedictis secundum formam compositionis prelocute, alioquin quod nostre incumbit officio faciemus. Dicimus etiam vobis quod compositionem predictam initiatam parati erimus confirmare, dummodo preambula quantum ad hujusmodi obediencie, presentationem er alia bona fide sicut mutuo condictam extitit ab initio, et dominus abbas vester adhuc scribit quod ita fiat, serventur — et sic dicti priores ab episcopo recesserunt. Die² vero Omnium Sanctorum anno domini M.CC. nonagesimo secundo, in parochiali ecclesia de Spaldewyk', post magnam missam de die celebratam, comparuit personaliter coram episcopo frater Gaufridus prior de Tykeford', et tactis sacrosanctis ewangeliis juravit se canonicam obedienciam ratione ecclesiarum prioratui de Tykeford' appropriatarum in diocese Lincoln' secundum formam compositionis predicte, presentibus Magistro Gocelino Archidiacono Stowe, Rogero de Sixil et Johanne de Scalleby capellanis, Hugone Duket et Hugone de Harewod' subdiaconis et pluribus aliis de familia dicti domini episcopi. Vide plus in hac parte ad hoc signum.³

SALDEN. Philip de Wulwardington' ch. p. by Sir Robert Fitz-Nigel (filius Nigelli) knight to the chapel of Salden vacant by the death of Richard. Inst. Spaldwick, Nov. 4, 1292.

TICKFORD (Tykeford').⁴ Note that on Dec. 11, 1292, the Prior of Tickford and William de Corberia, a monk of St. Martin's, Tours, brought to the bishop at Dorchester-on-Thames a letter from the A. and C. of St. Martin's defining the rights which he was prepared to concede to the bishop over Tickford Priory, together with a grant of the advowson of the church of Sherington. Dated St. Martin's, May 1, 1292. The bishop objected to certain words in the letter and to the fact that the proxies brought no charter of enfeoffment with the said avowson and deferred the matter until June 11, 1293.

Subsequenter vero III idus Decembris anno domini M.CC. nonagesimo secundo apud Dorkecestr' ubi episcopus ad tunc erat, ...⁵ prior de Tykeford' et frater Willelmus de Corberia

---

¹ Sic, a double negative.
² Marginal note 'Obediencia Prioris de Tykeford".
³ Marginal drawing of a rather grim face.
⁴ The drawing of a grim face is repeated.
⁵ Blank in MS.

monachus monasterii majoris Turon' personaliter comparentes exhibuerunt quamdam litteram sigillis abbatis et capituli dicti monasterii signatam pro reali confirmatione negotii penes episcopum residendam, cujus est talis tenor: ..8. Universis presentes litteras inspecturis, fratres capituli majoris monasterii Turon' et frater Robertus permissione divina minister humilis eorundem salutem in domino. Noverint universi quod cum inter reverendum in Christo patrem dominum Oliverum Dei gracia episcopum, et decanum et capitulum Lincoln' ex una parte, et nos abbatem [*f. 323v*] et conventum predictos ac ...[1] priorem et monachos prioratus nostri de Tykeford' juxta Neuportpaynel, Lincoln' diocesis, ad nostrum predictum monasterium pleno jure spectantes ex altera, super eo quod iidem episcopus, decanus et capitulum Lincoln' prioratum predictum et ipsius priorem et monachos in visitatione, institutione et destitutione ac ceteris omnibus juribus episcopalibus de jure communi dicebant predicto episcopo pleno jure subjectos, ac nos pretenderemus predictos prioratum, priorem et monachos nostros ab omni episcopali subjectione auctoritate sedis apostolice totaliter exemptos, suborta fuisset materia questionis, tandem considerantes quod lites non solum corporis inquietudinem set et mentium distractiones et rerum consumpsionem inducunt, et sic eas juxta consilium canonicarum et civilium sanctionem non immerito execrantes, ac pacis pulchritudinem acceptantes, prefatam questionem per amicabilem compositionem duximus terminandam, a litis strepitu tunc inter nos protinus inchoande nisi fuisset amicabiliter compositum recedentes penitus sub hac forma: ... videlicet quod idem episcopum Lincoln' qui pro tempore fuerit ad prioratum predictum de Tykeford' declinaverit, cum solempni processione ... prioris vel ejus locum tenentis ipso absente vel canonice impedit et monachorum in albis prima vice solummodo post ejus consecrationem sine procuratione et visitatione, et in aliis vicibus sine processione, procuratione et visitatione, reverenter tamen aliis admitteretur. Et si voluerit clero aut populo ibidem pro voto suo convocando aut invento verbum Dei proponere, hoc faciendi in navi ecclesie vel in cimiterio ejusdem extra claustrum et capitulum prout elegerit liberam habeat facultatem, et in eodem prioratu cum transitum per illas partes fecerit suis libere valeat sumptibus, et tunc ut dictum est recipiatur sine processione, alia tamen reverenter. In vacatione siquidem dicti prioratus imposterum[2] quotienscumque vacaverit ...[1] prios illuc destinandus Episcopo

---

[1] Blank in MS.
[2] Interlined.

Lincoln' pro tempore existenti litteratorie presentabitur per litteram ...[1] abbatis qui pro tempore fuerit, qui ipsum episcopum per litteram suam presentatoriam et patentem rogabit quod eundem presentatum ad dictum prioratum admittat, et sic presentatus per episcopum sine examinatione et difficultate ac dilatione qualibet admittetur. Et super hujuscemodi admissionem episcopi litteram sine difficultate et dilatione qualibet optinebit, ac canonicam sibi obedienciam ratione ecclesiarum dicto prioratui seu priori in Lincoln' diocese appropriatarum salvis privilegiis prefati monasterii nostri jurabit, nisi citra festum Omnium Sanctorum proxime futurum sufficientur docuerimus ipsum priorem ad hujusmodi obedienciam prestandam non teneri, ita quod per privilegia usque ad dictum festum impetranda in hoc casu non valeamus nos juvare. Licebitque nobis ...[1] abbati predicto et cuilibet successorum nostrorum qui pro tempore fuerit priorem dicti loci quandocumque voluerimus seu voluerit revocare. A visitatione autem et correctione de personis prioris et monachorum ac procuratione et visitatione episcopali infra dictum locum sint dicti prior et monachi exnunc liberi et exempti. Privilegiis nobis abbati et conventui, prioribus et monachis aliis nobis salvis quatenus de jure sunt salvanda. Ut autem honor debitus prefate Lincoln' ecclesie impendatur, ac ipsius et episcoporum ejusdem qui pro tempore fuerint indempnitati in hoc facto uberius prospiciatur, nos abbas et conventus, prior et monachi predicti advocationem sive jus patronatus ecclesie de Schirinton' que ad nos et prioratum predictum spectabat, in recompensationem procurationis et aliarum que dictus episcopus et predecessores sui in dicto prioratu percipere consueverant prefato episcopo et ipsius successoribus imperpetuum contulerimus et conferimus, assignavimus et assignamus, cum omni jure et possessione nobis competentibus in eadem, nichil juris omnino nobis retinentes. In cujus rei testimonium nostra sigilla una cum sigillo ...[1] prioris et monachorum de Tykeford' predictorum presentibus litteris duximus apponenda. Datum in nostro generali capitulo, anno domini M.CC. nonagesimo secundo, in festo beatorum Philippi et Jacobi apostolorum. ... Petebunt insuper ut episcopus sub sigillo suo et capituli sui consimilem litteram penes abbatem et conventum majoris monasterii remanandam ipsos habere faceret vice versa. Examinata igitur littera [*f. 324*] forma compositionis superius annotate in quam London' consensum fuerat inter episcopum et abbatem predictos ac consilium utriusque, inveniebatur in eadem littera plura fuerunt verba inserta que non erant in dicta

[1] Blank in MS.

compositione, et aliqua transposita et adjecta prout ex utriusque tenore colligere poterit qui diligenter advertit. Similiter cartam super feoffatione advocationis ecclesie de Schyrington' nullatenus exhibebant. Quibus die sequenti scilicet II idus Decembris priori et commonacho suo predicto expositis, petebant quod episcopus formam littere predicte, deletis verbis delendis, convenientam fieri[1] faceret rei geste una cum carta feoffamenti super advocatione predicta, et ipsi litteram hujusmodi dictorum abbatis et capituli, ac cartam prioris et commonachorum de Tykeford' sigillis facerent consignari. . . .

BRADENHAM. R. Thomas son of Thomas of Gaunt, clerk in minor orders p. by Simon FitzRobert lord of Bradenham to the church thereof vacant by the death of Adam of Warwick. Ordained subd. and inst. Dorchester-on-Thames, Dec. 20, 1292.

WENDOVER. V. Nicholas of London ch. p. by the P. and C. of Southwark to the vicarage of Wendover vacant by the res. of William of Leicester (Leyc'). Inst. London, Old Temple, Feb. 18, 1293, in the presence of Masters Jocelyn of Kirmington Archdeacon of Stow and John le Fleming, Sir Walter of Stockton, all canons of Lincoln, Sir John Maunsel and John de Scalleby priests, and John of Ferriby notary-public.

STOKE REGIS. V. William of Merstham ch. p. by the P. and C. of Southwark to the vicarage of Stoke Regis vacant by the res. of Nicholas of London on his institution to the vicarage of Wendover. Inst. London, Old Temple, Apr. 17, 1293.

HANSLOPE.[2] R. Peter le Blund subd. p. by William de Beauchamp Earl of Warwick to the church of Hanslope vacant by the death of Simon of Elsworth and the res. of Master Robert de Systerne first presented. Inst. Lincoln, Mar. 24, 1293.

———

QUARTODECIMO KALENDAS JUNII VIDELICET DIE SANCTI DUNSTANI ANNO DOMINI M.CC. NONAGESIMO TERTIO INCIPIT ANNUS PONTIFICATUS DOMINI OLIVERI LINCOLNIEN' EPISCOPI QUARTUSDECIMUS.

———

[1] Interlined.
[2] This entry has been inserted out of order at the bottom of the folio.

TICKFORD.[1] Note that in June 1293, at London, Old Temple, the priors of Rillé and Tickford produced sealed letters patent from the A. and C. of St. Martin's, Tours, dated May (1), 1293, ratifying the agreement made with the bishop and the dean and chapter over Tickford Priory, together with two other sealed letters patent, one of the said A. and C. dated May 1 and one of the P. and C. of Tickford dated June 2, granting to the bishop and his successors the advowson of the church of Sherington. The bishop on his side issued sealed letters patent, dated London, Old Temple, June 1293, ratifying the agreement.

Postmodum mense Junii anno domini M.CC. nonagesimo tertio apud Vetus Templum' London' venerunt ad episcopum fratres[2] Leodegarius prior de Releye et frater Gaufridus prior de Neuportpaynel' deferentes eidem episcopo litteram quamdam sigillis abbatis et capituli majoris monasterii ac prioris et monachorum de Neuportpaynel' signatam, necnon quamdam cartam sigillis dictorum abbatis et capituli ac prioris et monachorum, et quamdam aliam cartam sigillis dictorum prioris et monachorum tantum signatas pro reali consummatione negotii penes episcopum residendi sub continentiis infrascriptis: ... Universis[3] presentes litteras inspecturis, fratres capituli majoris monasterii Turon' et frater Robertus permissione divina minister humilis eorundem salutem in domino. Noverint universi quod cum inter reverendum in Christo patrem dominum Oliverum Dei gracia episcopum ac decanum et capitulum Lincoln ex una parte, et nos abbatem et conventum predictos ac priorem et monachos prioratus de Tykeford' juxta Neuportpaynel Lincoln' diocesis[4] ad nostrum predictum monasterium spectantis ex altera, super eo quod idem episcopus prioratum predictum et monachos in visitatione, institutione et destitutione ac ceteris omnibus juribus episcopalibus dicebat sibi pleno jure subjectos, ac nos pretenderemus predictos prioratum, priorem et monachos ab omni episcopali subjectione auctoritate sedis apostolice totaliter exemptos, suborta fuisset materia questionis, tandem considerantes quod lites non solum corporis inquietudinem set[5] et mentium distractiones ac rerum consumptionem inducunt,

---

[1] Marginal drawing of a grim-looking face.
[2] Sic, recte 'frater'.
[3] Marginal note in a fourteenth century hand 'Carta abbatis et conventus monasterii majoris Turon' super concordia inita inter ipsos et episcopum Lincoln' de subjectione prioratus de Tykeford'.
[4] Marginal note (as before) 'Vide consimilem cartam episcopi et decani et capituli Lincoln' super eadem concordia in folio proxime sequente'.
[5] Sic.

et sic eas juxta consilium canonicarum et civilium sanctionum non immerito execrantes, ac pacis pulcritudinem[1] affectantes, prefatam questionem per amicabilem compositionem duximus terminandam, a litis strepitu tunc inter nos protinus inchoande nisi sic inter nos fuisset amicabiliter compositumn recedentes penitus sub hac forma:[2] ... videlicet quod cum dominus Episcopus Lincoln' qui pro tempore fuerit ad Prioratum predictum de Tykeford' declinaverit, cum solempni processione prioris vel ejus locum tenentis ipso absente vel canonice impedito et monachorum in albis prima vice solummodo post ipsius consecrationem, sine procuratione, et aliis vicibus sine processione et procuratione, reverenter tamen alias admittatur. Et si voluerit clero aut populo ibidem pro voto suo convocando aut invento verbum Dei proponere,[3] hoc faciendi in navi ecclesia vel cimiterio ejusdem extra claustrum et capitulum prout elegerit liberam habeat facultatem, et in eodem prioratu cum transitum per illas partes fecerit suis libere valeat sumpitbus hospitari,[4] et tunc ut dictum est recipiatur sine processione, alias tamen reverenter. In vacatione siquidem dicti[5] prioratus quotienscumque vacaverit, prior illuc destinandus Episcopo Lincoln' pro tempore existente litteratorie presentabitur per abbatem majoris monasterii, qui ipsum episcopum per litteram suam presentatoriam rogabit quod eundem presentatum ad dictum prioratum admittat,[6] et sic presentatus per episcopum sine examinatione et difficultate ac dilatione qualibet admittetur, et super hujuscemodi admissionem episcopi litteram sine difficultate et dilatione qualibet optinebit, ac canonicam sibi obedienciam ratione ecclesiarum dicto prioratui in Lincoln' diocese appropriatarum salvis privilegiis prefati monasterii nostri[7] jurabit.[8] Licebitque nobis abbati predicto et cuilibet successorum nostrorum qui pro tempore fuerit priorem dicti loci quandocumque voluerimus seu voluerit revocare. A visitatione et correctione de personis prioris et monachorum ac procuratione et jurisdictione epicopali infra dictum locum sint dicti prior et monachi exnunc liberi et exempti. Ut autem

---

[1] Sic.
[2] Marginal note (as before) 'Episcopus Lincoln' prima vice post suam consecrationem cum processione solemni recipiatur'.
[3] Marginal note (as before) 'Qualiter poterat episcopus in dicto prioratui predicare'.
[4] Marginal note (as before) 'Qualiter possit ibidem episcopus hospitari'.
[5] Interlined.
[6] Marginal note (as before) 'De presentatione prioris ibidem, et sua admissione'.
[7] Interlined.
[8] Marginal note (as before), partly illegible, 'de obediencia prioris et de ...'.

honor debitus prefate Lincoln' ecclesie impendatur ac ipsius et episcoporum ejusdem qui pro tempore fuerint indempnitati in hoc 'cto uberius prospiciatur, nos abbas et conventus, prior et monachi predicti advocationem sive jus patronatus ecclesie de Schirington'[1] que ad nos et dictum prioratum spectabat, in recompensationem procurationis et aliorum que dictus episcopus et predecessores sui in dicto prioratu percipere consueverant, prefato episcopo et ipsius successoribus imperpetuum contulimus et conferimus, assignavimus et assignamus cum omni jure et possessione nobis competentibus in eadem, nichil juris omnino nobis retinentes, salvis in aliis privilegiis nostris quatenus de jure sunt salvanda. In cujus rei testimonium nostra sigilla una cum sigillis prioris et monachorum predictorum presentibus litteri duximus apponendum. Datum in nostro generali capitulo anno domini M.CC. nonagesimo tertio, mense Maii.[2]

CARTA SUPER DE ECCLESIAM SCHIRINGTON'. Sequitur carta: Universis presentes litteras inspecturis, fratres capituli majoris monasterii [f. 325] Turon', et frater Robertus permissione divina ministerii humilis eorundem, salutem in domino. Sciant presentes et futuri quod nos de assensu et voluntate prioris et conventus de Tikeford' juxta Neuport Paynel' advocationem sive jus patronatus ecclesie de Schirrinton' Lincoln' diocesis que ad nos et prioratum nostrum de Tikeford' hactenus spectabat, in recompensationem procurationis et aliorum que venerabilis pater dominus Oliverus Lincoln' episcopus et predecessores sui in dicto prioratu nostro percipere consueverant prefato episcopo et ipsius successoribus imperpetuum contulimus et conferimus, assignavimus et etiam assignamus, cum omni jure et possessione nobis competentibus in eadem, habendum et tenendum cum omnibus juribus et pertinenciis suis eidem episcopo et successoribus suis episcopis Lincolnien' de capitalibus dominis feodi, libere et quiete imperpetuum, nichil juris omnino nobis vel successoribus nostris in advocatione predicta retinentes, ita quod quotienscumque vel qualitercumque ipsam ecclesiam de Schirriton'[3] vacare contigerit in futurum liceat predictis episcopo et successoribus suis tanquam veris patronis et loci dyocesanis ipsam ecclesiam conferre cuique voluerint successive, vel suum comodum inde facere qualitercumque voluerint absque nostri vel dictorum prioris et conventus seu

---

[1] Marginal note (as before) 'Shyrington' ecclesie jus patronatu'.
[2] The general chapter met on the feast of SS. Philip and James, May 1. See above, p. 145.
[3] Sic.

successorum nostrorum aut ipsorum reclamatione vel contradictione quacumque imperpetuum. In cujus rei testimonium
tam nos quam predicti prior et conventus de Tikeford'
presenti carte sigilla nostra duximus apponenda. Datum in
nostro generali capitulo prima die Maii anno domini M.CC.
nonagesimo tertio. ... Sequitur alia carta.

ALIA CARTA SUPER ECCLESIAM DE SCHIRINGTON'. Sciant presentes
et futuri quod nos frater Gaufridus Prior de Tikeford' et
ejusdem loci[1] conventus dedimus, concessimus et hac presenti
carta nostra confirmavimus venerabili in Christo patri
domino Olivero Dei gracia Lincoln' Episcopo et successoribus
suis Lincolniens' Epicopis imperpetuum advocationem sive jus
patronatus ecclesie de Schyrington Lincoln' diocesis que ad
nos hactenus de jure spectabat, in recompensationem
procurationis et aliorum que dictus pater et predecessores sui
Lincoln' Episcopi in prioratu nostro de Tikeford percipere
consueverant, habendum et tenendum dictam advocationem
sive jus patronatus prefate ecclesie de Schirington' cum
omnibus juribus et pertinenciis suis eidem episcopo et
successoribus suis Lincoln' episcopis libere, quiete, bene et in
pace imperpetuum, nichil juris omnino nobis vel successoribus nostris in advocatione predicta retinentes, ita quod
quotienscumque vel qualitercumque ipsam ecclesiam de
Schirington' vacare contigerit in futurum, liceat predictis
episcopo et successoribus suis tanquam veris patronis et loci
diocesanis ipsam ecclesiam conferre cuicumque voluerint
successive, vel suum comodum inde facere qualitercumque
voluerint absque nostri vel successorum nostrorum reclamatione vel contradictione quacumque imperpetuum. Et nos
dicti prior et conventus predictam advocationem sive jus
patronatus prefato episcopo et successoribus suis episcopis
Lincoln' imperpetuum warantizabimus. In cujus rei testimonium sigilla nostra presenti carte sunt appensa. Hiis
testibus, dominis Reginaldo de Grey, Johanne filio ejusdem,
Thoma de Bray et Willelmo de Sauntresdon' militibus,
Magistro Waltero de Wutton' at aliis. Datum in prioratu
nostro de Tikeford' IIII nonas Junii anno gracie M.CC.
nonagesimo tertio. ... Dicti autem priores habuerunt[2] ab
episcopo quemdam litteram sigillo ipsius episcopi et capituli
Lincoln' signata sub hac forma: ... Universis[3] presentes
litteras inspecturis Oliverus permissione divina Lincoln

---

[1] Interlined.
[2] The 'h' of this word has been interlined.
[3] Marginal note (as before) 'Carta domini epicopi ac decani et capituli
Lincoln' super predicta concordia'.

Episcopus, et decanus et capitulum loci ejusdem, salutem in omnium salvatore. Noverit universitas vestra quod cum inter nos ex parte una ac abbatem et conventum majoris monasterii Turon', ac priorem et monachos prioratus de Tykeford' juxta Neuportpaynel Lincoln' diocesis ad predictum monasterium spectantis ex altera, super eo quod nos episcopus prioratum predictum ac ipsius priorem et monachos in visitatione, institutione et destitutione ac ceteris omnibus juribus episco-palibus de jure communi dicebamus nos pleno jure subjectos, ac abbas et conventus, prior et monachi supradicti preten-derent eosdem prioratum, priorem et monachos ab omni subjectione episcopali auctoritate sedis apostolice totaliter exemptos, suborta fuisset materia questionis, tandem con-siderantes quod lites non solum corporis inquietudinum set[1] et mentium distractiones ac rerum consuptionem inducunt, et sic eas juxta consilium canonicorum et civilium sanctionum non immeritu execrantes, [f. 325v] ac pacis pulcritudinem[1] affectantes, prefatam questionem per amicabilem com-positionem duximus terminandam, a litis strepitu tunc inter nos protinus inchoande nisi sic inter nos fuisset amicabiliter compositum recedentes penitus sub hac forma, videlicet quod cum dominus Lincoln' Episcopus ad prioratum predictum de Tykeford' declinaverit, cum solempni processione prioris vel ejus locum tenentis ipso absente vel canonice impedito et monachorum in albis prima vice solummodo post ejus con-secrationem sine procuratione, et aliis vicibus sine processione et procuratione, reverenter tamen alias, admittatur. Et si voluerit clero aut populo ibidem verbum Dei proponere, hoc faciendi in navi ecclesie vel cimiterio ejusdem extra claustrum et capitulum prout elegerit liberam habeat facultatem, et in eodem prioratu cum transitum per partes illas fecerit suis libere valeat sumptibus hospitari, et tunc ut dictum est recipiatur sine processione, alias tamen reverenter. In vacatione siquidem dicti prioratus imposterum quotiens-cumque vacaverit prior illuc destinandus episcopo Lincoln' pro tempore existenti litteratorie presentabitur per abbatem majoris monasterii, qui ipsum episcopum per litteram suam presentatoriam et patentem rogabit quod eundem presen-tatum ad dictum prioratum admittat, et sic presentatus per episcopum sine examinatione et difficultate et dilatione qualibet admittetur, et super hujusmodi comodi admissione episcopi litteram sine difficultate et dilatione qualibet optinebit, ac canonicam sibi obedienciam ratione ecclesiarum dicto prioratui in Lincoln' diocese appropriatarum, salvis privilegiis prefati monasterii, jurabit. Licebitque abbati

[1] Sic.

predicto et cuilibet successorum suorum qui pro tempore fuerit priorem dicti loci quandocumque voluerit revocare. A visitatione autem et correctione de personis prioris et monachorum ac procuratione et jurisdictione episcopali infra dictum locum sint dicti prior et monachi exnunc liberi et exempti. Ut autem honor debitus Lincoln' ecclesie impendatur ac ipsius et episcoporum ejusdem qui pro tempore fuerint indempnitati in hoc facto uberius prospiciatur, abbas et conventus, prior et monachi supradicti advocationem sive jus patronatus ecclesie de Schirington' que ad ipsos et dictum prioratum spectabat, in recompensationem procurationis et aliorum que nos episcopus et predecessores nostri in dicto prioratu percipere consueveramus, nobis episcopo et successoribus nostris imperpetuum contulerunt et etiam assignarunt cum omni jure et possessione sibi competentibus in eadem, salvis in aliis privilegiis eorundem quatenus de jure sunt salvanda. In cujus rei testimonium nos episcopus decanus et capitulum supradicti sigilla nostra presentibus litteris duximus apponenda. Datum mense Junii anno domini M.CC. nonagesimo tertio.

STEWKLEY (Stivecle). V. Richard of Ketton ch. p. by the P. and C. of Kenilworth to the vicarage of Stewkley vacant by the res. of Roger on being inst. to the church of Leamington Priors (Lemmington'). Inst. London, Old Temple, Oct. 22, 1293.

WENDOVER. V. Note of letters patent under the bishop's seal, dated London, Old Temple, Dec. 11, 1293, ratifying an agreement about the division of tithes in the parish of Wendover, made between Henry de Kersaunton, proctor of the P. and C. of St. Mary's Southwark, and Nicholas of London, vicar of Wendover. Henry de Kersaunton's letters of proxy, dated at Southwark Aug. 18, and the letters patent of the P. and C., accepting the agreement, dated at Southwark Nov. 11, 1293, are both given in full.

Memorandum quod contentionem diu habitam inter quosdam vicarios ecclesie de Wendovere ex parte una, ac ...[1] priorem et conventum de Suthwerk' eandem ecclesiam de Wendovere in usus proprios possidentes ex altera, super tertia parte decime garbarum parochie de Wendovere quam Hugo quondam vicarius ipsius ecclesie suo tempore possidebat, demum hujusmodi contentio conquievit sub forma contenta in littera que sequitur, cujus est talis tenor: ... Oliverus

[1] Blank in MS.

permissione divina Lincoln' Episcopus, ad perpetuam memoriam rei geste. Inter quosdam vicarios parochialis ecclesie de Wendovere ex parte una, circa tertiam partem decime garbarum parochie loci ejusdem, quam iidem vicarii ad se ratione vicarie sue juxta formam ordinationis auctoritate pontificali olim inde facte, que de matriculis predecessorum nostrorum in forma que sequitur est excerpta.[1] 'Vicaria in ecclesia de Wendovere que est prioris et conventus de Suthwerk' ex dudum ordinata consistit in toto altaragio et in tertio parte decime garbarum de tota parochia provenientis [*f. 326*] et sustinebit vicarius omnia onera illius ecclesie episcopalia et archidiaconalia debita et consueta', ac dictos ...[2] priorem et conventum ex altera, asserentes dictam ordin-ationem quoad tertiam partam decime garbarum predictam fuisse factum pro tempore quondam Hugonis vicarii loci predicti qui eam tenuit circiter per quinquaginta annos, post cujus mortem hujusmodi decimam de qua agitur portioni sue consolidari seu accrescere debere dicebant suborta dudum contentione perquamgravi, ex qua pericula corporum notorie contigerant et dispendium similiter animarum, tandem prefati prior personaliter et conventus per procuratorem, ac Nicholaus de London vicarius dicte ecclesie similiter presens erga nos instabant ut hujusmodi periculis et dampnis imposterum pro pace et quiete partis utriusque in premissis occurrere, et de remedio providere benignius curaremus, memoratis ...[2] priore et conventu in recompensationem dicte decime contentiose ad augmentum vicarie predicte terras, redditus, prata et pasturas, servicia tenentium suorum in Wendovere, et emendationem excessuum tenentium eorundem, et comoditatem bosci in bosco de Kyngeswode spectantem ad ipsos, una cum omnibus aliis sive nomine decimarum sive alio jure pertinerent ad eosdem in villa predicta, decima garbarum, feni et molendinorum dumtaxat excepta, pro bono pacis offerentibus libera sponte sua. Facta igitur super valore decime tertie partis garbarum predicte, necnon estimatione dictarum portionum oblatarum, et utrum petitionem nobis factam in premissis exaudire deceret vel etiam expediret, per archidiaconum loci inquisitione, acceptoque per idem quod decima tertie partis garbarum predicta deductis expensis valet decem marcas annuatim, quodque triginti due acras terre de dominica terra dicte ecclesie possunt ibidem seminari per annum, quarum quelibet valet sex denarios. Sunt etiam

---

[1] Hugh's institution by Grosseteste is recorded in C. and Y. Soc. X pp. 345 and 352. The exact wording of this extract occurs neither there nor in the register of Hugh of Wells.
[2] Blank in MS.

ibidem septem acre prati et pasture quarum quelibet valet communibus annis sexdecim denarios. Item, redditus assisus tenentium ecclesie una cum operibus suis per tresdecim dies in autumpno, et gallis et gallinis quos reddunt valet viginti solidos per annum, quodque una carettata bosci singulis diebus anni querenda in bosco de Kyngeswud' predicto valet per annum triginta solidos et IIII denarios. Item, pastura quatuor boum et duorum stottorum[1] cum pecoribus domini in ejusdem pastura in Wendovere valet per annum tres solidos. Item, decima piscarie, warencium et carbonum valet annuatim sex solidos, quodque prefatus archidiaconus sensit petitionem dictorum religiosorum in hac parte expedire plurimum exaudiri, nos ad devotam instanciam ... prioris et fratris Henrici de Kersaunton' concanonici sui procuratoris conventus et Nicholai vicarii predictorum, presentium coram nobis et jurantium ad sacra Dei ewangelia quod ordinationem nostram faciendam in hoc casu plenius observabunt deliber-atione previa duximus ordinandum, et salvis in omnibus jure episcopali et Lincoln' ecclesie dignitate ordinando statuimus quod vicaria dicte ecclesie decetero consistat in omnimodis decimis altaragii, necnon molendinorum et rerum qualincum-que aliarum, terris et redditibus, pratis, pascuis, pasturis, bosco et aliis juribus universis ad prefatos religiosos nomine dicte ecclesie de Wendovere pertinentibus quoquomodo, decima garbarum et feni dumtaxat excepta, quam prefati prior et conventus integraliter percipient in futuro, ita quod dictus vicarius sustinerit onera que prius portare solebat. Si vero circa hujusmodi ordinationem aliquod dubium vel obscurum oriri, aut portiones ad augmentum vicarie predicte assignatas decertiorari seu minorari aut earum aliquam vel aliquas casu quocumque decetero cessare contingat, nobis et successoribus nostris hujusmodi dubium et obscurum interpretandi et declarandi, necnon de prefatis portionibus dicte vicarie decertioratis seu minoratis aut cessantibus, ut debita compensatio fiat in hac parte ordinandi de plano et absque strepitu judiciali potestatem specialiter reservamus. In cujus rei testimonium sigillum nostrum presentibus est appensum. Actum et datum apud Vetus Templum London' IV idus Decembris anno domini M.CC. nonagesimo tertio et pontificatus nostri quartodecimo. ... Sequitur procuratorium fratris Henrici predicti: ... Venerabili in Christo patri domino Olivero Dei gracia Lincoln' Episcopo, sui humiles et devoti Willelmus Prior beate Marie de Suwerk' et ejusdem loci conventus Wynton' diocesis salutem et tanto patri tam debitam quam devotam in omnibus reverenciam, obedienciam

---

[1] 'Stot' is still used for 'bullock' in northern dialects.

pariter cum honore. Noverit paternitas vestra reverenda quod
nos facimus, ordinamus et constituimus dilectum nobis in
Christo fratrem Henricum de Kersaunton' concanonicum
nostrum procuratorem nostrum verum et legitimum ad
petendum nomine nostro et ecclesie nostre predicte a sancta
paternitate vestra confirmationem status nostri super
perceptione et possessione integre decime omnium garbarum
et feni et rerum aliarum quocumque censeantur provenientium
de terris existentibus infra limites parochialis ecclesie de
Wendovere vestre diocesis quam in usus proprios optinemus,
et ad concedendum pro nobis et ecclesie nostre predicte
vicario[1] qui pro tempore fuerit in eadem ecclesie de Wendovere decimam molendinorum provenientem de molendinis
in eadem parochia constitutis, ac alia omnia et singula que sibi
pro bono pacis optinendo videbitur expedire, et omnia alia et
singula facienda in premissis, et circa premissis que nos
faceremus si personaliter presentes essemus, ratum habituri et
gratum quicquid idem procurator noster in premissis et ea
contingentibus [*f. 326v*] duxerit faciendum, aliud mandatum
procuratorium eidem per nos alias factum per presentes
revocare minime intendentes. In cujus rei testimonium
sigillum nostrum commune presentibus duximus apponendum.
Datum in capitulo nostro apud Suwerk' XV kalendas
Septembris anno domini M.CC. nonagesimo tertio. ...
Postmodum siquidem dicti prior et conventus ordinationem
prescriptam approbarunt et acceptarunt per suas patentes
litteras, quarum talis est tenor: ... Universis sancte matris
ecclesie filiis ad quorum noticiam presentes littere pervenerint,
frater Willelmus prior ecclesie beate Marie de Suwerk' et
ejusdem loci conventus Wynton' diocesis salutem in domino
perpetuam. Noverit universitas vestra quod cum venerabilis
pater dominus Oliverus Dei gracia Lincoln' episcopus ordinationem vicarie ecclesie de Wendovere ad instanciam nostram
et vicarii loci ejusdem certa consideratione mutasset, illamque
noviter ordinasset sub hac forma, O. etc. nos ordinationem
prescriptam pro nobis expressius approbavimus et acceptavimus
eam, quam nobis approbatam tenore presentium acceptamus.
In cujus rei testimonium, sigillum nostrum commune presentibus apposuimus. Datum in capitulo nostro apud Suwerk III
idus Novembris anno domini M.CC. nonagesimo tertio. ...
Postmodum siquidem dicti prior et conventus ordinationem
prescriptam approbarunt et acceptarunt per suas patentes
litteras, quarum talis est tenor: ... Universis sancte matris
ecclesie filiis ad quorum noticiam presentes littere pervenerint, frater Willelmus prior ecclesie beate Marie de Suwerk'

---

[1] Interlined.

et ejusdem loci conventus Wynton' diocesis salutem in domino perpetuam. Noverit universitas vestra quod cum venerabilis pater dominus Oliverus Dei gracia Lincoln' episcopus ordinationem vicarie ecclesie de Wendovere ad instanciam nostram et vicarii loci ejusdem certa consideratione mutasset, illamque noviter ordinasset sub hac forma, O. etc. nos ordinationem prescriptam pro nobis expressius approbavimus et acceptavimus eam, quam nobis approbatam tenore presentium acceptamus. In cujus rei testimonium, sigillum nostrum commune presentibus apposuimus. Datum in capitulo nostro apud Suwerk III idus Novembris anno domini M.CC. nonagesimo tertio.

BEACONSFIELD. R. Geoffrey of Walden, clerk in minor orders, p. by Sir Thomas de Handeng' knight to the church of Beaconsfield vacant by the death of Sir Robert Marmiun. Had custody for a period. Ordained subd. and inst. Wycombe, Dec. 19, 1293.

ASTON SANDFORD. R. Robert de Stibenach', clerk in minor orders, p. by Robert de Vere, earl of Oxford, to the church of Aston Sandford vacant by the res. of Master Stephen of Haslingfield. Ordained subd. and inst. Wycombe, Dec. 19, 1293.

WESTBURY. V. William de Homeshend' ch. p. by the Abbess and C. of Elstow to the vicarage of Westbury vacant by the death of Hugh de Hekeney. Inst. Wooburn, Jan. 18, 1294.

NEWPORT PAGNELL. V. Robert called Gule ch. p. by the P. and C. of Tickford to the vicarage of Newport Pagnell vacant by the res. of William on being inst. to a living in the diocese of Lichfield and Coventry. Inst. London, Old Temple, Feb. 13, 1294.

CLIFTON REYNES. R. Roger of Granby ch. p. by Richard de Bois Roard to the church of Clifton Reynes vacant by the death of Ascelin. Inst. Banbury, Mar. 4, 1294.

TICKFORD.[1] Note of a formal record, drawn up by John of Ferriby notary-public, and witnessed by Masters Jocelyn of Kirmington and Walter of Wootton, Sir William of Stockton, John de Scalleby and Robert of Kilworth, of the proper ceremonial reception accorded to the bishop at Tickford Priory, Mar. 25, 1294.

[1] Marginal drawing of a grim-looking face.

Memorandum quod VIII kalendas Aprilis die annunciationis beate Marie anno domini M.CC. nonagesimo quarto domino Olivero Lincoln' episcopo tendente ad domum monachorum de Tykeford' juxta Neuportpaynel, occurrerent extra portam interiorem que ducit ad ecclesiam fratres Gaufridus dictus Vig' prior domus ejusdem, Willelmus Peytesin', Johannes dictus Blackberd', Walterus de Mauntes et quidam Stephanus, monachi commorantes ibidem, albis induti, deferentes textum et thurribulum cum incenso, precedentibus aliis ministris eorum aquam benedictam et cereos accensos portantibus, ipseque prior aquam benedictam tradidit episcopo juxta[1] morem in prelatorum admissione [*f. 327*] observatum, et eum reverenter cum thurribulo incensavit, ac statim postmodum idem prior et fratres sui predicti episcopum in ecclesiam introduxerunt cum cantu solempni, ubi dictus pater subsequenter eodem die missam in pontificalibus cum ministris suis presente populo celebravit, et eidem populo post missam hujusmodi in ecclesie predicavit publice verbum Dei. Acta fuerunt hec presentibus Magistris Gocelino Archidiacono Stowe. Waltero de Wutton' et domino Willelmo de Stockton' canonicis Lincoln', Johanne de Scalleby et Roberto de Kibwrth clericis episcopi et pluribus aliis, necnon Johanne de Feriby publico notario qui super hiis publicum instrumentum confecit.

DIE SANCTI DUNSTANI VIDELICET QUARTODECIMO KALENDAS JUNII ANNO DOMINI MILLESIMO DUCENTESIMO NONAGESIMO QUARTO INCIPIT ANNUS PONTIFICATUS DOMINI OLIVERI DEI GRACIA LINCOLN' EPISCOPI QUINTUSDECIMUS.

WALTON. R. Mediety. Robert of Mendham ch. p. by Roger of Brailesford and Margaret Rixbaud to the mediety of the church of Walton vacant by the res. of Richard of Ely. Inst. Edmonton near Tottenham, June 22, 1294.

CHICHELEY. V. Walter Goldsmith of Oxford d. p. by the P. and C. of Tickford to the vicarage of Chicheley vacant by the res. of Robert Goule on being inst. to the vicarage of Newport Pagnell. Inst. Edmonton, June 24, 1294.

[1] Interlined and far from clear.

AUGMENTATIO VICARIE DE AYLESBIR'.[1] Note of an agreement between Master Richard of Harrington, prebendary of Aylesbury, and his prebendal vicar, augmenting the vicarage by the addition of two parts of the tithe of mills in Aylesbury. Lincoln Cathedral, Dec. 12, 1290.

[f. 327v] BIERTON, QUARRENDON, BUCKLAND AND STOKE MANDEVILLE. (Burton' cum Querendon', Bokeland' et Stokes.) V. Adam of Berrington ch. p. by the dean and chapter of Lincoln to the vicarage to be set up in the chapels of Bierton, Quarrendon, Buckland and Stoke Mandeville, appropriated to the said dean and chapter. Robert of Thame, pr., first presented, resigned on accepting the living of St. Mary Magdalen's in the church yard of Lincoln Cathedral. Inst. Stow Park, Nov. 24, 1294. On the same day the bishop, as a result of an enquiry held by Master Richard of St. Frideswide, prebendary of Marston St. Lawrence, issued an ordinance setting up the said vicarage.

Roberto de Thame presbitero ad vicariam in capellis de Burton', Querendon', Bokeland' et Stokes juxta Aylesbir', commune capituli Lincoln' appropriatis, ordinandam, per ...[2] decanum et capitulum Lincoln presentato, factaque inquisitione per Magistrum Ricardum de sancta Fredeswyda prebendarium de Merston' secundum articulos consuetos et precipue de valore proventuum altaragii hujusmodi capellarum, per quam inter cetera acceptum fuit de valore proventuum prout inferius continetur, ac postmodum eodem Roberto presentationi de se facte renunciante per hoc quod ecclesiam beate Marie Magdalene in atrio ecclesie Lincoln' subsequenter admisit, dicti decanus et capitulum Adam de Berington' capellanum ad dictam vicariam taliter ordinandum iterum presentarunt, cujus presentatione recepta, episcopus post collationem cum capitulo suo predicto habitem VII kalendas Decembris anno domini M.CC. nonagesimo quarto apud Parcum Stowe vicariam hujusmodi ordinavit sub forma subscripta: ... Noverint universi quod nos Oliverus permissione divina Lincoln' Episcopus in capellis de Burton', Querendon', Bokeland' et Stok' nostre diocesis commune capituli Lincoln' appropriatis vicariam ordinari volentes hoc eidem capitulo nostro[3] expressimus viva voce, unde mediante presentatione eorundem inquiri fecimus per Magistrum

---

[1] In another hand, not that of B., and out of sequence in time. It was not, however, added to an already finished folio.
[2] Blank in MS.
[3] Interlined.

Ricardum de Sancta Fredeswida prebendarium de Merton' de valore proventuum altaragii hujusmodi capellarum. Acceptaque per inquisitionem eandem quod proventus altaragii capelle de Burton' valent communibus annis quindecim marcas, proventus altaragii capelle de Querendon' valent communibus annis octo marcas, proventus altaragii capelle de Bokeland' valent communibus annis sex marcas, et proventus altaragii capelle de Stok' valent communibus annis septem marcas, et consistunt ipsi proventus in omnimodis oblationibus, mortuariis, decima lane, agnorum, lactis, lini, canabi, porcellorum, aucarum, ovorum, pullorum equinorum, vitulorum, ortorum et croftorum que cum pedibus et vangiis[1] foduntur, et etiam in decima columbarum, quodque in parochia capelle de Burton' datur quoddam bladum pro sepultura parochianorum de Huccote[2] qui apud Burton' sepeliuntur, Puttecorne vulgariter nuncupatem, quod spectat ad altaragium de Burton', et quod sunt ibidem duo molendina, unum aquaticum et aliud equinum, quodque ipsa vicaria in dictis portionibus competentius poterit ordinari, et in villa de Burton' mansus vicarii assignari, nos advertentes quod in capellis de Querendon' unum, de Bokeland' alium et de Stok' tertium ministrare oportebit necessarie capellanos, sitque decens ut vicarius sacerdotem secum morantem habeat, ordinamus ut portio vicarii futuris temporibus instituendi consistat in omnibus et singulis portionibus suprascriptis et aliis consimilibus si que sint que debent altaragii nomine contineri, quodque dictum capitulum mansum competentem ad opus vicarii apud Burton' in fundo capelle ex parte occidentali suis sumptibus edificet competenter, salvis eidem capitulo decima garbarum et feni et omnibus terris et tenementis cum pertinenciis suis in pasturis et aliis quibuscumque spectantibus ad capellas easdem, necnon jurisdictione quam dudum prebendarii in ipsis capellis antiquitus habere solebant sine prejudicio juris pontificalis. Ordinamus insuper ut dictum capitulum libros et ornamenta congruentia pro statu dictarum capellarum ab initio inveniat honesta, que vicarii pro tempore succedentes ibidem eque honesta suis impediis sustentare et invenire, ministrosque idoneos ad ministrandum in omnibus capellis prefatis et cetera omnia que ad divinum obsequium quomodolibet requiruntur exhibere decetero teneantur, quodque dictum capitulum curet et vigilet diligenter ut hujusmodi ornamenta et libros per vicarios honeste custodiantur, et cum res exigent reparentur, alioquin si vicarius tempore existens

---

[1] Spades. A sort of market-garden, as opposed to an in-field which was ploughed.
[2] Hulcott.

fortasse non suffecerit ad reparationem seu emendationem eorum, in eo casu capitulum defectus hujusmodi emendare per sua negligencia teneatur. Constructio vero et reparatio cancellorum capellarum predictarum ad capitulum seu parochianos locorum juxta morem preteriti temporis sequatum spectare debebunt. Ordinamus itidem ut vicarius pro tempore existens in capellis pretactis ab omni onere ordinario preter reparationem et emendationem librorum et ornamentorum prescriptam immunis existat, pro portione tamen vicarie sue si illam exnunc ad aliquam decimam vel contributionem aliam in futurum taxari contingat dumtaxat respondere debebit. Si vero portio vicarii ut premittitur ordinata tanquam insufficiens processu temporis merito videatur augenda, hoc faciendi et etiam si quid dubium, obscurum aut interpretatione dignum in hujusmodi ordinationi apparuerit, illud declarandi et interpretandi nobis successoribus nostris potestatem specialiter reservamus. Actum apud Parcum Stowe VII kalendas Decembris anno domini M.CC. nonagesimo quarto. ... Deinde episcopus eidem anno et loco adherens inquisitioni prius facte, prefatum Adam, de natalibus, vita, moribus et conversatione a capitulo commendatum, ad dictam vicariam admisit et vicariam perpetuum cum onere personaliter ministrandi et continue residendi canonice instituit in eadem. Jurataque episcopo canonica obediencia in forma consueta, prestitoque a dicto Ada juramento de residendo in vicaria predicta secundum formam constitutionis edite super vicariis admittendis, scriptum fuit vicario de Aylesbir' quod eundem Adam corporalem possessionem dicte vicarie habere faceret in forma predicta. Et habuit dictus Adam nichilominus litteram de institutione patentem.

WADDESDON. Thomas of Onslow ch. p. by Eleanor widow of Sir Hugh de Courtenay knight to that portion in the church of Waddesdon held by William of Street (Strete), vacant by the res. of the said William. Inst. Riby, Jan. 28, 1295.

[f. 328] BROUGHTON. R. Master Benedict of Ferriby (Feriby), clerk in minor orders p. by the P. and C. of Caldwell to the church of Broughton vacant by the res. of Master Thomas on his being inst. to the church of Guilden Morden (Gilden Morton'). Ordained subd. and inst. Lincoln, Feb. 26, 1295.

WESTBURY (Westebir'). V. Master John of Northampton subd. p. by the Abbess and C. of Elstow to the vicarage of

Westbury vacant by the death of William. Ordained d. and inst. Nettleham[1] Feb. 26, 1295.

THORNBOROUGH. V. Henry of Buckingham ch. p. by the P. and C. of Luffield to the vicarage of Thornborough vacant by the death of Simon. Inst. Baumber, Mar. 13, 1295.

DIE SANCTI DUNSTANI EPISCOPI VIDELICET QUARTODECIMUS KALENDAS JUNII ANNO DOMINI M.CC. NONAGESIMO QUINTO INCIPIT ANNUS PONTIFICATUS DOMINI OLIVERI LINCOLN' EPISCOPI SEXTUS DECIMUS.

[f. 328v] CHENIES (Isenhamsted'). R. Master William of Weedon, clerk in minor orders p. by Bartholomew de Cheyne to the church of Chenies vacant by the death of Simon le Gode. Ordained subd. and inst. London, Old Temple, May 28, 1295.

IVER (Evere). R. Robert of Clavering d. p. by Sir Robert FitzRoger knight to the church of Iver vacant by the death of Ingram de Balliol. Inst. London, Old Temple, May 28, 1295.

CHOLESBURY (Chilwardebyr') R. Ralph of Ch(i)eveley (Chyvele) pr. collated to the church of Cholesbury, vacant for two years, saving the right of the patron.[2] Newnham, July 4, 1295.

MARLOW. R. Master Henry de Lancarvan' subd. p. by Gilbert de Clare, Earl of Gloucester and Hereford to the church of Marlow vacant by the death of Master Walter of Bath and the res. of Sir John of Langton, first presented. Henry resigned his livings of Alford and All Hallows the Great, London, according to the constitutions of Ottobono, and was inst. Theydon Mount, July 31, 1295.
    'Est est sciendum quod dictus Magister Henricus duas ecclesias quas prius tenuerat, scilicet ecclesiam de Allingford' in Somersete et ecclesiam Omnium Sanctorum ad Fenum London' abjuravit juxta formam constitutionis edite per Ottobonum legatum'.

[1] The ordinations took place in Lincoln Cathedral, but Sutton was staying at Nettleham, and John may have come thither to receive institution.
[2] The Hospitallers had presented in 1278, L.R.S. 20, p. 256.

IVINGHOE. Confirmation by the bishop of the election of Isolde de Beauchamp (Bello Campo), a nun of St. Margaret's, Ivinghoe, as prioress thereof in succession to Matilda of Hockliffe (Hocclive) who had died. By licence of the Bishop of Winchester, patron. London, Aug, 17, 1295.

MAIDS MORETON. R. Master Peter Passelewe subd. p. by Sir John Peyvre knight to the church of Maids Moreton vacant by the res. of Robert Inge. Inst. Banbury, Sept. 2, 1295.

NEWPORT PAGNELL. V. Geoffrey de Wenrich' ch. p. by the P. and C. of Tickford to the vicarage of Newport Pagnell vacant by the death of William. Inst. Stony Stratford, Sept. 22, 1295.

GAYHURST. R. Robert Barr', clerk in minor orders p. by Sir William de Nodariis knight to the church of Gayhurst vacant by the death of William. Had custody for a period. Ordained subd. and inst. Berkhampstead, Sept. 24, 1295.

[f. 329] SIMPSON. R. Roger of Newport, clerk in minor orders p. by Sir John de Grey, knight to the church of Simpson vacant by the death of Hugh de la Leye. Ordained subd. and inst. Berkhampstead, Sept. 24, 1295.

CHESHAM BOIS. R. Thomas of Little Linford ch. p. by Thomas de Hamul', as guardian of the lands and heir of Bartholomew de Breanzon, to the church of Chesham Bois vacant by the death of Hugh. Inst. Caistor near Peterborough, Oct. 20, 1295.

SAUNDERTON (Saundreston'). R. Ralph de Plummeyre, clerk in minor orders p. by Ralph called Brown (Brun) to the church of St. Nicholas, Saunderton, vacant by the res. of William of Swayfield (Swafeld') on his being inst. to the church of Theydon in the diocese of London. Ordained subd. and inst. Huntingdon, Dec. 17, 1295.

HAMBLEDEN. R. Richard of Waltham, clerk in minor orders p. by Edmund Earl of Cornwall to the church of Hambleden vacant by the death of Laurence of Burgh. Presentation disputed by Gilbert de Clare, Earl of Gloucester and Hereford, who p. Robert of St. Fagan, clerk in minor orders. Writ in favour of the Earl of Cornwall, witnessed by J. of Mettingham, Westminster, Nov. 24, 1295. Richard was ordained subd. and inst. Huntingdon, Dec. 17, 1295.

WADDESDON (Wuttesdon'). Edmund Bernard clerk in minor orders p. by King Edward to the third part of the church of Waddesdon vacant by the death of Ralph Bernard. Ordained subd. and inst. Huntingdon, Dec. 17, 1295.

RADCLIVE (Radeclive). R. Richard of Cornwall (Cornubia) clerk in minor orders p. by Andrew of St. Lys (sancto Licio) to the church of Radclive vacant by the death of John of Whitchurch. Ordained subd. and inst. Rothwell, Feb. 18, 1296.

———

[f. 329v] QUARTODECIMO KALENDAS JUNII VIDELICET DIE SANCTI DUNSTANI EPISCOPI ANNO DOMINI M.CC. NONAGESIMO SEXTO INCIPIT ANNUS PONTIFICATUS DOMINI OLIVERI LINCOLN' EPISCOPI SEPTIMUS-DECIMUS.

———

EDGCOTT (Achecote). R. John Walclin of Brightwell (Brictewell') ch. p. by Roger of Englefield (Englefeud') to the church of Edgcott vacant by the death of Andrew of Englefield. Inst. Sleaford, July 31, 1296.

STANTONBURY (Stonton'). V. Henry of Bishopstone ch. p. by the Prioress and C. of Goring to the vicarage of Stantonbury vacant by the death of Gervase. Inst. Nettleham, Sept. 20, 1296.

LITTLE MARLOW (Parva Merlawe). Mediety. Robert Daunvers clerk in minor orders p. by William Daunvers to the mediety of the church of Little Marlow vacant by the res. of Walter of Grindale. Ordained subd. and inst. Lincoln, Sept. 22, 1296.

BRADENHAM. R. Richard de Wottesdon' ch. p. by Simon FitzRobert, Lord of Bradenham, to the church thereof, vacant by the death of Thomas de Davent. Inst. Nettleham, Sept. 27, 1296.

EAST CLAYDON. R. Robert of Lavington ch. p. by Lady Joan de Valoyne to the church of East Claydon vacant by the death of Wiliam FitzNigel. Inst. Stow Park, Oct. 14, 1296.

RADCLIVE. R. Richard of Cornwall subd. re-presented by Andrew of St. Lys to the church of Radclive vacant by the fact that the said Richard had not been ordained priest within a year of institution. Inst. Wooburn, Apr. 26, 1296.

HANSLOPE.[1] R. Peter le Blunt, subd. p. by William de Beauchamp, Earl of Warwick, to the church of Hanslope vacant by
the death of Simon of Elsworth. Inst. London, Mar. 25, 1296.

QUARTODECIMO KALENDAS JUNII VIDELICET DIE SANCTI DUNSTANI
ANNO DOMINI M.CC. NONAGESIMO SEPTIMO INCIPIT ANNUS PONTI-
FICATUS DOMINI OLIVERI DEI GRACIA LINCOLN' EPISCOPI OCTAVUS-
DECIMUS.

[f. 330] ASHRIDGE (Asserugge).[2] Note that on the res. of
Richard of Watford, head of the house of Bonshommes at
Ashridge, the community elected William of Harrold. The
bishop appointed the Archdeacon of Huntingdon as his
commissary to investigate the election, in a letter dated
Theydon Mount, May 24, 1297. Election quashed for faulty
procedure, May 27. The bishop then summoned five
members of the community to appear before him and
appointed one of them, Ralph of Aston, giving him letters
patent. Theydon Mount, June 4, 1297.

Vacante domo de Asserugge per cessionem fratris Ricardi de
Watford' ultimi prioris ejusdem factam in manibus Magistri
Walteri Archidiaconi Hunt' commissarii episcopi ad hoc vive
vocis oraculo deputati, et per eundem commissarium
admissam fratreque Willelmo de Harewold in ipsius domus
rectorem ut dicebatur electo, episcopus fratrum dicte domus
parcere volens laboribus et expensis dictum archidiaconum ad
eandem domum destinavit, committens sibi vices suas in
hujusmodi electionis negotio sub hac forma: ... Oliverus
permissione divina Lincoln' Episcopus dilecto in Christo filio
...[3] Archidiacono Hunt' salutem, graciam et benedictionem.
Ne ...[3] electus domus de Asserugge vel fratres loci ejusdem in
veniendo ad nos pro presentatione negotii electionis inibi
facte sicut dicitur difficultate laboris vel incomodo expensarum
gravari contingat, vel domum eandem per diutinam vacationem

---

[1] This entry has been crowded into the space left at the end of the year.
[2] Ashridge lies in Hertfordshire (Archdeaconry of Huntingdon) although
very close to the Buckinghamshire border. Scalleby has not marked it as
belonging to the Archdeaconry of Huntingdon. It is noteworthy that
although Sutton deputed the Archdeacon of Huntingdon to act as his
commissary in this case, he ordered the Archdeacon of Buckingham to
induct.
[3] Blank in MS.

incurrat grave dispendium vel jacturam, ad examinandum in
dicta domo processum electionis pretacte et recipiendum in
forma juris testes procedendos, ac quascumque probationes
legitimas exhibendas, necnon omnia et singula que juxta
qualitatem et naturam hujusmodi negotii requiruntur, sive de
plano sive judicialiter faciendum, et etiam ad statuendum,
decernendum, pronunciandum, diffiniendum et reservandum
nobis jus nostrum in eventu prout justum fuerit in hac parte,
vobis certa consideratione vices nostras committimus cum
cohercionis canonice potestate. Valete. Datum apud Theydon'
ad Montem IX kalendas Junii anno domini M.CC. nonagesimo
septimo. ... Coram quo quidem commissario in dicta domo
VIII kalendas Junii anno domini supradicto personaliter
constituto processu electionis predicte per fratrem Walterum
de Dunstaple procuratorem conventus ad hoc constitutum
exhibito, et ad probationem ipsius quatuor de fratribus dicte
domus productis in testes, juratis et die sequente examinatis
ac dictis[1] eorum[1] postmodum pupplicatis et copia eorundem
dicto procuratori nomine dominorum suorum oblata et ab eo
recusata, cum idem procurator nichil aliud vellet proponere
in hac parte, dictus commissarius inveniens ad electionem
faciendam per viam scrutinii fuisse processum, reperiensque
in forma processus predicti defectus varios qui[1] ipsam[1]
electionem[1] cassam et irritam reddebant ipso jure, eandem
electionem ex causis hujusmodi et non propter defectum
persone electe VI kalendas Junii anno domini memorato
pronunciavit finaliter esse irritam et inanem, ipsamque
quatenus de facto processit cassavit et etiam irritavit, electores
propter culpam suam eligendi ea vice potestate privando,
facultatemque providendi dicte domui de rectore dicto patri
specialiter reservando. Deinde votis singulorum de conditionibus et meritis personarum loci ejusdem secretius
examinatis per commissarium antedictum, quod invenerat
idem[1] commissarius[1] episcopo exponebat, unde scriptum fuit
per episcopum ...[2] correctori et confratribus dicte domus
quod fratres Radulphum de Aston' et Johannem de Tilton',
associatis eis tribus aliis de conventu quos magis decreverent
expedire, ad episcopum apud Theydon' ad Montem in
Essexia ad diem martis in septimana Pentecostis ad audiendum
provisionem seu prefectionem ipsius episcopi de persona
ydonea in dicta domo faciendam mitterent tempestive. Quo
die martis scilicet II nonas Junii apud Theydon' fratribus
Radulpho de Aston' et Johanne de Tilton' predictis, necnon
Johanne le Enveyse, Johanne de Hamelhamsted' et Waltero

[1] Interlined.
[2] Blank in MS.

de Dunstaple coram episcopo constitutis et per ipsum de conditionibus ac meritis personarum dicte domus ex habundante examinatis singillatim, demum conditionibus omnium confratrum ejusdem domus ipsiusque qualitate pensatis, quia fratri Radulpho de Aston' confratri dicte domus de honestate vite et meritis graciosis invenit laudabile testimonium perhiberi, eundem in rectorem ejusdem domus jure ad ipsum ea vice devoluto auctoritate pontificali prefecit, curam et administrationem spiritualium et temporalium ipsius domus eidem plenius committendo Jurataque per eundem rectorem episcopo et officialibus suis canonica obediencia in forma consueta, scriptum fuit Archidiacono Buck' vel ejus officiali quod id quod suum esset circa ipsius rectoris installationem exequeretur sine mora, et quod injungeret, etc. Habuit insuper idem rector quamdam patentem litteram sub hac forma: ... Universis pateat per presentes quod licet jure providendi domui de Asserugge vacanti de rectore, propter culpam fratrum ejusdem domus in electione rectoris in eadem nuper minus canonice celebrata evidenter commissam, et non propter defectum persone electe, ad nos Oliverum permissione divina Lincoln' episcopum legitime devoluto hac vice, eidem domui de fratre Radulpho de Aston' ipsius domus confratre ad presens duxerimus providendum, ipsum in rectorem dicte domus auctoritate pontificali preficientes, eisdem tamen fratribus et eorum successoribus per hoc factum nostrum quin hoc non obstante liberam electionem habeant in futurum prejudiccare non intendimus quoquo modo. In cujus rei testimonium litteras nostras dictis fratribus ad eorum instanciam concessimus has patentes. Actum et datum apud Theydon' ad Montem II nonas Junii anno domini M.CC. nonagesimo septimo.

MARSWORTH (Messeworth'). V. Robert of Malton d. p. by the P. and C. of Caldwell to the vicarage of Marsworth vacant by the res. of Richard of Bromham. Inst. London, Old Temple, July 7, 1297.

[f. 330v] WADDESDON. William of Rogate, clerk in minor orders p. by King Edward as guardian of the lands and heir of Sir Hugh de Courtenay to the portion in the church of Waddesdon lately held by Edmund Bernard, vacant by the res. of the said Edmund. Inst. London, Old Temple, July 10, 1297.

KINGSEY. V. Master John of Haddenham pr. p. by the P. and C. of Rochester to the vicarage of the chapel of Kingsey vacant by the death of John. Inst. Kilworth, Sept. 20, 1297.

NEWTON BLOSSOMVILLE. R. William Druel, clerk in minor orders p. by Sir John Druel knight to the church of Newton Blossomville vacant by the res. of Robert de Rugemund' on being inst. to the living of Chishall in the diocese of London. Ordained subd. and inst. Leicester, Sept. 21, 1297.

WOLVERTON. V. John of Ely d. p. by the P. and C. of Bradwell to the vicarage of Wolverton vacant by the death of Ralph of Wolverton. Ordained pr. and inst. Leicester, Sept. 21, 1297.

RADCLIVE. R. Robert of Luffenham ch. p. by Andrew of St. Lys to the church of Radeclive vacant by the res. of Richard of Cornwall on being inst. to the church of Frodingham (Frothingham). Inst. Stow Park, Nov. 10, 1297.

QUAINTON (Quenton'). R. Master Peter of Askern ch. p. by Robert Malet to the church of Quainton vacant by the res. of Walter Hachard. Inst. Thornholm, Jan. 25, 1298.

RADCLIVE. William of Warwick ch. p. by Andrew of St. Lys to the chapel of St. Michael at Radclive vacant by the res. of Robert of Luffenham. Inst. Nettleham, Feb. 27, 1298.

LITTLE KIMBLE. R. Hugh of Berkhamstead clerk in minor orders p. by the A. and C. of St. Albans to the church of Little Kimble vacant by the res. of John of Baldock. Ordained subd. and inst. Lincoln, Mar. 22, 1298.

[*f. 331*] MENTMORE. V. Stephen of Bennington (Beniton') ch. p. by the P. and C. of St. Bartholomew's, London, to the vicarage of Mentmore vacant by the death of Robert. Inst. Newark, Apr. 21, 1298.

LAVENDON. V. Simon of Lavendon ch. p. by the A. and C. of Lavendon to the vicarage thereof vacant by the death of Richard. Inst. Liddington, May 7, 1298.

CAVERSFIELD. V. John of Ascot ch. p. by the A. and C. of Missenden to the vicarage of Caverfield vacant by the death of John Fraunceys. Inst. Liddington, May 8, 1298.

———

QUARTODECIMO KALENDAS JUNII VIDELICET DIE SANCTI DUNSTANI ANNO DOMINI M.CC. NONAGESIMO OCTAVO INCIPIT ANNUS PONTIFICATUS DOMINI OLIVERI EPISCOPI LINCOLN NONUSDECIMUS.

———

PITSTONE (Pichelsthorn'). R. Thomas Neirnut, clerk in minor orders p. by Sir John Neirnut knight to the church of Pitstone vacant by the death of Fulk Neirnut. Ordained subd. and inst. Brampton near Huntingdon, June 12,[1] 1298.

OAKLEY with BRILL (Acle cum Brehull'). R. William of Wrotham, clerk in minor orders p. by King Edward to the church of Oakley with Brill, vacant because Richard of Louth had been deprived of his living for misconduct by Archbishop Winchelsey (letter given in full and dated Wingham, Mar. 1, 1297). Ordained subd. and inst. Brampton near Huntingdon, May 31, 1297, with the warning that Richard had appealed to Rome.

Memorandum quod cum venerabilis pater dominus Robertus Cantuar' Archiepiscopus contra Ricardum de Luda clericum ex officii sui debito processisset prout continetur in littera ejusdem domini archiepiscopi episcopo Lincoln' missa, cujus est talis tenor: ... Robertus permissione divina Cantuar' Archiepiscopus, totius Anglie primas, venerabili fratri domino Dei gracia Lincoln' Episcopo salutem et fraternam in Deo caritatem. Cum in negotio correctionis moto judicialiter ex officio nostro contra Ricardum de Luda clericum in sub-diaconatus ordine constitutum, ecclesiasticaque beneficia in vestra diocese prout intelleximus optinentem, nobis legitime constiterit per confessionem ejusdem Ricardi sepius coram nobis in judicio sponte factam, ipsum cum Juliana relicta quondam Henrici Box civis London' vidua in subdiaconatus ordine infra dimidium annum proxime jam preteritum de facto matrimonium contraxisse, et postmodum eandem se carnaliter cognovisse, ac cum Mergeria Skyp et cum Johanna uxore Ricardi Peysoner de Cant' fornicationem et adulterium pupplice commisisse, necnon sponte et scienter in respon-sionibus coram nobis factis sepius perjurium incurrisse, sicut ex confessionibus suis et responsionibus in virtute juramenti sui de veritate dicenda coram nobis prestiti judicialiter ad interrogatoria nostra factis plenius continentur, nosque consideratis [f. 331v] premissis ex hujusmodi temerario contractu cum vidua propter affectum intentionis, cum opere subsecuto ac ratione multiplicati perjurii, et ex aliis certis causis coram nobis sufficienter detectis, advertentes ipsum Ricardum notam irregularitatis proculdubio incurrisse, et omni beneficio ecclesiastico se indignem totaliter reddidisse, pronunciaverimus eundem Ricardum inhabilem esse ad

[1] This date is wrongly given, it should be May 31. See register folio 407, and the following entry.

quodcumque beneficium ecclesiasticum optinendum imposterum seu aliqualiter retinendum. Insuper et omni
beneficio ecclesiastico si quod haberet ipsum privandum fore
decreverimus, et de premissis excessibus conjunctim ecclesia
per sentenciam privaverimus, justicia suadente, fraternitati
vestre mandamus quatinus dictum Ricardum sic inhabilem et
privatum pupplicetis et pupplicari solmpniter faciatis locis et
temporibus quibus videritis expedire. Denuncietis insuper
patronis beneficiorum suorum ecclesiasticorum si que optinet
in vestra diocese quod eisdem tanquam vacantibus de personis
ydoneis sine mora dispendio quatenus ad eos attinet provideant
competenter. Et vos quoad amotionem Ricardi quatenus de
facto eorum possessione incumbit officii vestri debitum
exequamini cum effectu. Et quid feceritis de premissis nos
quamcitius poteritis opportune per litteras vestras patentes
harum tenorem habentes certiores reddatis. Datum apud
Wengham kalendis Martii anno domini M.CC. nonagesimo
septimo, consecrationis nostre quarto. ... Episcopus mandatum hujusmodi quantum ad ecclesiam de Acle cum Brehull'
quam dictus Ricardus in diocese Lincoln' tenebat, pro eo
quod idem Ricardus commiserat cum Juliana predicta in
jurisdictione dicti domini archiepiscopi exempta, scilicet in
decanatu ecclesie beate Marie de Arcubus London' com-
morante de quo in mandato suo mentio nulla fiebat, fecit
executioni debite demandari, et dominus Edwardus Dei gracia
illustratis Rex Anglie patronus dicte ecclesie de Acle Willelmum
de Wroteham clericum ad eandem ecclesiam presentavit,
justaque inquisitione per ...[1] officialem Archidiaconi Buck'
per quam etc., idem Willelmus II kalendas Junii anno XIX
apud Brampton' juxta Hunt' in subdiaconatum ordinatus, ad
dictam ecclesiam est admissus, eisdem die, anno et loco et
rector canonice institutus in eadem, jurataque episcopo
canonica obediencia in forma consueta, scriptum est dicto
archidiacono vel ejus officiali quod, etc. Et est sciendum quod
ante ordinationem et institutionem dicti Willelmi, cum
diceretur sibi per episcopum prefatum Ricardum a sentencia
dicti archiepiscopi ad sedem apostolicam appellasse et eam
episcopo notificasse, sibique prospiceret contra eandem
antequam ordinem sacrum et institutionem admitteret in
ecclesia memorata, idem Willelmus dicebat se velle periculo
suo ordinari et institui, appellatione hujusmodi non obstante.[2]

---

[1] Blank in MS.
[2] The next entry, referring to Glatton, is described in a marginal note as 'in archidiaconatu Hunt'. It has been transferred to the manuscripts of that archdeaconry, above, p. 90.

TWYFORD. R. John of Sutton subd. collated by the bishop to the church of Twyford vacant by the res. of Master Nicholas of Appletree (Apiltr') on his being inst. to the church of Barnack. Buckden, Sept. 20, 1298.

LITTLE MARLOW. Julian of Hampton, precentrix of Little Marlow, elected prioress thereof in succession to Agnes of Clivedon who had res. Licence obtained from the patrons, the Earl of Gloucester (by his proctor Sir William of Hambledon (Hameldon) and William d'Anvers. Election confirmed Crowland, Oct. 4, 1298.

[*f. 332*] ASTON CLINTON. Henry of Risborough ch. p. by Sir Simon Montague (de Monte Acuto) knight to the chapel of St. Leonard in the parish of Aston Clinton vacant by the death of Randulph. Inst. Nettleham, Nov. 25, 1298.

PADBURY. V. Ralph of Lutterworth (Luttrewurth') ch. p. by the P. and C. of Bradwell to the vicarage of Padbury vacant by the death of John of Pury (Pyrie) and the res. of John of Lutterworth first presented. Inst. Liddington, Dec. 11, 1298.

EMBERTON. R. John of Heslerton pr. p. by Sir Roger of Tyringham knight to the church of Emberton vacant by the res. of Sir Walter of Amersham on being inst. to the church of Glatton. Presentation disputed by Thomas of Furness. Writ in favour of Sir Roger, York, Jan. 28, 1299, witnessed by J. of Mettingham. John of Heslerton inst. Liddington, Feb. 3, 1299.

CALVERTON. R. John of Felsham acolyte p. by Sir Hugh de Vere knight to the church of Calverton, vacant by the death of Sir William de Percy. Inst. Buckden, Apr. 22, 1299.

QUARTODECIMUS KALENDAS JUNII VIDELICET DIE SANCTI DUNSTANI ANNO DOMINI M.CC. NONAGESIMO NONO INCIPIT ANNUS PONTI-FICATUS DOMINI OLIVERI EPISCOPI LINCOLN' VICESIMUS.

HANSLOPE. R. Master Thurstan of Hanslope acolyte p. by Guy de Beauchamp Earl of Warwick to the church of Hanslope vacant because Peter le Blunt had not been ordained pr. within a year of institution. Inst. Buckden, June 3, 1299.

HUGHENDEN (Huchenden') V. Robert of Bowells ch. p. by the P. and C. of Kenilworth to the vicarage of Hughenden vacant by the death of Richard of Saddington. Inst. Buckden July 15, 1299.

HANSLOPE. R. Peter le Blund[1] sub. d. p. by Guy de Beauchamp Earl of Warwick to the church of Hanslope vacant by the res. of Thirston. Inst. Buckden, June 23, 1299.[2]

LITTLE MARLOW. R. Edmund Attenok' acolyte p. by Sir Milo de Beauchamp knight to the church of Little Marlow vacant by the death of Richard Nernut. Inst. Sleaford, July 24, 1299.

HARDWICK. R. Roger Cantok', clerk in minor orders p. by Sir John de Moeles knight to the church of Hardwick vacant by the res. of Master Thomas Cantok'. Inst. Nettleham, Nov. 5, 1299, with the provision that he be ordained in due time.

ASTON CLINTON. R. William Gacelyn pr. p. by Sir John of Droxford (Drokenesford'), clerk to the church of Aston Clinton by the res. of Sir Walter of Wimborne (Wyneburn'). Had custody for a period. Inst. Nettleham, Nov. 4, 1299.

WRAYSBURY (Wyrardesbury).[3] R. Robert le Wyse of Gloucester (Gloucestr') subd. p. by the A. and C. of Gloucester to the church of Wraysbury with the chapel of Langley Marish vacant by the res. of Master Richard of Gloucester. Inst. (after making proof of age) Nettleham, Nov. 11, 1299.

'Es est sciendum quod quia dicebatur dictum Robertum non esse legitime etatis ad ecclesiasticum beneficium optinendum, idem Robertus ante admissionem suam exhibuit litteram officialis Wygorn' sub data VII die Novembris anno domini M.CC. nonagesimo octavo testificante ipsum Robertum vicesimum quintum annum attigisse. Exhibuit etiam litteras domini Episcopi Hereford'testificantes eundem Robertum XI kalendas Decembris anno domini M.CC. nonagesimo octavo tanquam majorem ad ecclesiam de Rudeford'[4] Hereford' diocesis fuisse admissum et etiam institutum in ea'.

---

[1] Sic.
[2] This entry is slightly out of order. There is no evidence as to why the Earl changed his mind about getting rid of Peter.
[3] Sutton's last official act, he died two days later.
[4] Rudford.

ARCHDEACONRY OF OXFORD 1290–99

[*f. 335*] INSTITUTIONES OXON' ANNO XI

———

QUARTODECIMO KALENDAS JUNII DIE SANCTI DUNSTANI ANNO DOMINI M.CC. NONAGESIMO INCIPIT ANNUS PONTIFICATUS DOMINI OLIVERI EPISCOPI LINCOLN' UNDECIMUS.

———

CORNWELL. R. Roger of Kilworth (Kyvelingwrth') ch. p. by the A. and C. of Osney to the church of Cornwell, vacant because Adam of Kilworth had been inst. to the church of Donington (Dunington'). Inst. Notley, June 4, 1290.

NORTH STOKE (Stokebasset). R. Roger de Bikkerwyk' subd. p. by Edmund Earl of Cornwell to the church of North Stoke, vacant because Roger had not been ordained pr. within a year. Inst. Sleaford, July 28, 1290.

ALL SAINTS', OXFORD. R. John of Churchill ch. p. by the P. and C. of St. Frideswide's, Oxford, to the church of All Saints, vacant by the death of Master William. Inst. Skillington, Sept. 20, 1290.

GREAT TEW (Tywe) R. Master Robert of Thorpe subd. p. by Sir John de Preus knight to the church of Great Tew, vacant by the death of Richard. Inst. Buckden, Oct. 21, 1290.

ST. MICHAEL AT THE NORTH GATE, OXFORD. R. Richard of Ewelme ch. p. by the P. and C. of St. Frideswide's, Oxford, to the church of St. Michael, vacant because John of Churchill (Certelle) had been inst. to the church of All Saints. Inst. Buckden, Oct. 26, 1290.

LOWER HEYFORD. Mediety. R. Simon of Wells, clerk in minor orders p. by the A. and C. of Eynsham to the mediety of the church of Lower Heyford, vacant by the death of Master W. Ordained subd. and inst. Wycombe, Dec. 23, 1290.

CHURCHILL (Certell') R. Oliver Sutton ch. p. by the P. and C. of St. Frideswide's, Oxford to the church of Churchill, vacant because Master Richard of St. Frideswide had become

Archdeacon of Buckingham. Inst. (after six months *in commendam*)[1] Wooburn, Jan. 25, 1291.

[*f. 335v*] SOMERTON. R. Robert Trevet, d. p. by Thomas de Gardino to the church of Somerton vacant by the death of Walter of Cotes. Inst. Fingest, Jan. 28, 1291.

TACKLEY. R. Roger le Mareschal, clerk in minor orders, p. by Roger, Bishop of Lichfield and Coventry, and Walter Douvile to the church of Tackley, vacant by the res. of Master Stephen of Codnor to become a Dominican. The presentation was opposed in the King's court by the Prioress and C. of Studley. Roger, after having custody for a period, was ordained subd. and inst. Northampton, Mar. 17, 1291.

BECKLEY (Bekkele). R. Master Philip de Hoddeshovere, clerk in minor orders, p. by Edmund Earl of Cornwall to the church of Beckley, vacant because Master Richard of Sotwell had been inst. to the church of Frodingham. Ordained subd. Northampton, Mar. 17, 1291, and inst. next day, saving to the Prioress and C. of Studley, the A. and C. of Osney and the P. and C. of St Frideswide's Oxford their customary tithes in the parish.

ST. PETER AT THE EAST GATE, OXFORD. V. William Batayle subd. p. by Sir Bogo de Clare, rector of St. Peter's, to the vicarage thereof vacant by the death of Philip Poer. Ordained subd. Northampton, Mar. 17, 1291, and inst. next day.

EWELME. R. Master Robert Bakun, clerk in minor orders p. by Sir Adam le Despenser, knight to the church of Ewelme vacant by the death of Ingram. Ordained subd. and inst. Northampton, Mar. 17, 1291.

MINSTER LOVELL. Stephen d'Ivry p. by the P. and C. of St. Mary's Ivry, (the abbot being detained on business at the papal curia) to the office of Prior of Minster Lovell, vacant by the death of John. Letter of presentation dated at Ivry Feb. 22, 1291, and accepted without dispute by the bishop. Admitted Corby, Apr. 4, 1291.

COKETHORPE. Note that on the death of Ralph of Dunwich, chaplain of Cokethorpe, the chapel was reunited to the church of Ducklington on the plea of Philip Dyve its rector, provided that he should arrange for a chaplain to serve it.

---

[1] '*as noted in the custody roll*'. This roll is not extant.

The results of the Archdeacon's inquisition are given in full. Banbury, Apr. 5, 1290.[1]

... per quas quidem inquisitiones videbatur inventum quod capella de Cokthrop' predicta reputabitur spectare ad ecclesiam de Dukelington' tanquam pars et membrum ejusdem, hoc tamen salvo quod quidem capellanus rector de Cokthrop' et de Herdewyk'[2] in divinis officiis et sacramentis ecclesiasticis exhibendis apud Cokthrop' continue et personaliter ministrare solebat, et hoc excepto quod defuncti de villula de Herdewyk' apud Bampton' et illi de Cokthrop' apud Dukelington' sepeliri et pro eis mortuaria consueta vere prestari, quodque rectores seu capellani dicte capelle rectoribus ecclesie de Dukelington' aliquod annuum, ut nunc unam libram incensi, nunc tres solidi et unam libram incensi, nunc decem solidos, in universo solvisse dicebantur temporibus successivis, quodque ante tempus quondam Willelmi Child' qui ex collatione germani sui tunc rectoris ecclesie de Dukelington' dictam capellam de Cokthrop' optinebat circiter per quinquaginta annos, necnon ante tempus predicti Radulphi qui ad presentationem cujusdam domini Willelmi Dyve patroni ecclesie de Dukelington' predicte contra ipsius ecclesie tunc rectorem volentem retinuisse in manu sua prefatam capellam tanquam portionem ecclesie sue pro jure patronatus ejusdem capelle divisim habendo ab advocatione ecclesie de Dukelington' in curia regia litigantis et pro se sentenciam optinentis, de dicti rectoris voluntate quasi coacta, per oppressione sine presentatione episcopo facta et sine auctoritate pontificali ipsam capellam tenuit per quadraginta annos ut dicebatur, capellani deservientes eidem capelle per rectores ecclesie de Dukelington' pro libito ponebantur et amovebantur ad votum. Nec potuit ullimoda certitudo haberi per depositiones juratorum vel registra episcoporum precedentium, licet inde perscrutatio fieret exquisita, quod unquam aliquis in dicta capella de Cokkethrop' auctoritate pontificali fuerat institutus vel ad illam aliter admissus. Verumptamen archidiaconi loci de dicta capella quinque solidos annuos nomine procurationis dicebantur ex consuetudine percepisse. Demum hujusmodi inquisitionibus factis et aliis concurrentibus, circumstanciis ac dicte capelle qualitate pensatis, et ex hiis una cum hoc quod venerabilis pater dominus Robertus dei gracia Bathon' et Wellen' episcopus custos terrarum et heredis Johannes Dyve redintegrationem

[1] The date is correct, and the displacement of the entry remains unexplained.
[2] Hardwick near Velford.

dicte capelle cum ecclesia de Dukelington' si forte prius separati et diversi[1] jure [*f. 336v*] fuissent quoad curam spiritualem de quo non constat consensit, Philippum Dyve rectorem ecclesie de Dukelington' predicte ad eandem capellam nobis presentans, motum animi nostri informantes decetero sustinemus quantum in nobis est quod rector ecclesie de Dukelington' de dicta capella de Cokkethrop' et pertinentibus ad eam tanquam de parte parochie sue in spiritualibus et temporalibus curet et ordinet in futurum, jure heredis Johannes Dyve nunc minoris si pro se cum ad etatem legitimam pervenerit proponere voluerit cum effectu quare hujusmodi consolidatio ut premittitur facta minime debeat tolerari, et etiam archidiaconi loci ac omnium quorum interest in omnibus semper salvo, et hoc specialiter addito quod rector ecclesie de Dukelington' pro tempore existens dicte capelle de Cokkethrop' per capellanum honestum ibidem continue residentem ac personaliter ministrantem faciat plenius deserviri sicut consuevit fieri temporibus retroactis. Actum apud Bannebir' nonis Aprilis anno domini M.CC. nonagesimo.

XII QUARTODECIMO KALENDAS JUNII VIDELICET DIE SANCTI DUNSTANI ANNO DOMINI M.CC. NONAGESIMO PRIMO INCIPIT ANNUS PONTIFICATUS DOMINI OLIVERI EPISCOPI LINCOLN' DUODECIMUS.

FRINGFORD (Feringford'). R. Robert of Houghton ch. p. by Sir Robert de Grey, knight, to the church of Fringford vacant by the death of Thomas of Idmiston. Inst. Louth, June 6, 1291.

SOUTH STOKE (Stok Abbatis'). R. Simon of Wells (Welles), clerk in minor orders, p. by the A. and C. of Eynsham to the church of South Stoke vacant by the res. of Jordan de la Pomereye on joining the Cistercians. Ordained subd. and inst. Boston, June 16, 1291.

CROPREDY (Cropperye). V. William of Cottenham pr. collated by the bishop to the prebendal vicarage of Cropredy, from which he had resigned, in virtue of a papal dispensation for his birth of unmarried parents dated at Orvieto Mar. 28, 1291, and subject to certain conditions. Collation by letters

---

[1] Sic. For 'separate et diverse'.

patent under the bishop's seal, Spaldwick, July 2, 1291, witnessed by Master Jocelyn of Kirmington, Walter of Wootton, John de Scalleby, Robert of Kibworth, John of Ferriby and others.

[*f. 337v*] GLYMPTON. R. Nicholas of Saltford subd. p. by the P. and C. of Kenilworth to the church of Glympton' vacant by the death of Robert called Schirlok'. Inst. Spaldwick, July 15, 1291.

COGGES. Mathew Dupont, p. by the Abbot of Fécamp to the office of prior of Cogges vacant by the res. of Stephen de Alba Malla. Admitted at the second attempt, the first letters of presentation having proved incorrect, Biggleswade, Aug. 28, 1291.

LOWER HEYFORD, Mediety. R. Master Hugh of Thurlby (Thurleby) clerk in minor orders p. by the A. and C. of Eynsham to the mediety of Lower Heyford, vacant by the res. of Simon of Wells to become a Dominican. Ordained subd. and inst. Grantham, Sept. 22, 1291.

HETHE. R. Master William of Chadshunt (Chadelshunt')[1] re-presented by the P. and C. of Kenilworth to the church of Hethe vacant because the said William had not been ordained pr. within a year of institution. Inst. Stow Park, Oct. 9, 1291.

NORTH STOKE. R. Roger de Bykkerwyk' subd. represented by Edmund Earl of Cornwall to the church of North Stoke vacant because the said Roger had not been ordained pr. within a year of institution. Inst. London, O.T., Dec. 6, 1291.

COTTISFORD. R. Odo of Down Ampney p. by Thibaut de Cambrai proctor of the Abbey of Bec to the church of Cottisford vacant because John de Cusanc' had been inst. to a church in the diocese of London. Inst. Dec. 16, 1291 (place not given).[2]

[*f. 338*] ALKERTON (Alcrinton'). R. Master Robert of Clifton, clerk in minor orders, p. by Amaury de St. Amand to the church of Alkerton vacant by the death of Peter of Linwood. Ordained subd. and inst. Wycombe, Dec. 22, 1291.

---

[1] Status not given.
[2] Sutton was at Wooburn on this date.

ADDERBURY. R. Sir Edmund of Maidstone pr. p. by J. Bishop of Winchester to the church of Adderbury vacant by the death of Master Nicholas. Inst. Wooburn, Feb. 2, 1292.

GREAT TEW. R. Simon Meadows (de Pratellis), clerk in minor orders, p. by Sir John Meadows knight to the church of Great Tew vacant by the death of Master Robert of Thorpe. Ordained subd., after giving proof of age, and inst. Wycombe, Mar. 1, 1292.

BROUGHTON POGGS. R. William le Ireys, clerk in minor orders p. by Sir John Maudut, knight, to the church of Broughton Poggs vacant by the death of Robert of Southrop. Ordained subd., after giving proof of age, and inst. Wycombe, Mar. 1, 1292.

STUDLEY. Clemency Sweyn, appointed by the bishop to be prioress of Studley in succession to Mabel, who had died. The nuns' attempt to elect a successor had been a failure, as was reported by the bishop's commissaries Master John le Fleming and Walter of Wootton. Fingest, Apr. 8, 1292.

KIDLINGTON. (Chadelington'). Letters patent of the bishop, declaring that Master Philip of Barton, rector of Charlbury, had been inducted to the chapel of Kidlington in accordance with the decision of the papal judges-delegate. London, Apr. 18, 1292.

BUCKNELL. R. Ithel of Caerwent (Kayrwent') subd. p. by Richard de Aumorri to the church of Bucknell vacant by the death of Roger de Aumorry. Inst. South Stoke, May 12, 1292. 'De Johanne vero de Aumorry ad prefatam ecclesiam primitus presentato actum est prout in rotulo custodiarum continetur'.

DEDDINGTON. R. William of Holcot pr. p. by Sir Osbert Gifford, knight, to the church of Deddington vacant by the death of Master Nicholas of Marnham. Presentation opposed by the King, who in right of custody of the lands and heir of Henry Dyve presented Walter of Amersham clerk, but later withdrew his claim, saving his right to put it forward at a subsequent vacancy. William was inst. Dorchester, May 12, 1292, in the person of Henry Tilley pr. his proctor, with a papal dispensation to hold in plurality the church of Catworth.

ST. PETER-LE-BAILEY, OXFORD. R. Alexander of Hemingby (Hemmingby) p. by the P. and C. of St. Frideswide's Oxford to the church of St. Peter-le-Bailey, vacant by the death of Master Ralph. Master Roger Mymkan, first presented, renounced his claim by letters patent. Inst. Osney, May 17, 1292.

DIE SANCTI DUNSTANI VIDELICET QUARTODECIMO KALENDAS JUNII ANNO DOMINI M.CC. NONAGESIMO SECUNDO INCIPIT ANNUS PONTI-FICATUS DOMINI OLIVERI EPISCOPI LINCOLN' TERTIUSDECIMUS.

DUNS TEW (Dunstywe, Donstywe). V. Robert of Milcombe ch. p. by the P. and C. of Merton to the vicarage of Duns Tew vacant by the death of John. Inst. Thornton Curtis, June 30, 1292.

[f. 339] ROUSHAM. R. James of Berkhamstead (Berkhamsted'), clerk in minor orders p. by Edmund Earl of Cornwall to the church of Rousham vacant because William Heath (de Brueria) had been inst. to the church of All Saints Hemswell. Ordained subd. and inst. Northampton, Sept. 22, 1292.

HETHE. R. Henry of Dunton, ch. p. by the P. and C. of Kenilworth to the church of Hethe vacant by the res. of Master William of Chadshunt. Inst. Banbury, Oct. 3, 1292.

LAUNTON. R. Master John of Denby pr. p. by the A. and C. of Westminster to the church of Launton vacant by the death of Master Roger Baret. Inst. Banbury, Oct. 6, 1292.

FRITWELL (Frettewell'). V. John of Sherington ch. p. by the P. and C. of St. Fridewide's Oxford to the vicarage of Fritwell vacant by the res. of Edmund of Ringstead. Inst. Spaldwick, Oct. 17, 1292. 'Et est sciendum quod licet littere resignatorie predicte sigillum decani de Burnecestr' una cum sigillo quod dicebatur resignantis esset filo mediante per modum collationis appensum, prefatus tamen Johannes illam ad sancta Dei ewangelia veram esse juravit.'

COLD NORTON. Robert of Ravesden, canon of Canons' Ashby, collated by the bishop to the office of prior of Cold Norton in succession to Walter who had resigned, at the request of the subprior and community. Licence to elect had been obtained from the Bishop of Bath and Wells, and from Richard Breton, who together farmed the vill of Chipping Norton. No place or date (Autumn, 1292)

ELSFIELD. V. William of Rollright ch. p. by the P. and C. of St. Frideswide's Oxford to the vicarage of Elsfield vacant by the death of William. Inst. Biggleswade, Dec. 1, 1292.

[*f. 339v*] SWALCLIFFE. V. Walter of Alkerton ch. p. by Thomas of Wickham rector of Swalcliffe to the vicarage thereof, vacant as Peter of Shenington had been inst. to the vicarage of Wetwang in the diocese of York. Inst. Dorchester, Dec. 18, 1292.

LOWER HEYFORD, Mediety. R. Master Alexander of Whaplode, clerk in minor orders p. by the A. and C. of Eynsham to the mediety of Lower Heyford vacant by the death of Hugh of Thurlby. Had custody for a period. Ordained subd. and inst. Dorchester, Dec. 18, 1292.

MERTON. R. Roger of Kilworth ch. p. by the A. and C. of Eynsham to the church of Merton vacant by the res. of Master Robert of Kilworth. Inst. Fingest, Jan. 15, 1293.

NUNEHAM COURTENAY. R. Maynard of Colham ch. p. by the A. and C. of Abingdon to the church of Nuneham Courtenay vacant by the death of Master Peter of Lockinge. Inst. London, Old Temple, Feb. 21, 1293.

LEWKNOR. V. Robert of Hendred ch. p. by the A. and C. of Abingdon to the vicarage of Lewknor vacant because William of Grave had been inst. to a vicarage in Abingdon. Inst. London, Old Temple, Mar. 1, 1293.

———

DIE SANCTI DUNSTANI VIDELICET QUARTODECIMUS KALENDAS JUNII ANNO DOMINI M.CC. NONAGESIMO TERTIO INCIPIT ANNUS PONTI-FICATUS DOMINI OLIVERI LINCOLNIEN' EPISCOPI QUARTUSDECIMUS.

———

CORNWELL. R. Master Geoffrey of Belgrave, clerk in minor orders p. by the A. and C. of Osney to the church of Cornwell vacant because Roger of Kilworth had been inst. to the church of Merton. Ordained subd. (by licence of the Bishop of London) and inst. London, Old Temple, May 23, 1293.

[*f. 340*] NORTH STOKE. R. Master John of Everdon, clerk in minor orders p. by Edmund Earl of Cornwall to the church of North Stoke vacant by the res. of Roger de Bikerwyk'.

Ordained subd. (by licence of the Bishop of London) and inst. London, Old Temple, May 23, 1293.

ROTHERFIELD PEPPARD. R. Master Walter of Wycombe p. by Sir Ralph Peppard knight to the church of Rotherfield Peppard vacant by the death of John Daryel. Inst. Fingest, June 25, 1293.

NOKE (Oke) Richard of Shirburn ch. p. by Sir Henry Thyes knight to the chapel of Noke vacant by the death of John of Draycott. Inst. Dorchester, July 1, 1293.

LITTLEMORE. Emma of Wantage appointed by the bishop to the office of prioress of Littlemore in succession to Matilda of Gloucester who had died. An attempt by the nuns to elect was quashed for faulty procedure (*multiplex vitium processus*) but the nuns were unanimous in their support of Emma. Dorchester, July 1, 1293.

THAME. V. James of Frieston ch. p. by Master Thomas of Sutton, prebendary of Thame, to the vicarage thereof vacant by the death of William. A special inquiry was held at the request of Master John of Monmouth canon of Lincoln and prebendary of Milton, who acted as the bishop's commissary in the matter of institution. Inst Thame, July 17, 1293.

'Et est sciendum quod hujosmodi inquisitio demandata fuit dicto Magistro Johanne facienda certa de causa, ita quod per hoc decano et capitulo super[1] jure inquirendi sibi competenti in hac parte nullum prejudicium generaretur'.

MARSH BALDON. Hugh of Bacton ch. p. by Master William de Montfort dean of St. Paul's, by reason of his custody of the lands and heir of Sir Peter de la Mare, to the chapel of Marsh Baldon, with cure of souls, vacant by the death of Robert of Kington. Inst. Banbury, July 21, 1293.

[*f. 340v*] CHARLBURY. Letters patent granting to the A. and C. of Eynsham licence to appropriate the church of Charlbury with the dependent chapels of Kidlington and Shorthampton, saving to the Archdeacon of Oxford an annual payment of half-a-mark. Until the church of Charlbury should fall vacant the A. and C. were to enjoy some extra tithes from the parish of Banbury. Under the bishop's seal, Banbury, July 21, 1293. The statement of their case by the A. and C. is given in full, and dated at Eynsham 'in the month of July'.

[1] Underlined.

APPROPRIATIO ECCLESIE DE CHERLEBIR'. Universis, etc. Oliverus permissione divina Lincoln' episcopus salutem etc. Nos qui ex debito officii pastoralis religiosorum omnium nobis subditorum prospicere tenemur utilitati pariter et quieti, dilectis in Christo filiis ...[1] abbati et conventui de Eynesham ex certis causis obligatos nos reputamus specialibus in hac parte. Hinc est quod cum iidem abbas et conventus ecclesiam de Cherlebir' cum suis pertinenciis, necnon et decimas quas in parochiis de Cherlebir' et Bannebir' solent percipere, nostre ordinationi pure, sponte, simpliciter et absolute per omnia submiserint prout in littera super eorum submissione confecta plenius continetur. Attendentes eorum indigenciam qua non satis sufficiunt eis ad sui sustentationem et alia onera eisdem incumbentia bona sua temporalia quin necesse habeant pro suis suplendis[2] necessitatibus nimis multiplicari secularibus occupationibus et per consequens a celestium contemplatione que a religiosis precipue requiritur plurimum impediri, quodque de obventionibus ad dictam ecclesiam de Cherlebir' spectantes magnam perceperunt hactenus portionem, per quod videbantur quasi secte obventiones que videntur potius uniende, quod etiam dictis considerationibus pro salute animarum et statu parochie de qua agitur in spiritualibus et temporalibus magis expedire videtur quod fiat appropriatio et vicaria competens ordinetur quam nomine rectoris preficiatur aliquis in eadem, Deum habentibus pre oculis prefatam ecclesiam de Cherlebir' cum suis de Chadelington' et Schorthampton' capellis cujus esse noscuntur absque qualibet dubitatione patroni, necnon cum omnibus suis juribus et pertinenciis, seu fructus, proventus et obventiones ejusdem ecclesie qualescumque, rectore ipsius factum nostrum approbante et plenius collaudante cedente vel decedente, auctoritate pontificali, concurrenteque consensu ...[1] decani et capituli nostre Lincoln' ecclesie, prefatis abbati et conventui ac monasterio suo concedimus et assignamus in usus proprios perpetuo convertendos, salva portione congrua pro vicaria in ipsa ecclesia una cum domo seu manso congruo pro nostra arbitrio ordinanda. Ordinamus insuper et diffinimus quod Archidiacono Oxon' qui pro tempore fuerit pro comodo sequestri quod tempore vacationum ipsius ecclesie percipere consuevit dimidiam marcam in festo Pasche annuatim solvere teneantur. De decimis vero quas in parochia de Bannebir' impresenciarum percipiunt et hactenus pacifice perceperunt volumus et tenore presentium ordinamus quod earundem gaudeant possessione quieta quousque ut premittitur ecclesie

---

[1] Blank in MS.
[2] Sic.

de Cherlebir' cedente vel decendente rectore ipsius ecclesie
fructuum et obventionum possessionem pacificam nacti
fuerint et quietam, qua adepta et optenta pacifice solis illis
decimis sint contenti que de terris nostris dominicis in
parochia de Bannebir' provenunt, nullam decimam aliam sibi
vendicare in eadem parochia presumentes, omnes etiam alias
decimas ejusdem parochie ad ecclesiam de Bannebir' extunc
pertinere volumus et tenore presentium diffinimus, ut sic
ecclesie que in facultatibus a statu pristino multum decidit
prospiciatur in tanto et sepedicti abbas et conventus de statu
suo securiores effecti litem minus timere valeant in futurum.
Premissa autem omnia sic ordinate intelligimus salvis episcopalibus consuetudinibus et Lincoln' ecclesie dignitate. In cujus
rei testimonium sigillum nostrum presentibus est appensum.
Datum apud Bannebir' XII kalendas Augusti anno domini
M.CC. nonagesimo tertio et pontificatus nostri quartodecimo.
Sequitur Submissio.[1] Universis sancte matris ecclesie filiis ad quos
presentes littere pervenerint, frater Thomas abbas monasterii
de Eynesham et ejusdem loci conventus salutem in vero
salutari. Ad universitatis vestre noticiam volumus pervenire
quod cum nos et monasterium nostrum plures decimas tam
majores quam minores de manerio et dominicis terris
venerabilis patris domini Lincoln' episcopi ac etiam de terris
et possessionibus quorundam aliorum infra parochiam
prebendalis ecclesie de Bannebir' necnon et in parochia de
Cherlebir' cum suis capellis de Chadelington' et Schorthampton'
hactenus pacifice possiderimus canonice in presenti ac
tendentes ex quibusdam verisimilibus conjecturis quod super
eisdem decimis vel eorum aliquibus lis contra nos saltem de
facto proximus retroactis temporibus fuisset subporta, nisi
prius pater dominus. Oliverus Dei gracia Lincoln' episcopus
monasterii nostri patronus defensionis clipeo nobis in hac
parte adversari volentibus restituisset, quodque preteritorum
exempla in consimilibus cavere nos admoneret in futurum, et
affectionem sincerem quam dictus pater erga nostrum et
suum peculiare monasterium predictum semper gessit et
adhuc gerere comprobatur plenius advertentes, et sic de
ipsius patris benevolencia confidentes ad plenum, quoad
omnes decimas predictas quas infra dictam parochiam de
Bannebir' optinemus et quoad jus ac possessionem omni-
modam quod et quam habuimus, habemus seu habere
poterimus in eisdem, necnon et ecclesiam predictam de
Cherlebir' cum suis capellis antedictis que de nostro patronatu
existit nos ac monasterium nostrum et ipsas decimas omnes et
predictam ecclesiam cum suis capellis dicti patris ordinationi

[1] In the margin 'Submissio abbatis et conventus de Eynesham'.

pure, sponte et simpliciter submittimus per presentes, ratum habituri et firmum quicquid dictus pater de premissis qualitercumque duxerit ordinandum. In cujus rei testimonium sigillum nostrum commune presentibus est appensum. Datum in capitulo nostro de Eynesham manse Julii anno domini M.CC. nonagesimo tertio.[1]

[*f. 341*] WOOD EATON. R. John of Winchelsea, clerk in minor orders p. by the A. and C. of Eynsham to the church of Wood Eaton vacant by the res. of Master Robert of Winchelsea. Had custody for a period. Ordained subd. and inst. Lincoln, Sept. 19, 1293.

MINSTER LOVELL. Ralph de Montfort p. by the A. and C. of St. Mary's, Ivry, to the office of prior of Minster Lovell vacant by the res. of Stephen de Habitu.[2] Letter of presentation given in full but undated. Stephen's letter of resignation given in full and dated Minster Lovell, Oct. 4, 1293, under the seal of the dean of Wytton, his own seal being unknown to many. Admitted London, Old Temple, Oct. 7, 1293, without dispute.

ST. FRIDESWIDE, OXFORD. V. John of Aldbourne (Aldburn') ch. p. by the P. and C. of St. Frideswide's to the vicarage thereof, vacant by the res. of Thomas of Hungerford. Inst. London, Old Temple, Oct. 19, 1293.

SHIRBURN. V. Gilbert of Stanwick ch. p. by the A. and C. of Dorchester to the vicarage of Shirburn vacant because Richard of Easter [sic] had been inst. to the church of Noke (Ake). Inst. London, Old Temple, Oct. 19, 1293.

BLOXHAM. V. John of Marston ch. p. by the Abbess and C. of Godstow to the vicarage of Bloxham vacant by the death of Philip. Inst. London, Old Temple, Nov. 3, 1293.

ROUSHAM (Roulesham). R. Peter of Wallingford subd. p. by Edmund Earl of Cornwell to the church of Rousham vacant by the res. of James of Berkhampstead, reported by Master Richard of Sotwell. Inst. London, Old Temple, Nov. 24, 1293. 'Et est sciendum quod de modo vacationis ejusdem ecclesie suprascripto constabat tantum per assertionem Magistri Ricardi de Sottewell' asserentis se velle super sacrosancta jurare quod dictus Jacobus aliam ecclesiam

---

[1] Marginal note 'Vide plus in quaterno sequenti.' See pp. 190–92.
[2] Alias Stephen d'Ivry.

admisit ut est dictum, et quod in presencia domini ...[1] comitis supradicti dictam ecclesiam de Roulesham resignavit expresse, et de hoc se velle cavere sub privatione beneficii sui, et nichilominus continebatur in littera domini comitis presentatoria dictam ecclesiam esse vacantem per dicti Jacobi resignationem expressam'.

STOKE TALMAGE. R. Master Richard of Battle, clerk in minor orders p. by the A. and C. of Thame to the church of Stoke Talmage vacant by the death of John. Had custody for a period after being ordained subd. Inst. Fingest, Jan. 4, 1294.

DORCHESTER-ON-THAMES (Dorkecestr'). William of Rofford canon of Dorchester, elected to the position of abbot in succession to Ralph of Didcot who had died. Election confirmed Dorchester, Jan. 28, 1294. The letters of the P. and C. asking for licence to elect and the bishop's reply are given in full, dated respectively Dorchester, Jan. 21 and Fingest, Jan. 22, 1294.

CLANFIELD. V. Master Robert son of Maurice of Elstow (Elnestowe) ch. p. by the Abbess and C. of Elstow to the vicarage of Clanfield vacant by the res. of John of Wilsamstead. Inst. Banbury, Mar. 15, 1294.

[f. 342] BRIGHTWELL BALDWIN. R. Master William of Apperley clerk in minor orders p. by Sir Thomas Park knight to the church of Brightwell Baldwin vacant by the death of John of Blewbury. Had custody for a period. Ordained subd. and inst. Banbury, Mar. 13, 1294.

ST. FRIDEWIDE, OXFORD. Alexander of Sutton, subprior of St. Frideswide's, elected *per viam compromissi* to the office of prior in succession to Robert of Ewelme who had resigned. Election confirmed Biggleswade, Apr. 24, 1294. Note that although the bishop had written testifying to Robert's resignation, the king took no notice of this letter, the licence to elect referring only to that of the canons of St. Frideswide's.
'Et habuit dictus prior quamdam litteram episcopi patentem domino Regi directam pro testificanda confirmatione predicta sub forma quam habuit abbas de Thornton', que est in primo folio hujus libri.[2] Et est sciendum quod quando canonici dicte domus adierunt dominum Regem pro petenda licencia eligendi, habuerunt litteram episcopi patentem

---

[1] Blank in MS.
[2] L.R.S. vol. 39, pp. 141–2.

testimonialem de admissione cessionis fratris predicti
universis directam, que est in libro memorandorum de anno
pontificatus predicto[1] set[2] eam reportarunt asserentes eam
fuisse cancellario domini Regis ostensam et eis retraditam per
eundem. Et in littera domini Regis de licencia eligendi
concessa, nulla fiebat mentio de dicta littera testimoniali
cessionis, set[2] tantum de litteris capituli sancte Fredeswyde
testificantibus cessionem eandem. Et sic videtur quod curia
Regis de talibus litteris episcoporum testificantibus hujusmodi
cessiones non curat, set[2] stat litteris capitulorum'.[3]

DIE SANCTI DUNSTANI EPISCOPI VIDELICET QUARTODECIMO
KALENDAS JUNII ANNO DOMINI MILLESIMO DUCENTESIMO NONAGESIMO
QUARTO INCIPIT ANNUS PONTIFICATUS DOMINI OLIVERI DEI GRACIA
LINCOLNIEN' EPISCOPI QUINTUSDECIMUS.

NORTH STOKE. R. Master John of Everdon d. re-presented by
Edmund Earl of Cornwall to the church of North Stoke
vacant because the said Master John had not been ordained
pr. within a year of institution. Inst. Biggleswade, June 29,
1294.

[f. 342v] NORTHMORE (Mera, La Mere). R. William of Down
Ampney ch. p.by Stephen, prior of Deerhurst in the diocese
of Worcester, to the church of Northmore vacant by the
death of Hugh of Clifford. Inst. Dorchester, Sept. 12, 1294.

GLYMPTON. R. Ralph de Salle, clerk in minor orders, p. by the
P. and C. of Kenilworth to the church of Glympton vacant by
the death of Nicholas of Saltford. Ordained subd. and inst.
Dunstable, Sept. 18, 1294.

ST. PETER AT THE EAST GATE, OXFORD.[4] Approval by the
bishop of the appropriation of the church of St. Peter at the
East Gate, vacant by the death of Master Bogo de Clare, by
the scholars and brethren of Merton College, in virtue of a
licence granted by Bishop Richard Gravesend at Spaldwick,

---

[1] L.R.S. vol. 52, pp. 182–3.
[2] Sic.
[3] This seems to have annoyed Sutton, as well it might.
[4] In the margin, in a fourteenth-century hand, 'Appropriatio ecclesie S.
Petri orientalis in Oxon'.

Sept. 13, 1266. A letter was sent to the Archdeacon of Oxford ordering him to put the grant into effect. Liddington, Nov. 2, 1294.

Vacante ecclesia sancti Petri versus orientem Oxon' per mortem domini Bogonis de Clara qui ultimo tenebat eandem ex parte scolarium et fratrum domus de Merton' Oxon' IIII nonas Novembris anno domini M.CC. nonagesimo quarto apud Lydington' exhibita fuit episcopo quedam littera domini Ricardi proximi predecessoris sui, appropriationem ejusdem ecclesie cum suis capellis et pertinenciis universis per ipsum eis factam continens, cujus est talis tenor: ... Omnibus Christi fidelibus ad quos presentes littere pervenerint, Ricardus miseratione divina Lincoln' episcopus salutem in domino sempiternam. Officii nostri debitum suasu pietatis exposcit ut quod subditorum nostrorum devotio ad laudem sui con-ditoris prona disponit, auxilio salubri nostra sollicitudo studeat promovere.

Cum igitur dilectus filius nobis et ecclesie nostre devotus dominus Walterus de Merton' illustris domini H. Regis Anglie quondam cancellarius, domum que scolarium de Merton' nuncupatur apud Maldon' Wynton' diocesis ad sustentationem perpetuam scolarium in scolis degentium et ministrorum altaris Christi in dicto domo residentium pia consideratione stabilierit et fundaverit ad honorem divini nominis et ecclesie sacrosancte profectum, nos ob Dei omnipotentis intuitum et pium dicti Regis necnon et fundatoris ipsius interventum, in nomine sancte et individue trinitatis ecclesiam S. Petri Oxon' versus orientem in qua dicti scolares et fratres ex collatione dicti domini Regis jus optinent patronatus dictorum scolarium et fratrum usus,[1] interveniente in hoc assensu W. decani et capituli nostri Lincoln', damus, assignamus, concedimus, statuentes ut eam quamprimum vacaverit libere et absque difficultatis obstaculo auctoritate presentium ingredi valeant, ipsamque cum suis capellis, juribus et pertinencis omnibus propriis eorum usibus habeant et possideant imperpetuum, salva rationabili vicaria ad quam custos domus supradicte idoneos vicarios vice scolarium et fratrum predictorum nobis et successoribus nostris quotiens eam vacare contigerit presentabit, ecclesiam insuper sancte Johannis Baptiste Oxon'[2] in qua ex collatione religiosorum virorum ...[3] abbatis et conventus Rading' jus patronatus optinent, eorundem

---

[1] sic, recte 'usibus'?
[2] In the margin, in a fourteenth-century hand 'Appropriatio ecclesie S. Johannis Baptiste in Oxon'.
[3] Blank in MS.

scolarium et fratrum usibus ob Dei intuitum assignamus, concedimus et confirmamus, statuentes ut et ipsam quam-primum vacaverit libere et absque difficultatis obstaculo ingredi valeant, et eam cum suis pertinenciis habeant et possideant imperpetuum, salva rationibili vicaria aut alia sustentatione ministrorum ejusdem per nos vel successores nostros providenda, ad quam custos dicte domus nobis et successoribus nostris vice scolarium et fratrum ipsorum ministros ydoneos similiter presentabit, salvis etiam in omnibus episcopalibus consuetudinibus et Lincoln' ecclesie jure et dignitate. In cujus rei testimonium sigillum nostrum una cum sigillo capituli nostri Lincoln' presentibus est appensum. Datum apud Spaldewyk' idibus Septembris anno domini M.CC. LX sexto et pontificatus nostri octavo.[1] ... Cujus quidem appropriationis pretextu et parte dictorum scolarium et fratrem petitum fuit ab episcopo ut eos induceret vel induci faceret in corporalem possessionem dicte ecclesie cum capellis et pertinenciis suis sic vacantis. Episcopus vero appropriationem predictam ex pia causa laudibiliter factam approbans, constante sufficienter jus patronatus dicte ecclesie ad dictos scolares ex collatione quondam domini Henrici Regis Anglie filii Regis Johannis, et confirmatione domini Edwardi Regis filii ejusdem Henrici secuta pertinere, constante etiam sufficienter de morte domini Bogonis predicti, Archi-diacono Oxon' vel ejus officiali mandavit protinus sub hac forma: ... O. etc., archidiacono Oxon' vel ejus officiali salutem etc. Cum bone memorie dominus Ricardus proximus predecessor noster, concurrente ad hoc consensu ...[2] decani et capituli ecclesie nostre Lincoln', ecclesiam sancti Petri versus orientem Oxon', in qua ecclesia [*f. 343*] cum suis capellis, juribus et pertinenciis universis scolares et fratres domus de Merton' ex collatione clare memorie domini Henrici patris domini Edwardi Dei gracia illustris Regis Anglie, et etiam confirmatione ejusdem domini nostri domini Edwardi Regis predicti jus optinent patronatus, eisdem scolaribus et fratribus dudum sub data idibus Septembris anno domini M.CC. sexagesimo appropriare curavit, ita ut in eventu vacationis ejusdem ecclesie proxime post appropri-ationem eandem ipsa ecclesia cum suis pertinenciis supratactis usibus perpetuis cedat scolarium predictorum, salva ration-

---

[1] Gravesend's original licence is now in Merton College and has been printed by J. R. L. Highfield in *The Early Rolls of Merton College*, pp. 405–6. Slight textual variations (e.g. Maldon' for Meaudon', Spaldewyk' for Spaldewik') suggest that Scalleby copied, as one would expect, not the original licence but the copy enrolled among Gravesend's memoranda, now lost.
[2] Blank in MS.

abili vicaria ad quam custos domus predicte idoneos vicarios vice scolarium et fratrum predictorum nobis et successoribus nostris quotiens eam vacare contigerit presentabit, episcopalibus etiam consuetudinibus et Lincoln' ecclesie jure et dignitate in omnibus semper salvis, sicut in instrumentis autenticis nobis super hoc exhibitis vidimus plenius contineri, ac prefata ecclesia sancti Petri vacat ad presens per mortem domini Bogonis de Clara qui tempore appropriationis predicte ecclesiam tenebat eandem, nos hujusmodi appropriationem ex pia causa factam laudabiliter approbantes vobis mandamus quatinus dictos scolares in corporalem possessionem dicte ecclesie taliter appropriate et omnium spectantium ad eam inducere non tardetis, contradictores vobis et rebelles per censuram ecclesiasticam canonice compescentes. Valete. Datum apud Lydington' IIII nonas Novembris anno domini M.CC. nonagesimo quarto et pontificatus nostri quintodecimo.

DIE SANCTI DUNSTANI EPISCOPI VIDELICET QUARTODECIMO KALENDAS JUNII ANNO DOMINI NONAGESIMO QUINTO INCIPIT ANNUS PONTIFICATUS DOMINI OLIVERI EPISCOPI LINCOLN' SEXTUSDECIMUS.

STANTON HARCOURT. R. Master Hugh of Stamford, clerk in minor orders p. by the A. and C. of Reading to the church of Stanton Harcourt vacant by the death of Sir Hugh de la Penne. Ordained subd. (by licence of the Bishop of London) and inst. London, Old Temple, May 28, 1295.

CROWELL. R. John de Verny, clerk in minor orders, p. by Sir John of St. Helen *alias* St. Agatha knight to the church of Crowell vacant by the death of Adam of Stratton. Ordained subd. (by licence of the Bishop of London) and inst. London, Old Temple, May 28, 1295. Presentation opposed by the King, who p. Peter of Guildford as guardian of the lands and heir of Isabel de Fortibus, Countess of Albemarle. Case settled in favour of Sir John, Westminster, Apr. 30, 1295, witnessed by John of Mettingham (Metingham).

[*f. 343v*] LOWER HEYFORD Mediety. R. Robert de la Kerneyl, clerk in minor orders, p. by Sir Roger Delisle knight to the mediety of the church of Lower Heyford vacant by the res. of William of Brampton. Had custody for a period. Ordained subd. (by licence of the Bishop of London) and inst. London, Old Temple, May 28, 1295.

CHARLBURY. Mandate to the Archdeacon of Oxford to induct the A. and C. of Eynsham into possession of the church of Charlbury which they were licensed to appropriate, together with its dependent chapels of Kidlington and Shorthampton, after the resignation of its rector Philip of Barton (whose letter of resignation, under his own seal and that of the official-principal of Winchester, is given in full and dated at Eynsham, May 22, 1295). London, Old Temple, May 30, 1295. Note of a mandate to the Constable of Banbury to divert to the prebendal church of Banbury all those tithes which the said A. and C. had been accustomed to receive, except those from the demesne lands of the bishop. London, Old Temple, July 16, 1295.

ST. MARTIN, OXFORD. R. Walter de la Rye, ch. p. by the A. and C. of Abingdon to the church of St. Martin vacant by the death of John de Estewode'. Inst. London, Old Temple, Aug. 6, 1295.

[*f. 344*] BAMPTON. V. Master Richard of Beeston ch. p. by the D. and C. of Exeter to the vicarage of Bampton vacant by the papal provision of Master William of Bodmin to the church of Towcester. Inst. Stony Stratford, Sept. 22, 1295.

TADMARTON. R. William of Culham subd. p. by the A. and C. of Abingdon to the church of Tadmarton vacant by the death of Ralph. Ordained d. and inst. Berkhampstead, Sept. 24, 1295.

GODSTOW. Alice de Gorges, nun of Godstow, elected to the office of prioress *per viam inspirationis* in succession to Annabel who had resigned. Election confirmed by the bishop, Spalding Oct. 22, 1295. Licence to elect had been obtained from the King as patron.

ST. MARTIN, OXFORD. R. William of Wycombe (Wycumb) d. p. by the A. and C. of Abingdon to the church of St. Martin vacant by the res. of Walter de la Rye. Inst. Market Deeping, Oct. 29, 1295.

DUCKLINGTON. R. Robert of Ashby subd. p. by the King as guardian of the lands and heir of Henry Dyve to the church of Ducklington vacant by the death of Philip Dyve. Had custody for a period. Inst. London, Old Temple, Nov. 27, 1295. Presentation opposed by John Dyve who claimed to be of age when the church fell vacant. Case settled in favour of the King, Westminster, Oct. 30, 1295, witnessed by R. le Brabazoun.

MIDDLETON STONEY. R. William of Louth clerk in minor orders, p. by the A. and C. of Barlings to the church of Middleton Stoney vacant by the death of Master Peter Durandus and the withdrawal of Richard of Louth, first presented. Ordained subd. and inst. Huntingdon, Dec. 17, 1295.

[*f. 344v*] ALVESCOT. R. Hugh de la Penne, clerk in minor orders, p. by the King to the church of Alvescot vacant by the res. of Ralph de Watervill'. Had custody for a period. Ordained subd. and inst. Rothwell, Feb. 18, 1296.

———

DIE SANCTI DUNSTANI EPISCOPI VIDELICET QUARTODECIMO KALENDAS JUNII ANNO DOMINI M.CC. NONAGESIMO SEXTO, INCIPIT ANNUS PONTIFICATUS DOMINII OLIVERI LINCOLN' EPISCOPI SEPTIMUS-DECIMUS.

———

HAMPTON POYLE. R. Master Richard of Wellingborough, clerk in minor orders p. by Sir Walter de la Puyle knight to the church of Hampton Poyle vacant by the death of John of Burton. Ordained subd. and inst. Lincoln, May 19, 1296.

NORTHMORE. R. Valentine of Tangley ch. p. by the prior of Deerhurst to the church of Northmore vacant by the death of William of Down Ampney. Inst. Eresby, May 30, 1296.

EASINGTON. R. John of Tormarton ch. p. by the Abbess and C. of Godstow to the church of Easington vacant by the death of Robert de Dolouhton'. Inst. Louth, June 4, 1296.

CHARLBURY. V. Record of the setting-up of a vicarage in the church of Charlbury, with its dependent chapels of Kidlington and Shorthampton, on the occasion of its appropriation by the A. and C. of Eynsham. Provision was made for a manse for the vicar in Charlbury and one for his chaplain serving Kidlington. Right of augmentation and interpretation reserved to the bishop and his successors. In the presence of John of Cheltenham and Robert of Maidenhead, monks of Eynsham, and Richard of Berwick, vicar-designate. Stow Park, June 19, 1296. Richard was allowed to wait until Michaelmas before deciding whether or not to be instituted, and meanwhile the A. and C. were to pay his chaplains and build him a manse.

ORDINATIO VICARIE DE CHERLEBIR'. Memorandum quod XIII
kalendas Julii anno domini M.CC. nonagesimo sexto apud
Parcum Stowe episcopus vicariam in ecclesie de Cherlebir' ...[1]
abbati et conventui de Eynesham appropriata de novo
habendam in presencia fratrum Johannis de Chiltenham et
Roberti de Maidenhide commonachorum ejusdem domus de
Eynesham et procuratorum ...[1] abbatis et conventus predictorum ad audiendum et recipiendum ordinationem
hujusmodi vicarie per episcopum faciendum deputatorum
specialiter, necnon in presencia Ricardi de Berewyk' ad
eandem vicariam ordinandum per eosdem abbatem et
conventum presentati, ordinavit sub continentia infrascripta:
... In dei nomine amen. Constante per inquisitionem ad
mandatum nostrum factam per dilectum in Christo filium S.
Archidiacono Oxon' super vero valore omnium proventuum
ecclesie de Cherlebir' cum suis capellis de Chadelington' et
Schorthampton' ut sit ad vicariam in dicta ecclesia, ...[1] abbati
et conventui de Eynesham appropriata, per nos Oliverum
permissione divina Lincoln' episcopum ordinandam, certius
posset procedi, quod dictus proventus preter quasdam
decimas in parochia ejusdem ecclesie quas una cum pensione
quinque marcaram in ipsa ecclesia iidem religiosi solebant
percipere ab antiquo valent per annum C marcas, quodque
altaragium de Cherlebir' cum capella de Schorthampton' valet
per annum XVIII marcas, et fenum decimale valet per annum
IX marcas. Item totum altaragium de Chadlington' ad VIII
marcas estimatur, et fenum decimale ibidem valet XL solidos
annuatim, quodque in dicta ecclesia de Cherlebir' solebant esse
duo capellani ad minus et hoc pro capella de Schorthampton'
in qua ter in singulis septimanis divina sunt celebranda, et duo
[f. 345] clerici ministrantes, et in capella de Chadlington' unus
capellanus parochialis cum clerico continue moram trahens,
nos ad valorem dicte ecclesie et onera ministrorum ejusdem
oculos convertentes, vicariam in dicta ecclesia de Cherlebir',
vocatis hiis quorum interest et sufficienter competentibus, ex
nunc esse debere perpetuo ordinamus, proventus altaragiorum predictorum et totum fenum decimale tam apud
Cherlebir' et Schorthampton' quam apud Chadlington',
necnon sexaginta quinque acras terre arabilis que sunt de
dominice dicte ecclesie de Cherlebir' cum omnibus pertinenciis suis et commoditatibus quibuscumque, ad sustentationem
vicarii pro tempore inibi instituendi, ac unius capellani secum
moraturi quamdiu idem vicarius poterit personaliter ministrare,
et duorum capellanorum si ad celebrandum forsan impotens
efficiatur, scilicet pro ecclesia de Cherlebir' et capella de

[1] Blank in MS.

Schorthampton' predicta in qua ter in ebdomada vicarius faciet celebrari, et etiam unius capellani parochialis ad capellam de Chadlington' residenciam continue facturi, et clericorum sufficientium, et omnium aliorum sive pro luminaribus sive pro aliis ad divinum ministerium requirendis que per rectorem consueverant exhiberi inveniendorum per vicarium in futuro assignantes, ita quod nec idem vicarius aliquas decimas de dictis terris prefatis religiosis seu iidem religioso vice versa de suis bonis aut proventibus quibuscumque eidem vicario solverc teneantur. Ordinando etiam statuimus quod vicarius in dicta ecclesia omnimoda ornamenta in cancello quocumque nomine censeantur que rector invenire solet et debet, et etiam libros, teneatur decetero invenire, ita tamen quod dicti abbas et conventus ea omnia hac vice juxta ordinationem ... archidiaconi loci reparent seu faciant fieri in bono statu, sed iidem religiosi quotiens res exegerit reficiant et reparabunt cancellum. Ordinamus insuper quod vicarius sinodalia et Letare Jerusalem et hiis similia ordinaria consueta persolvet, sed religiosi archidiaconum procurabunt. Onera vero dedicationis et reconciliationis si ex causa sine culpa vicarii et suorum in futuro contingant, quod absit, dicti religiosi quoad procurationem et alia tenebantur subire. Alia autem onera contributionum sive in subsidium terre sancte sive alio modo dictam ecclesiam qualitercumque contingentium in futuro vicarius pro rata portionis sue sicut equum fuerit declaranda pro tempore, et similiter iidem religiosi pro rata portionis sue agnoscent. Demum volumus et ordinamus quod vicarius in ecclesia de Cherleby in fundo ecclesie dotali mansum habeat competentem, et per prefatum archidiaconum vice nostra in presencia et sub testimonio virorum fidedignorum de parochia pro vitanda contentione in posterum certius limitandis sumptibus quod dictorum religiosorum ab initio cum omnibus edificiis necessariis edificandis ut decet, et in villa de Chadlington' pro capellano ibidem moraturo mansum similiter congruum in fundo dotali ecclesie designandum per archidiaconum et edificandum ut supra. Ceterum quod secundum diversitatem temporum status rerum variatur quandoque, et ex factis hominum dubietates interpretatione digne oriuntur frequenter, ad augmentandum dictam vicariam si ad illius augmentationem nobis et successoribus nostris visum fuerit procedi debere, necnon ad declarandum et interpretandum de plano si quid dubium obscurumve in premissis emerserit in futurum potestatem nobis et successoribus est appensum. Actum et datum apud Parcum Stowe XIII kalendas Julii, anno domini M.CC. nonagesimo sexto et pontificatus nostri XVII. ... Qua quidam ordinatione recitata et serio promulgata dictus presentatus asseruit se velle deliberare utrum institutionem admittere vellet in dicta vicaria vel non, tum pro eo quod videbatur sibi altaragia ecclesie de Cherlebir' et capelle de Chadlington' ultra valorem communem estimata, tum pro eo quod abbas et conventus predicti quasi totum emolumentum dictorum altaragiorum anni instantis perceperant ut dicebat, et oportebat ipsum capellanis stipendiariis solvere quatuor marcas citra festum sancti Michaelis si statim institueretur, tum pro eo quod non sunt edificia pro eo parata, in quibus capud[1] reclinaret, propter quod episcopus ordinavit quod fenum decimale dicte parochie per dictos abbatem et conventum colligeretur ad opus vicarii futuri, quodque pro emolumento percepto capellanis satisfaciant de quatuor marcis supradictis, et domos necessarias pro statu vicarii competentes edificarent, et dictus presentatus usque ad festum sancti Michaelis deliberaret utrum vellet institui in vicaria predicta vel non.[2]

CROWMARSH GIFFORD. V. William of Wolston ch. p. by the Prioress and C. of Goring to the vicarage of Crowmarsh Gifford vacant by the res. of Simon. Inst. Sleaford, July 19, 1296.

[*f. 345v*] CHARLBURY.[3] V. Richard of Berwick. Inst. Nettleham, Sept. 25, 1296.

STOKE TALMAGE (Stok' Talmach'). R. Walter de la Kaleng' clerk in minor orders, p. by the A. and C. of Thame to the church of Stoke Talmage vacant by the res. of Master Richard of Battle (Bello). Ordained subd. and inst. Lincoln, Sept. 22, 1296.

MERTON (Meriton'). R. Master Robert of Kilworth (Kevelingwurth') ch. p. by the A. and C. of Eynsham to the church of Merton vacant by the res. of Roger of Kilworth. Held the church *in commendam* for a period. Inst. Stoww Park, Oct. 9, 1296.

SPELSBURY. R. Paul of Brailes ch. p. by William de Beauchamp Earl of Warwick to the church of Spelsbury vacant by

---

[1] Sic, recte, 'caput'.
[2] In the margin a cross, with a note in Scalleby's hand 'ex alia parte folii'. See below, next entry but one.
[3] A cross in the margin. See the last entry but one.

the death of Master Peter of Taunton. Inst. Stow Park, Oct. 11, 1296.

YARNTON (Erdington). V. Walter of Kingham ch. p. by the A. and C. of Eynsham to the vicarage of Yarnton vacant because Richard of Berwick had been inst. to the vicarage of Charlbury. Inst. Buckden, Nov. 4, 1296.

SHIPLAKE. V. Peter of Hadenham ch. p. by the A. and C. of Missenden to the vicarage of Shiplake vacant by the res. of Alexander. Inst. Spaldwick, Dec. 19, 1296.

ISLIP (Islep') R. Master Robert de Leyam clerk in minor orders p. by the A. and C. of Westminster to the church of Islip vacant by the death of Walter of Cuddington. Ordained subd. and inst. Buckden, Dec. 22, 1296.

MINSTER LOVELL. Thomas of Finchampstead ch. p. by Sir John Lovell knight to the chantry in the chapel of St. Cecilia in the churchyard of Minster Lovell, vacant by the death of John of Chalgrove. An inquiry by the official of the Archdeacon of Oxford showed that the chapel had been founded by Sir John Lovell in the time of Bishop Gravesend and that the annual endowments were worth six marks and more.[1] Inst. Buckden, Feb. 5, 1297.

WROXTON. V. William of Weldon ch. p. by the P. and C. of Wroxton to the vicarage thereof vacant by the death of John. Inst. London, Mar. 24, 1297.

LEWKNOR. R. Master Simon of St. John (de sancto Johanne) pr. p. by the A. and C. of Abingdon to the church of Lewknor vacant by the death of John of Colchester. Inst. London, Apr. 2, 1297.

OSNEY. John of Bibury (Bebur') canon of Osney, elected *per viam compromissi* to the position of abbot, vacant by the death of Roger. Election confirmed Wooburn near Wycombe, May 2, 1297. Letters to the King in the same form as those issued on behalf of the Abbot of Thornton.[2] Solemn benediction of the abbot in Wooburn church, May 3.

---

[1] L.R.S. vol. 20, p. 224.
[2] L.R.S. vol. 39, pp. 141–2.

QUARTODECIMO KALENDAS JUNII VIDELICET DIE SANCTI DUNSTANI
ANNO DOMINI M.CC. NONAGESIMO SEPTIMO INCIPIT ANNUS PONTI-
FICATUS DOMINI OLIVERI DEI GRACIA LINCOLN' EPISCOPI OCTAVUS-
DECIMUS.

SHIPTON-UNDER-WYCHWOOD. V. Ralph of Ardley (Ardufle) ch. p. by Sir Roger of Frampton (Frompton') rector of Shipton-under-Wychwood to the vicarage thereof vacant by the death of Peter. Inst. London, Old Temple, July 15, 1297.

MARSTON. V. Stephen of Livermere ch. p. by P. and C. of St. Frideswide's Oxford to the vicarage of Marston vacant by the death of Adam of Wolford. Inst. Banbury, Sept. 16, 1297.

[*f. 346v*] COLD NORTON. William of Tew, canon of Cold Norton, appointed by the bishop to the office of prior in succession to Robert of Ravensden who had resigned. Licence to elect had been obtained from Henry son of William le Espicer who farmed the manor of Chipping Norton from the Earl of Arundel. William's election *per viam scrutinii* was quashed for faulty procedure, Sleaford, Oct. 7, 1297, after being reported at Panton on the previous day.

ST. PETER AT THE EAST GATE, OXFORD. V. Ordinance, under the bishop's seal, defining the payments due to the arch-deacon of Oxford from Merton College, in respect of the college's appropriation (by licence from Bishop Gravesend) of the church of St. Peter at the East Gate, with its dependent chapels of Holy Cross and Wolvercote. Leicester, Sept. 23, 1297. the letter of John de la More, *custos*, and the scholars and brethren of Merton, appointing Master John of Wendover and William of Walcot as proctors is given in full and dated Osney, Sept. 20, 1297. Similar letters were received from Master Simon of Ghent, Archdeacon of Oxford, appointing John de Scalleby and Robert of Kilworth as proctors.

ORDINATIO FACTA INTER MAGISTRUM SIMONEM DE GANDAVO ARCHIDIACONUM ET SCOLARES DOMUS DE MERTON'. Ad perpetuam rei memoriam, nos Oliverus permissione divina Lincoln' episcopus notum esse volumus universis quod cum inter dilectos in Christo filios magistrum Simonem de Gandavo archidiaconum Oxon' ex parte una, et magistrum Johannem de la More custodem et scolares et fratres domus de Merton' in Oxon' ecclesiam sancti Petri in oriente ejusdem municipii cum capellis de sancta Cruce et de Wulgercotes ab eadem ecclesia dependentibus eisdem scolaribus per bone memorie dominum Ricardum predecessorum nostrum dudum appropriatum nunc de novo possidentes ex altera, super jure et comodo sequestri quod dictus archidiaconus et sui predecessores in dicta ecclesia cum suis capellis tempore vacationis ejusdem ecclesie ante tempus appropriationis hujusmodi consueverant percipere et habere, quodque ipse et sui predecessores in casu consimili percipere possent in futurum, suborta fuisset materia questionis movende, tandem prefati partes dispendia litium attendentes, et ob hoc volentes hujusmodi questionis materia potius per pacis pulchritudinem quadam equitatis statera liberandam quam per dubios lites amfractus consultius terminari se nostre ordinationi, dispositioni, dicto seu laudo literatorie submiserunt, promittentes utrimque se fideliter servaturos quicquid ordinandum, disponendum, dicendum vel laudandum duxerimus in hac parte prout per earundem partium litteras patentes residentes penes nos plene liquet, unde nos optentu quietis subditorum nostrorum dictam submissionem suscipientes in nos, et super premissis deliberantes solerter auditis propositis utrobique, votisque partium utrarumque cautius exquisitis et pensatis diligenter in hac parte pensandis, ut dictis scolaribus sic sua jura servemus quod status archidiaconalis in hoc prout possumus illesus existat, dicimus et ordinamus quod predicti custos ac scolares et eorum successores imperpetuum prefato archidiacono et suis successoribus quatuor solidos annuatim die sinodi post festum sancti Michaelis[1] Oxon' pro jure et comodo sequestri predictis, quod dictus archidiaconus et sui successores tempore vacationis dicte ecclesie ut premittitur forent percepturi persolvantperpetuis temporibus in futuro, salvis prefato archidiacono et suis successoribus procuratione ratione visitationis de dicta ecclesia, sibi debita ac juribus et consuetudinibus archidiaconalibus quibuscumque aliis a comodo sequestri predicto. Si vero dicti scolares in solutione hujusmodi prestationis annue facienda cessarint, volumus et ordinamus quod archidiaconus pro tempore existens eosdem scolares ad dictam pecunie summam prestandam per sequestrationem fructuum dicte ecclesie et aliam cohercionem canonicam prout expedire decreverit compellere valeat et de plano. In cujus rei testimonium sigillum nostrum presentibus est appensum. Actum apud Leyc' IX kalendas Octobris anno domini M.CC. nonagesimo septimo. ... Sequitur submissio scolarium de Merton'. ... Pateat universis quod cum inter nos Johannem de la More custodem domus scolarium de Merton' in Oxon', scolares et fratres ejusdem domus ecclesiam beati

---

[1] Marginal drawing of a flag.

Petri in oriente Oxon' cum suis capellis adjacentibus in usus proprios ex parte una, et reverendum virum, magistrum Simonem de Gandavo archidiaconum Oxon' Lincoln' diocesis ex altera, super jure et comodo sequestri quod sibi in dicta ecclesia per vacationem ipsius futuris temporibus obvenire posset, si ea propriis usibus ut premittitur deputata non esset contentionis occasio oriretur, nos dicti custos, scolares et fratres discordiarum materiam amputare et amfractus litium evitare volentes in [*f. 347*] reverendum patrem dominum Oliverum Dei gracia Lincoln' episcopum pro decidenda hujusmodi controversia duximus consentiendum, et cujus ordinationi, dispositioni, dicto vel laudo nos super premissis concorditer submittimus per presentes, promittentes insuper nos fideliter servaturos quicquid dictus pater ordinandum, disponendum, dicendum vel laudandum duxerit in hac parte. In dicto vero submissionis negotio pro dicti patris ordinatione, dispositione vel laudo subeundo, dilectos nobis in Christo magistros Johannem de Wendovere et Willelmum de Walcote clericos procuratores nostros facimus, constituimus ac tenore presentium ordinamus, dantes eisdem conjunctim et alteri eorundem divisim plenariam potestatem et speciale mandatum dictas submissionem et ordinationem ac dispositionem pena seu juramento nomine nostro vallendi, aliasque si necesse fuerit jurandi et cetera omnia faciendi sine quibus submissio, ordinatio et dispositio supradicte subsistere non poterunt aut valere. Pro eisdem etiam procuratoribus nostris et eorum altero rem ratam haberi et judicatum solvi sub ypotheca rerum nostrarum promittimus et exponimus cautionem. In testimonium omnium premissorum commune sigillum domus nostre ad ea fecimus litteris hiis apponi. Datum Osen' XII kalendas Octobris anno domini M.CC. nonagesimo septimo. ... Sub consimili forma submisit se dictus archidiaconus terminis mutatis, et ad subeundum ordinationem predictum suos constituit procuratores Johannem de Scalleby et Robertum de Kybwurth' conjunctim et divisim. Tenores autem submissionum sunt inter presentationes clericorum ad ecclesias.

GORING (Garing'). Agatha of Oxford, a nun of Goring, appointed by the bishop as prioress in succession to Sara of Oxford who had died. Licence to elect had been obtained from the Earl of Cornwall, because the house lay in the honour of Wallingford, but the ensuing election was quashed by the bishop on account of extremely incorrect procedure, without prejudice to the character of Agatha who was elected. Louth, Jan. 13. 1298.

Vacante prioratu de Garing' per mortem Sarre de Oxon' ultime priorisse loci ejusdem, idibus Januarii anno domini M.CC. nonagesimo septimo apud Ludam presentata fuit episcopo Agatha de Oxon' tanquam electa. Demum productis duabus monialibus ad probandum processum electionis, exhibitaque quadam cedula sine sigillo continente formam scrutinii facti, admisse fuerunt dicte testes et examinate. Constabat quidem per attestationes earum de die mortis dicte priorisse et ejus sepultura, necnon de sola petitione legitime a domino comite Cornubie eligendi, ea sola ratione quod dicta domus sita est infra honorem Walingford' nichil habens alias de eodem, quodque omnes que debebant, poterant et volebant processui electionis hujusmodi interfuerant, idem processus tanquam multipliciter viciosus, tum pro eo quod scrutator votorum conventus non erat de voluntate omnium deputatis,[1] tum pro eo quod in pupplicatione scrutinii facta fuit collectio solius numeri ad numerum, propriis nominibus monialium omnino suppressis, tum pro eo quod tres erant nominate a pluribus quarum nulla habuit votes majoris partis conventus, licet aliqua haberet majoritatem partium comparatione minorum, tum pro eo quod dicta Agatha non premissa de ea aliqua electione in communi fuit ad altare tanquam electa solempniter deportata, erat nullus et viribus vacuus declaratus, fama dicte Agathe cui nichil obviat integra reservata, monialesque dicti collegii propter culpam suam ea vice eligendi fuerunt potestate private, facultate providendi eidem domui episcopo specialiter reservata, demum episcopus habita deliberatione de meritis personarum monialium dicte domus, dictam Agatham tanquem ydoneam et humano judicio morigeratam, religiosam, et bene meritam, jure ad ipsum devoluto solempniter in priorissam prefecit, unde jurata ab eadem priorissa episcopo et officialibus suis canonica obediencia, scriptum fuit ...[2] decano de Henle,[3] archidiaconatu Oxon' vacante, quod eam vice et auctoritate episcopi installaret, etc.

KINGHAM (Keynsham). R. John of Halstead (Hallested') ch. p. by the A. and C. of Walden to the church of Kingham vacant by the death of Master Richard Ash (de Fraxino). Inst. Wellow near Grimsby, Jan. 18, 1298.

DORCHESTER-ON-THAMES. Alexander of Waltham, canon of Dorchester, elected **per viam compromissi** to be abbot in

---

[1] Sic, although presumably it was a scrutatrix.
[2] Blank in MS.
[3] Henley.

succession to William of Rofford (Ropford') who had died. Election confirmed Nettleham, Feb. 7, 1298. Solemn benediction Nettleham, Feb. 9, 1298. Letters issued on the same day to the rural dean of Cuddesdon (the archdeaconry being vacant) for induction and to the bailiff of Thame for handing-over of temporalities.

[*f. 347v*] ALKERTON (Alcrinton') R. Henry of Aston ch. p. by Sir Amaury de St. Amand knight to the church of Alkerton vacant because Master Robert of Clifton had been inst. to a living in the diocese of Bath and Wells. Inst. Nettleham, Feb. 9, 1298.

BEGBROOKE. R. Henry of Combrook ch. p. by John de Lyuns to the church of Begbrooke vacant by the death of Richard de Lyuns. Inst Nettleham, Feb. 15, 1298.[1]

ADDERBURY. R. Robert of Maidstone pr. provided by Boniface VIII to the church of Adderbury vacant by the death of Edmund of Maidstone in the course of a journey to Rome. Rome, St. Peter's, Feb. 15, 1298.

BLETCHINGDON. R. Richard of Musgrave clerk in minor orders, p. by Hugh of Musgrave and Matilda his wife to the church of Bletchingdon vacant because Thomas Chapel (de Capella) had been inst. to a living in the diocese of Canterbury. Presentation opposed in the King's court by Nicholas Trimenel and Mabel his wife. Writ in favour of Hugh and Matilda, Westminster, Jan. 24, 1298, witnessed by J. of Mettingham (Metingham). Richard was ordained subd. and inst. Lincoln, Mar. 22, 1298.

? BURTON (Bourton') V. William de Torkeden' ch. p. by the A. and C. of Osney to the vicarage of the chapel of ? Burton vacant by the death of John. Inst. Stamford, May 11, 1298.

QUARTODECIMO KALENDAS JUNII VIDELICET DIE SANCTI DUNSTANI ANNO DOMINI M.CC. NONAGESIMO OCTAVO, INCIPIT ANNUS PONTI-FICATUS DOMINI OLIVERI EPISCOPI LINCOLN' NONUSDECIMUS.

------

[1] The next entry, referring to Adderbury, is cancelled and has been re-written.

[*f. 348*] ST. CLEMENTS, OXFORD. R. Henry of Norton ch. p. by the P. and C. of St. Frideswide's Oxford to the church of St. Clement beyond the little bridge at Oxford, vacant by the death of Hugh. Inst. London, Old Temple, June 24, 1298.

ST. EDWARD'S, OXFORD. Note that the ordinance uniting St. Edward's with St. Frideswide's, Oxford, is in the memoranda records of the nineteenth year.[1]

SHIPTON-ON-CHERWELL. R. Roger of Penton ch. p. by John of Penton to the church of Shipton-on-Cherwell vacant by the death of William de Wyteweye. held *in commendam* for a term. Inst. Buckden, Sept. 13, 1298.

BIX GIBWYN. R. James Paynel, clerk in minor orders, p. by Sir Giles Delisle knight to the church of Bix Gibwyn vacant by the death of Ralph. Presentation opposed by Peter Brian of Middleton who withdrew on condition that he might present on alternate occasions. Ordained subd. and inst. Brampton, Sept. 21, 1298.

BRIZE NORTON (Norton' Bronn'). V. Roger of Oundle ch. p. by the A. and C. of Eynsham to the vicarage of Brize Norton vacant by the death of John of Poulton. Inst. Mere, Oct. 16, 1298.

WENDLEBURY. R. William of Blackthorn subd. p. by Sir Laurence de Pavely knight to the church of Wendlebury vacant by the death of Henry de Pavely. Inst. Stow Park, Nov. 14, 1298.

ST. PETER LE BAILEY, OXFORD. R. Master James of Dover subd. p. by the P. and C. of St. Frideswide's Oxford to the church of St. Peter-le-Bailey, vacant by the res. of Alexander of Hemingby. Inst. in the person of Augustine of Thornton his proctor, Newark, Nov. 30, 1298.

AMBROSDEN. R. Master John le Fleming ch. p. by the rector and brethren of the house of Ashridge to the church of Ambrosden vacant by the death of Master Ralph de Martival. Inst. in the person of John de Scalleby his proctor, Empringham, Dec. 20, 1298.

ALBURY (Aldebury). R. William, called le Despenser, clerk in minor orders, p. by John of London to the church of Albury

---

[1] See L.R.S. vol. 65, pp. 106–7.

vacant by the death of Master Hugh of Langley. Ordained subd. and inst. Liddington, Dec. 20, 1298.

LOWER HEYFORD Mediety. R. John de la Carnayle, clerk in minor orders, p. by Sir John Delisle (de Insula) knight to the mediety of the church of Lower Heyford vacant by the death of Robert de la Carnayle. Presentation opposed by John of Shilton who afterwards withdrew his claim. Ordained subd. and inst. Liddington, Dec. 20, 1298.

[*f. 348v*] SOUTH WESTON. R. Nicholas of Sotwell ch. p. by Sir John FitzGuy knight to the church of South Weston vacant because Roger had been inst. to the living of Shipton-on-Cherwell. Inst. Liddington, Dec. 22, 1298.

BECKLEY. R. Henry of Exeter subd. and p. by Edmund Earl of Cornwall to the church of Beckley vacant by the death of Master Philip of Hedsor. Inst. Liddington, Jan. 27, 1299, and promised not to vex the Prioress and C. of Studley with claims to the tithes formerly granted to them by Bishop Hugh of Wells with the consent of the chapter. Hugh's grant, with the chapter's seal appended, was read to Henry on the day of his institution.

QUARTODECIMO KALENDAS JUNII VIDELICET DIE SANCTI DUNSTANI ANNO DOMINI M.CC. NONAGESIMO NONO INCIPIT ANNUS PONTIFICATUS DOMINI OLIVERI EPISCOPI LINCOLN' VICESIMUS.

COWLEY (Covele). V. John of Sutton ch. p. by the A. and C. of Osney to the vicarage of Cowley vacant by the death of Thomas. Inst. Buckden, May 23, 1299.

COGGES. Roger called Hardy, monk of Fécamp, p. by Thomas Abbot of Fécamp to the office of prior of Cogges, vacant by the res. of Matthew Dupont. Admitted Buckden, May 29, 1299. Both the letter of presentation (dated at St. Gervais near Rouen, Apr. 30, 1299) and Matthew's letter of resignation (sealed with the seal of the dean of Oxford and dated at Oxford, May 24, 1299) are given in full.

WOOD EATON. R. William de Estmore subd. p. by the A. and C. of Eynsham to the church of Wood Eaton vacant by the res. of Master John of Winchelsea. Inst. Buckden, June 21, 1299.

ST. ALDGATE'S, OXFORD. R. William le Clere of Oxford p. by the A. and C. of Abingdon and the P. and C. of St. Frideswide's to the church of St. Aldgate vacant by the death of Master Hugh of Lincoln. Inst. Spaldwick, June 28, 1299.

WESTCOTT BARTON (Barton' Parva). R. Nicholas of Clanfield (Clanefeld') ch. p. by the A. and C. of Eynsham to the church of Westcott Barton vacant by the death of Robert de la Pomeray. Inst. Nettleham, July 30, 1299.

FINMERE. R. John of Langton clerk in minor orders, p. by the A. and C. of St. Augustine's Bristol to the church of Finmere vacant by the death of Master Ralph of Oxford. Ordained subd. (date not given). Inst. Stow Park, Oct. 2, 1299.

LANGFORD. V. Robert of Highworth (Hegwurth') ch. p. by Sir Adam Blessingle and Sir John de Chyssebecch', who were farming the prebendal church of Langford for a term of four years dating from Easter (Apr. 19) 1299, to the prebendal vicarage thereof vacant by the death of Master Henry of Fotheringhay. Inst. Stow Park, Oct. 3, 1299.

TACKLEY. V. Consolidation of the vicarage of Tackley, vacant by the institution of Nicholas of Clanfield to the church of Westcott Barton, to the rectory thereof, at the request of Master Roger the rector. Louth, Oct. 17, 1299.

Vacante vicaria que fuerat in ecclesia de Tackele per hoc quod Nicholaus ultimus vicarius ejusdem post institutionem suam in eadem vicaria ecclesiam de Parva Barton' curam animarum habentem titulo institutionis admisit, Magister Rogerus rector ecclesie de Tackele ad episcopum personaliter accedens et asserens dictam vicariam non fuisse perpetuo ordinatam de consensu [f. 349v] eorum quorum interest, instanter petiit ut dicta vicaria rectorie ecclesie predicte consolidaretur. Unde facta inquisitione per officialem archidiaconi Oxon' super statu dictarum ecclesie et vicarie per quam acceptum extitit inter cetera dictam ecclesiam ad octodecim marcas secundum taxationem Norwyc' esse taxatam, et vicariam ad duas marcas, ac vicarios in dicta ecclesia pro tempore administrantes ex sola voluntate rectorum loci ejusdem sine ordinatione diocesani ut credebatur fuisse admissos, examinato insuper registro de admissionibus clericorum ad beneficia ecclesiastica in diocese Lincoln'[1] per quod apparebat vicarios qui pro tempore fuerant in ecclesia predicta ad solam presentationem rectorum

---

[1] See L.R.S. vol. 20, p. 219 for a description of the vicar's portion.

ejusdem ecclesie fuisse admissos et institutos, de consensu eorum quorum intererat nulla in eadem registro facta penitus mentione, episcopus premissis et aliis rationibus motus prefatam vicariam cum pertinenciis rectorie dicte ecclesie consolidavit XVI kalendas Novembris anno XX apud Ludam, ipsam ecclesiam per ipsius rectorem et successores suos canonice instituendos regendam fore imposterum statuendo, ita tamen quod dictus Magister Rogerus suo perpetuo residenciam in dicta ecclesia faceret corporalem sicut ante hujusmodi consolidationem sepius optulerat se facturum. Et super hoc scriptum fuit ...[1] officiali Archidiaconi Oxon' quod dictum rectorem fructus et proventus prefate ecclesie integre percepire permitteret, et premissa in dicta ecclesia de Tackele et locis aliis in quibus expedire videret publicaret.

MINSTER LOVELL. John de Mont Calvet monk of Ivry p. by John, Abbot, and the community of Ivry to the office of prior of Minster Lovell, vacant by the res. of Ralph de Montfort. Admitted Nettleham, Nov. 10, 1299.[2] Both the letter of presentation (dated at Ivry July 25, 1299) and Ralph's letter of resignation (sealed with seal of the dean of Witney and dated at Taynton Sept. 18, 1299) are given in full.

COLLATIONS TO PREBENDS 1290–99

[f. 353] ARCHDEACONRY OF BUCKINGHAM, with prebends of Aylesbury (Aylesbir') and MILTON ECCLESIA. Note that on the death, at the Papal Curia, of Sir Percival de Lavania (Lavannia), Pope Nicholas IV in a letter (given in full and dated Rome, Santa Maria Maggiore, April 22, 1290) empowered Bishop Sutton to divide the prebend of Aylesbury into two, and to collate to these, with the archdeaconry, persons of English birth who were distinguished in theology or in civil and canon law. The bishop thereupon collated to the archdeaconry Master Richard of St. Frideswide (Fredeswyda) D.C.L., with

---

[1] Blank in MS.
[2] Three days before Sutton's death. He was still at work a day later, Reg. f. 332v.

letters patent under the episcopal seal, witnessed by Masters Jocelyn of Kirmington and Walter of Wootton, canons of Lincoln, and Sirs William of Stockton, Roger of Sixhills and John de Scalleby, chaplains and clerks of the bishop. Newark, the bishop's chamber, July 11, 1290, about the third hour.

Afterwards the bishop divided the prebend into two, Aylesbury and Milton Ecclesia. To Aylesbury (saving to the chapter of Lincoln the chapels of Quarrendon, Bierton, Stoke Mandeville and Buckland) he collated Master Richard of Harrington (Hetherington') D.D., Nettleham, August, 16, 1290.

To Milton Ecclesia he collated Master John of Monmouth D.D., Nettleham, Aug. 18, 1290.

Both had letters patent under the bishop's seal.

[f. 354] NORTON EPISCOPI. Sir Philip of Willoughby, dean of Lincoln, to the prebend of Norton Episcopi, vacant by the consecration of Master William of Louth to the see of Ely. Ely, the bishop's lodging, Oct. 2, 1290, after the day's mass. Witnessed by Masters Durand, Archdeacon of Stow, Henry of Nassington, John le Flemeng, Jocelyn of Kirmington, Walter of Wootton and Stephen of Tathwell, canons of Lincoln.

WELTON PAYNSHALL (Welleton'). Sir Roger of Rothwell (Rowell'), canon of Lincoln, to the prebend of Welton Paynshall, vacant by the collation of Sir Philip of Willoughby to the prebend of Norton Episcopi. Fingest, Dec. 9, 1290. Witnessed by Masters John le Flemeng, Jocelyn of Kirmington and Walter of Wootton, canons of Lincoln, and John de Scalleby, priest. Note[1] that a letter ordering his installation was sent to the D. and C. of Lincoln.

ARCHDEACONRY OF LINCOLN with prebend of CORRINGHAM. Sir William de Estiniaco, provided by the pope to the next vacancy in the chapter of Lincoln, collated in the person of William de Grandisson (Grandisono) his proctor by the Bishop of Bath and Wells,[2] acting as executor of the papal provision, to the archdeaconry of Lincoln and the prebend of Corringham, vacant by the death of Master William de la Gare. Date not given.[3]

ARCHDEACONRY OF NORTHAMPTON. Master Thomas of Sutton, canon of Lincoln, with Master William of Langworth

---

[1] Interlined.
[2] Robert Burnell.
[3] Dec. 1290 or Jan. 1291.

as his proctor for installation, to the archdeaconry of Northampton vacant by the death of Sir Stephen of Sutton. Fingest, Jan. 9, 1291, about the hour of sunrise. Witnessed by Masters Durand Archdeacon of Stow, John le Fleming, Jocelyn of Kirmington and Walter of Wootton, canons of Lincoln.

EMPINGHAM. Master Jocelyn of Kirmington, with William of Anlaby as his proctor for installation, to the prebend of Empingham vacant by the death of Sir Stephen of Sutton. Place, date, time and witnesses (except for the said Jocelyn) as above.

BUCKDEN. Master Stephen of Tathwell, canon of Lincoln, to the prebend of Buckden vacant by the collation of Master Jocelyn of Kirmington to the prebend of Empingham. Fingest, in the bishop's chamber, Jan. 19, 1291, about the third hour. Witnessed by Master Durand Archdeacon of Stow, John le Fleming and Jocelyn of Kirmington, canons of Lincoln, and Robert of Sixhills and John de Scalleby, priests.

[*f. 354v*] BEDFORD MAJOR. Sir William of Stockton to the prebend of Bedford Major, vacant by the collation of Master Stephen of Tathwell to the prebend of Buckden. Place, time, date and witnesses as above.

AYLESBURY. Note of a letter from Bishop Sutton to Pope Nicholas IV, certifying that the said pope's injunctions concerning the archdeaconry of Buckingham and the division of the prebend of Aylesbury had been duly carried out. Stow Park, Sept. 13, 1290.[1] A note is added to say that the pope's ruling about residence appears on the next folio but one.[2]

SOUTH SCARLE. Master William de Montfort, canon of Lincoln, to the prebend of South Scarle vacant by the death of Master Durand of Lincoln. London, O.T., the bishop's chamber, Dec. 4, 1291. Witnessed by Masters Henry of Nassington, John le Fleming, Jocelyn of Kirmington, Walter of Wootton and Robert of Kilworth, canons of Lincoln. A letter on the said William's behalf was sent to Master John of Creacombe (Craucomb'), vicar-general of the Archbishop of York, dated London, O.T., Dec. 6, 1291.

ARCHDEACONRY OF STOW. Master Jocelyn of Kirmington to the archdeaconry of Stow, vacant by the death of Master

---

[1] See above, p. 203.
[2] See below, p. 208.

Durand of Lincoln. Fingest, the bishops's chamber, Dec. 30, 1291, about the time of vespers. Witnessed by Ralph of Toft (Toftes), Franciscan, and Masters Henry of Nassington, John le Fleming and William of Stockton, canons of Lincoln.

[*f. 355*] ARCHDEACONRY OF BEDFORD. Master Roger of Rothwell D.C.L. to the archdeaconry of Bedford, vacant by the death of Master John Hook. Place, date and time as above. Witnessed by the same, with the addition of Roger of Sixhills and John de Scalleby, priests.

LIDDINGTON (Lidington'). Master Robert of Kilworth (Kivelingwrth') canon of Lincoln, to the prebend of Liddington vacant by the death of Master John Hook. Place, date, time and witnesses as above.

MARSTON ST. LAWRENCE. Sir Peter of Savoy to the prebend of Marston St. Lawrence vacant by the collation of Master Robert of Kilworth to the prebend of Liddington. Place, date, time and witnesses as above.

WELTON RYVAL (Welleton' cum Kirketon'). Master Walter of Wootton, canon of Lincoln, · to the prebend of Welton Ryval vacant by the death of Master Salomon of Northbourne. Ware, the chamber of the prior, in which the bishop was lodging, Apr. 22, 1292, about the third hour. Witnessed by Jocelyn, Archdeacon of Stow, and Sir William of Stockton, canon of Lincoln, and Sirs John Maunsel, Roger of Sixhills, Robert of Kibworth and John de Scalleby, priests.

[*f. 355v*] DIE SANCTI DUNSTANI VIDELICET QUARTODECIMO KALENDAS JUNII ANNO DOMINI MILLESIMO DUCENTESIMO NONAGESIMO SECUNDO INCIPIT ANNUS PONTIFICATUS DOMINI OLIVERI EPISCOPI LINCOLN' TERTIUSDECIMUS.

THAME. Master Thomas of Sutton, Archdeacon of Northampton, to the prebend of Thame vacant by the death of Sir William Ferre. Liddington, Sept. 11, 1292. Witnessed by Masters Henry of Nassington, official-principal, Jocelyn, Archdeacon of Stow and John le Fleming, canon of Lincoln.

LEIGHTON BUZZARD. Master John le Fleming to the prebend of Leighton Buzzard, vacant by the collation of Master

Thomas of Sutton to the prebend of Thame. Place and date as above. Witnesses not mentioned, presumably Masters Henry of Nassington and Jocelyn of Kirmington.

LANGFORD MANOR. Sir Peter of Savoy to the prebend of Langford Manor, vacant by the res. of Sir Robert of Swillington (Swylington'). Fingest, the bishop's chamber, Dec. 23, 1292. Witnessed by Masters Jocelyn of Kirmington, John le Fleming, Walter of Wootton, Robert of Kilworth and William of Stockton, canons of Lincoln.

GRETTON. Sir Robert of Swillington canon of Lincoln to the prebend of Gretton, vacant by the collation of Master John le Fleming to the prebend of Leighton Buzzard. Place and date as above, about the hour of vespers. Witnesses as above.

MARSTON ST. LAWRENCE. Master Richard of St. Frideswide, Archdeacon of Buckingham, to the prebend of Marston St. Lawrence, vacant by the collation of Sir Peter of Savoy to the prebend of Langford Manor. Fingest, the bishop's chamber, Dec. 24, 1292, about the third hour. Witnesses as above.

ST. MARY CRACKPOLE. Master Henry of Benniworth, D.C.L., to the prebend of St. Mary Crackpole vacant by the collation of Master Walter of Wootton to the prebend of Welton Ryval with the portions of Kirton in Lindsey and Hibaldstow. Fingest, the bishop's chamber, Dec. 31, 1292, about the third hour. Witnessed by Masters Jocelyn of Kirmington, Henry of Nassington, John le Fleming, Walter of Wootton, and Sir William of Stockton, canons of Lincoln.

SCAMBLESBY with MELTON ROSS. John de Vere to the prebend of Scamblesby with Melton Ross, vacant by the death, at the papal curia, of Master Andrew de Candulphis, about the feast of St. Lawrence[1] 1292. The bishop declared that he meant no disrespect to the pope by this collation, made in accordance with a decree of Gregory X concerning failure to provide after the lapse of one month. London O.T., Feb. 11, 1293. Witnessed by Master Jocelyn of Kirmington, Henry of Nassington, John le Fleming, Walter of Wootton, Robert of Kilworth and William of Stockton, canons of Lincoln, and John de Scalleby and Robert of Kibworth, priests.

[1] August 10.

[*f. 356*] ST. HUGH'S ALTAR, LINCOLN CATHEDRAL. William of Gayton, pr. to St. Hugh's Altar in Lincoln Cathedral, vacant by the death of John of Cadney. Biggleswade, Mar. 24, 1293.

———

QUARTODECIMO KALENDAS JUNII VIDELICET DIE SANCTI DUNSTANI ANNO DOMINI M.CC. NONAGESIMO TERTIO INCIPIT ANNUS PONTIFICATUS DOMINI OLIVERI LINCOLNIENSIS EPISCOPI QUARTODECIMUS.

———

DECLARATION CONCERNING THE RESIDENCE OF THE PREBENDARIES OF AYLESBURY AND MILTON ECCLESIA (Declaratio residencie prebendariorum de Aylesbir' et de Milton).[1] Copy of a bull of Pope Nicholas IV addressed to Bishop Sutton and dated Orvieto, Sept. 22, 1291. After re-iterating his permission to collate to the archdeaconry of Buckingham and the prebends of Aylesbury and Milton Ecclesia,[2] the pope replies to a question put by the bishop as to whether the prebendaries should keep normal residence at Lincoln and in their prebends, or reside in their prebends and serve the parochial churches annexed to them. He rules that they should keep normal residence and present suitable vicars to the parochial churches. A note by Master Stephen of Tathwell, the bishop's proctor at the curia, quotes the legal basis for this ruling.[3] ... Juxta bullam predictam scripsit Magister Stephanus de Tawell' qui bullam impetraret eandem quamdam clausulam infrascripti tenoris, ... Quia forsan aliquis emulus vel scripture simplex indagator diceret quod hec declaratio est minus valida cum ipse ecclesie sint vel dicantur prebende, et sic facta esset impetratio tacita veritate, ideo oppositionem eorum sic[4] excludo. ... Prebenda quoque nomen juris est, et constituuntur tamen ex possessionibus, set[5] ex quodam jure spirituali cui annexa est possessio seu prebenda, et hoc habetur expressum per dominum Innocentium in glosis suis *Extra* de prebendis et dignitatibus majoribus.

[*f. 356v*] THORNGATE. Master Richard of Plymstock to the prebend of Thorngate vacant by the collation of Master Richard of St. Frideswide to the prebend of Marston St.

---

[1] Marginal drawing of a face in profile.
[2] Above, p. 203.
[3] Apparatus Innocencii Decretalium. Lib.III, t.v.c. xxvii [Venice, 1491].
[4] Interlined.
[5] Sic.

Lawrence. Newark, Aug. 9, in the morning after Mass. Witnessed by Masters Walter of Wootton and Robert of Kilworth, canons of Lincoln, and John de Scalleby, priest.

SCAMBLESBY with MELTON ROSS. Master Richard of Plymstock to the prebend of Scamblesby with Melton Ross, vacant by the death of John de Vere. Stow Park, Aug. 25, 1293, in the morning after Mass. Witnessed by Jocelyn of Kirmington, Walter of Wootton, Robert of Kilworth and William of Stockton, canons of Lincoln.

CAISTOR, LAFFORD AND BEDFORD MAJOR. Master Roger de Martivall to the prebend of Caistor vacant by the death of Master Adam of Brampton. Also Sir William of Stockton (Stokton') to the prebend of Lafford, vacant by the collation of Master Roger de Martivall to Caistor, and Sir William of Heanor (Henevere) to Bedford Major, vacant by the collation of Sir William of Stockton to Lafford. London O.T., Nov. 18, 1293, in the morning after Mass. Witnessed by Jocelyn of Kirmington, Walter of Wootton and, in the cases of Caistor and Bedford Major, by Sir Walter of Stockton, canons of Lincoln.

PRECENTORSHIP (Precentoria). Sir Peter of Savoy, in virtue of a provision made for him by Pope Nicholas IV of some position in the chapter of Lincoln Cathedral, to the office of precentor, vacant by the death of Master Adam of Brampton. London, O.T., Nov. 29, 1293.

[f. 357] SUBDEANERY (Subdecanatus) with the prebend of WELTON WESTHALL. Master Henry of Benniworth D.C.L. to the office of subdean and the prebend customarily associated with it, vacant by the death of Master Gilbert of Stratton. Banbury, Mar. 15, 1294. Witnessed by Masters Jocelyn of Kirmington and Sirs Robert of Swillington and William of Stockton, canons of Lincoln, John Maunsel, Robert of Warsop and Robert of Kibworth, priests, and John of Ferriby, notary-public.

ST. MARY CRACKPOLE. Sir John Maunsel pr. to the prebend of St. Mary Crackpole, vacant by the collation of Master Henry of Benniworth to the office of subdean and the prebend of Welton Westhall. Place, date and witnesses (with the exception of the said John Maunsel) as above.

———

DIE SANCTI DUNSTANI EPISCOPI VIDELICET QUARTODECIMO KALENDAS
JUNII ANNO DOMINI MILLESIMO DUCENTESIMO NONAGESIMO QUARTO
INCIPIT ANNUS PONTIFICATUS DOMINI OLIVERI DEI GRACIA LINCOLN'
EPISCOPI QUINTUSDECIMUS.

———

SOUTH SCARLE.[1] Edward son of Sir John of St. John (de
Sancto Johanne) to the prebend of South Scarle, vacant by
the death of Master William de Montfort, with letters patent
dated London, O.T., Sept. 23, 1294. Edward resigned his
claim to the prebend of Thame by a letter (given in full but
not dated) under his seal.

... Pateat universis quod cum felicis recordationis dominus
Nicholaus papa quartus mihi Edwardo nato domini Johannis
de Sancto Johanne militis providisset de canonicatu et
prebenda integra non sacerdotali, nulli alii debita, in ecclesia
Lincoln' si qua tunc vacabat, alioquin prebendam hujusmodi,
proximo inibi vacaturam, conferendam mihi cum vacaret,
donationi apostolice reservasset, reverendis patribus dominis
Dunelm'[2] et Bathon'[3] episcopis ac venerabili viro magistro
Ramicano de Murro archidiacono Vervetonensi in ecclesia
Burgense[4] executoribus deputatis ita quod per se vel per
alios juxta dicte provisionis effectum facerent me recipi in
canonicum et in fratrem dicte ecclesie, stallum in choro,
locum in capitulo assignando, et mihi de prebenda in eadem
ecclesia provideri, Magister Thomas de Luggovere[5] canonicus
Wellens' cui et [f. 357v] dominis decano et Archidiacono
Lichefeld ac domino Willelmo de Weybolt'[6] cum illa clausula
Quod si non omnes, duo vel unus vestrum etc., archidiaconus memoratus in dicte provisionis negotio commiserat vices suas mihi
de prebenda de Thame in Lincoln' ecclesia per mortem
quondam Willelmi Ferre vacante providit, credens ipsam in
virtute dicte provisionis competere. Cumque super ipsa
prebenda de Thame inter venerabilem patrem dominum O.
dei gracia Linc' Episcopum et Magistrum Thomam de Sutton'
Archidiaconum Norhamt' cui dictus pater ipsam prebendam
prius suo jure contulerat ex una parte, et me ex altera, esset

---

[1] This entry may have been cancelled. The syllable 'cat' appears at the end
but I cannot find the corresponding 'va' at the beginning. There are some
illegible marginal notes in a later hand.
[2] Anthony Bek.
[3] Robert Burnell.
[4] Ranuccius de Murro, canon of Burgos and archdeacon of ?Briviesca.
[5] Lewknor.
[6] Unidentified.

materia questionis suborta, ego ductus consilio saniori mera et spontanea voluntate pure, simpliciter et absolute omni jure si quod mihi comperit in eadem prebenda de Thame vel ad eam, necnon omni liti, questioni et controversie ex parte mea qualitercumque mote occasione ipsius prebende contra reverendum patrem et Archidiaconum Norhamt' predictos, ac omni processui habito, et cuicumque appellatione meo nomine interposite et imponende ratione prefate prebende renuncio, litique cedo et juro me contra premissa imposterum non venturum. In cujus rei testimonium sigillum meum duxi presentibus apponendum.

DECEM LIBRARUM. Sir John of Langton (Langeton') to the prebend of Decem Librarum vacant because Sir Amaury de Montfort had resigned in order to become a knight, and Edward son of Sir John of St. John had been provided by the pope to the prebend of South Scarle. London, O.T., the bishop's chamber, Oct. 2, 1294. Witnessed by Masters Jocelyn of Kirmington, Henry of Nassington, Walter of Wootton and Robert of Kilworth, Sirs Robert of Swillington, William of Stockton and John Maunsel, canons of Lincoln, and John of Ferriby, notary-public.

THORNGATE. Oliver, son of the late Sir William of Sutton, knight, to the prebend of Thorngate vacant by the collation of Master Richard of Plymstock to the prebend of Scamblesby. Had letters patent. Thame, in the bishop's chapel within the rector's manse, Oct. 14, 1294, about the third hour. Witnessed by Masters Thomas of Sutton, Jocelyn of Kirmington, Sirs Roger of Sixhills and John de Scalleby, priests and John of Ferriby, notary-public.

ARCHDEACONRY OF LEICESTER with prebend of LEICESTER ST. MARGARET. Master Roger de Martivall to the archdeaconry of Leicester and the prebend of Leicester St. Margaret, vacant by the death of Master Roger of Saxenhurst. Louth, in the bishop's chamber, Jan. 16, 1295, about the first hour. Witnessed by Master Jocelyn of Kirmington, Sir Robert of Swillington, Master Walter of Wootton and Sir William of Stockton, canons of Lincoln, Roger of Sixhills, Robert of Kibworth and John de Scalleby, priests, and John of Ferriby and John of Clipston(e), notaries-public. Afterwards, at Riby near Ailby, on Jan. 28, Master Roger resigned the prebend while accepting the archdeaconry.

LEICESTER ST. MARGARET. Sir John Maunsel, canon of Lincoln, to the prebend of Leicester St. Margaret, vacant by the death of Master Roger of Saxenhurst. Riby near Ailby, Jan. 28, 1295.

[*f. 358*] LEIGHTON MANOR.[1] Note that Jonet Romey, clerk, proctor legally substituted by Vanno Jacobi, citizen of Florence and principal proctor of John son of Sir John son of Sir John de Colonna de Urbe (Columpna) and brother of Sir Peter cardinal-deacon of St. Eustace, presented to the bishop letters of Pope Celestine V providing the said John to the prebend lately held by Archbishop Robert Winchelsey. The bishop in letters to the D. and C. of Lincoln signified his acceptance of the provision without dispute, Newark, Feb. 18, 1295. John by his proctor was collated to the prebend of Leighton Manor and the archdeaconry of Huntingdon, and letters patent were issued on his behalf, Nettleham, Mar. 15, 1295.

PROVISIO OPPIZONIS DE BUSNATE. Note that Master John de Lucobincas, proctor of Sir Oppizo de Busnate, presented to the bishop letters of Pope Celestine V providing the said Oppizo to a prebend in the church of Lincoln. The bishop signified to the D. and C. his acceptance of the provision, but nothing further was done. Nettleham, Mar. 15, 1295.[2]

———

[*f. 358v*] DIE SANCTI DUNSTANI EPISCOPI VIDELICET QUARTODECIMO KALENDAS JUNII ANNO DOMINI MILLESIMO DUCENTESIMO NONAGESIMO QUINTO INCIPIT ANNUS PONTIFICATUS DOMINI OLIVERI DEI GRACIA LINCOLNIENSIS EPISCOPI SEXTUSDECIMUS.

———

ESTABLISHMENT OF THE BISHOP'S CHANTRY IN LINCOLN CATHEDRAL (Cantaria pro episcopo Olivero una cum ipsius obitu in Lincoln' ecclesia facienda). Record of three letters of the bishop, dated Theydon Mount, June 25, 1295, as follows:
(1) Letters patent under the seals of the bishop and the D. and C. of Lincoln, establishing and describing in full detail a perpetual chantry in the cathedral for the said bishop, to be supported from lands and tenements worth at least twelve marks a year. Witnessed by the dean, chancellor, treasurer, subdean, Archdeacon of Bedford, and other canons of Lincoln.

[1] Despite the heading, this entry deals also with the archdeaconry of Huntingdon.
[2] In the margin, 'can' ...akepole' and some illegible notes. Oppizo never held the prebend of St. Mary Crackpole.

(2) Indenture under the seals of the bishop and D. and C. of Lincoln, granting (under licence from the King to alienate in mortma   certain lands and tenements for the maintenance of the said chantry. Witnessed by John Bek, Robert le Venur, Richard of Buslingthorpe, John of Holland, Walter of Lowdham, John Burdun and Robert of Saundby, knights, and many others.

(3) Letters patent of the bishop, collating John of Utterby, priest, to the said chantry.

Octavo kalendas Julii anno xvi Theyden' ad Montem contulit episcopus Johanni de Utterby presbitero cantariam pro ipso episcopo perpetuo[1] una cum obitu suo cum decesserit annis singulis faciendam in ecclesia Linc' per ipsum episcopum ordinatam noviter sub hac forma:

In Dei nomine amen. Pateat universis quod cum nos Oliverus permissione divina Linc' episcopus ad unam cantariam pro nobis perpetuo[1] et obitum nostrum cum decesserimus annis singulis faciendum terras quasdam et tenementa cum pertin- enciis decano et capitulo nostre Linc' ecclesie contulerimus valencia duodecim marcas per annum ad minus, que sunt in carta a nobis super hac collatione confecta expressius et nominata, de illis duodecim marcis per nos et dictos decanum et capitulum ita est ordinatum: ... quod capellanus debens cantariam facere memoratam ad sui sustentationem percipiat a decano et capitulo annuatim sex marcas. In die vero obitus nostri distribuantur sexaginta solidi secundum modum inferius annotatum, et residui viginti solidi usibus capituli deputentur, ita tamen quod per ipsum provideatur capellano de ministratione et aliis omnibus que ad missam celebrandam necessario requiruntur. Per nos vero et nostros executores dum vixerint conferetur cantaria prefata, post quorum mortem vel si executores in conferendo per mensem fuerint necgligentes, ad decanum et capitulum collatio devolvetur, qui si per quindecim dies necgligentes fuerint, ad episcopum providere de capellano de eo pertinebit. Capellanus vero sive fuerit vicarius sive non interfuerit quando a choro dicitur officio mortuorum per se dicendo suplebit.[2] Tenebitur siquidem diebus singulis dicere *Placebo, Dirige* et *Commen- dationem*,[3] exceptis majoribus solempnitatibus, quibus est ob earum reverenciam quoad hujusmodi dicere deferendum. Ipse quidem diebus continuis celebraturus divina, in casu egritudinis vel alterius justi impedimenti corporalis quod per se non potest per alium supplere curabit, sed si perpetua

[1] Sic, recte 'perpetuam'.
[2] Sic, recte 'supplebit'.
[3] The Office for the Dead.

impotencia, vel non convenit honeste, non licebit ei cantariam de qua agitur retinere. Idem autem capellanus quotiens de novo assumetur juramentum corporale prestabit quod impositum sibi officium fideliter exequetur. Et est sciendum quod de stipendio prenotato recipiet in festo Sancti Michaelis unam marcam, in festo Sancti Thome Apostoli unam marcam, in festo Annunciationis Beate Virginis unam marcam, in festo Pentecostis unam marcam, in festo Sancti Petri ad Vincula unam marcam, et unam marcam in festo Nativitatis Virginis Gloriose. Assignabitur quoque decano et capitulo ad hanc cantariam faciendam certum altare, et celebrabit sepedictus capellanus pro nobis Olivero episcopo sive vivo sive defuncto, et pro animabus patris et matris nostre, et pro aliis vivis et defunctis, specialius quibus nos dum viximus sive ex debito sive ex voto nos reputavimus specialius obligatos, ac pro ceteris vivis et defunctis fidelibus universis. De sexaginta solidos obitui assignatis habeant canonici triginta duos solidos, ita quod quilibet habere possit duos solidos si fuerint sexdecim anumerato custode altaris Beati Petri, si vero plures fuerint, fiat defalcatio de duobus solidis ita quod distributio omnibus equalis fiat, si autem fuerint pauciores illud quod superest ultra duos solidos cuilibet assignatos pauperibus erogetur. Vicarii octodecim solidos percipiant inter se equaliter dividendos. Pauperes clerici tres solidos. Clericus hospitalis quatuor denarios. Pueri duos solidos. Sacrista, si non sit vicarius, octo denarios. Clericus suus tres denarios. Clericus commune octo denarios. Clericus capituli sex denarios. Capellani celebrantes pro animabus Ricardi de Faldingworth' sex denarios. Sacrista laicus quatuor denarios. Garcio suus duos denarios. Vigillarius tres denarios. Scoparius duos denarios. Pulsantes classicum sex denarios. Custos capitis et feretri Beati Hugonis quatuor denarios, et custos tumbe Beati Roberti quatuor denarios, si non sunt de previis nominatis. Attendendum quoque est de prefata distributione nullus portantium habitum aliquid debet recipere nisi presens fuerit in officio pro obitu celebrando dummodo non fuerit per infirmitatem vel aliud impedimentum legitimum excusatus, et de impedimento, utrum legitimum sit, erit capituli judicare. Idem intelligendum est de ministris eundem habitum non portantibus qui presentes non fuerint et in ecclesia suis ministris intendentes. Si quid autem superfluerit de sexaginta solidis supradictus quod non fuerit per distributionem modo prefato ordinatam consumptum, totum pauperibus fideliter erogetur. ... Ad hanc igitur ordinationem perpetuis temporibus inviolabiliter reservandam, nos decanus et capitulum pro nobis et successoribus nostris nos obligatos esse fatemur et cohercemur, episcopo qui pro

tempore fuerit nos submittimus ut possit nos per quam-
cumque viam decreverit si necesse fuerit ad ipsius observationem cohercere. In quorum omnium testimonium et robur
perpetuum tam nos Oliverus episcopus quam [*f. 359*] quam[1]
predicti decanus et capitulum sigilla nostra presentibus
duximus apponenda. Hiis testibus, Philippo decano, Johanne
cancellario, Ricardo thesaurario, Rogero Archidiacono
Bedeford', Henrico subdecano et aliis pluribus Lincoln'
ecclesie canonicis.

Universis[2] sancte matris ecclesie filiis ad quos presentes
littere pervenerint, Oliverus etc. Noveritis nos de licencia et
concessione domini Edwardi Regis Anglie illustris dedisse,
concessisse et hac presenti carta mea confirmasse ... decano et
capitulo nostre Linc' ecclesie omnes terras et tenementa, que
habuimus ex dono et feoffamento domine Alicie de Marton',
videlicet unum messuagium, duo tofta, unam carucatam terre
et novem denaratos[3] redditus in Marton', unum messuagium
et quatuor bovatas in Wyhum, unum messuagium et sex
bovatas terre in Ormesby et Utterby, cum villanis et villenagiis
et omnibus aliis pertinentiis ad predicta tenementa spectantibus,
tenenda et habenda predictis decano et capitulo libere, quiete,
bene et in pace, faciendo inde nobis et successoribus nostris
omnia servicia que predicta Alicia et antecessores sui nobis et
predecessoribus nostris pro predictis tenementis facere
solebant, et solvendo ad sustentationem unius capellani, pro
nobis in ecclesia predicta divina perpetuo celebraturi, et ad
obitum nostrum die anniversarii nostri annis singulis faciendum,
duodecim marcas secundum formam que in quodam scripto
inter nos et predictos decanum et capitulum cirographato
plenius continetur. Et nos Oliverus et heredes nostri omnes
predictas terras et tenementa predictis decano et capitulo
contra omnes homines warantizabimus in perpetuum. In
cujus rei testimonium tam nos Oliverus quam predicti
decanus et capitulum huic presenti scripto in modum
cirographi confecto sigilla nostra alternatim apposuimus. Hiis
testibus, dominis Johanne Bek', Roberto le Venur, Ricardo de
Buslingthorp', Johanne de Hoyland', Waltero de Ludeham,
Johanne Burdun', Roberto de Saundeby, militibus, et multis
aliis. ... Deinde scriptum fuit decano et capitulo Linc' sub hac
forma:
    O. etc. Quia cantariam pro nobis perpetuam una cum obitu
nostro cum decesserimus annis singulis faciendam in ecclesia

---

[1] bis.
[2] The word *Carta* appears in the margin.
[3] Sic, recte *denariatos*.

nostris Linc' predicta per nos noviter ordinatam dilecto in Christo filio Johanni de Utterby presbitero duxerimus conferendum, vobis mandamus quatinus eundem Johannem ad cantariam hujusmodi admittatis de hiis que pro suis stipendiis percipere debet juxta formam ordinationis super hoc per nos facta decetero respondentes eidem. Datum apud Theyden' VIII kalendas Julii, pontificatus nostri anno XVI.

ARCHDEACONRY OF HUNTINGDON. Commendation for a period of six months to Master Walter of Wootton, canon of Lincoln, to the archdeaconry of Huntingdon, vacant by the collation, on Jan. 28, 1294, of Master Roger de Martivall to the archdeaconry of Leicester, and the fact that Pope Boniface VIII had revoked the provision made by his predecessor Celestine V in favour of John son of Sir John de Colonna de Urbe, canon of Lincoln. Witnessed by Masters Jocelyn of Kirmington, Robert of Kilworth, Sirs William of Stockton and William of Heanor, canons of Lincoln, John de Scalleby, priest, John of Ferriby and John of Clipston, notaries-public. Letters patent, given in full, were issued on Master Walter's behalf to the clergy and people of the said archdeaconry, under the bishop's seal. Biggleswade, the bishop's chamber, June 30, 1295, after his (mid-day) sleep.[1]

ST. MARY CRACKPOLE (Crakepole). Sir Oliver Sutton, canon of Lincoln, to the prebend of St. Mary Crackpole, vacant by the collation of Sir John Maunsel to the prebend of Leicester St. Margaret. Place, date, time and witnesses as above.

[*f. 359v*] SCAMBLESBY. Note that at the O.T. London on July 15, 1295, John Nannius, merchant of the *Società* of Lambertucio de Frescobaldis of Florence, and proctor of Sir Thomas son of Sir Peter Conti de Cantansano, appeared before the bishop, claiming the prebend of Scamblesby by virtue of a provision made by Celestine V as pope-elect. Celestine had invested Sir Thomas by ring (*per anulum*) and committed the execution of his mandate to the Archdeacon of [?] (Bantesio) and Master Geoffrey de Vezano. After some consideration, the bishop accepted this provision, notwithstanding his previous collation of Master Richard of Plymstock to the prebend. London O.T., July 21, 1295. A letter (given in full) was sent on behalf of Sir Thomas to the D. and C. of Lincoln. London O.T., July 22, 1295.

[1] The words 'Vide plus in folio sequente' are interlined.

THORNGATE. Sir Hugh of Normanton to the prebend of Thorngate, vacant by the collation of Sir Oliver of Sutton to the prebend of St. Mary Crackpole, Buckden, Nov. 7, 1295, after morning Mass. Witnessed by Masters Walter of Wootton, Jocelyn of Kirmington, and by Robert of Kibworth and Roger of Sixhills, priests, John of Bayton and Hugh of Harewood clerks, and John of Clipston notary-public.

[*f. 360*] BANBURY. Sir Theobald de Barre,[1] brother of the Count of Bar, to the prebend of Banbury vacant by the death of Master Nicholas of Waltham. Spaldwick, Nov. 1, 1295, immediately after the mid-day meal. Witnessed by Master Walter of Wootton, Jocelyn of Kirmington, Hugh of Normanton, Robert of Warsop, Roger of Sixhills and Robert of Kibworth, priests, John of Bayton, clerk, and John of Clipston, notary-public. Letters on Sir Theobald's behalf sent to the D. and C. of Lincoln. Buckden, Nov. 15, 1295.

WELTON BRINKHALL (Welleton'). Master Nicholas of Whitchurch D.C.L. to the prebend of Welton Brinkhall vacant by the death of Master Hugh of Collingham. Biggleswade, Dec. 20, 1295, after morning Mass. Witnessed by Masters Jocelyn of Kirmington and Robert of Kilworth, canons of Lincoln, and Sirs Roger of Sixhills and William of Ham(m)erton (Hamerton'), priests.

ARCHDEACONRY OF HUNTINGDON. Master Walter of Wootton to the archdeaconry of Huntingdon, which he had *held in commendam* since June 20, 1295. Fingest, the bishop's chamber, Dec. 26, 1295, about the third hour. Witnessed by Masters Simon Archdeacon of Oxford, Jocelyn of Kirmington, and Robert of Kilworth, canons of Lincoln, John de Scalleby, priest, and John of Clipston, notary-public. Custody of the sequestrations of the church of Marston Mortayne, of which the said Master Walter had been rector, were committed to him. Place, date and time as above.

LEIGHTON ECCLESIA. Sir Oliver son of Sir William of Sutton, canon of Lincoln, to the prebend of Leighton Ecclesia vacant by the death of Master William of Malling. Lincoln Cathedral, in chapter, Apr. 9, 1296, about the first hour of the day. Witnessed by Masters Henry the subdean, Jocelyn of Kirmington, Nicholas of Whitchurch, official-principal, John le Fleming and William of Thornton, and Sirs William of Stockton, John Maunsel and Richard of Winchcomb, canons

---

[1] Bar-le-Duc.

of Lincoln, Master Walter of Fotheringhay and John of Clipston, notary-public. Had letters patent.

ST. MARY CRACKPOLE. Sir Hugh of Normanton to the prebend of St. Mary Crackpole vacant by the collation of Sir Oliver of Sutton to the prebend of Leighton Ecclesia. Place, date, time and witnesses as above.

[f. 360v] ST. HUGH'S ALTAR, LINCOLN CATHEDRAL. William of Swineshead chaplain to the altar of St. Hugh in Lincoln Cathedral, vacant because William of Gayton had received another benefice. Lincoln Cathedral, in chapter, Apr. 7, 1296. Witnessed by Masters John of Dalderby, chancellor, Henry of Benniworth subdean, Jocelyn of Kirmington, Nicholas of Whitchurch and other canons.

THORNGATE. Amadeus of Savoy (in the person of Henry called de Cameys his proctor) to the prebend of Thorngate formerly held by Sir Hugh of Normanton, in virtue of a provision of Boniface VIII dated Sept. 1, 1295. Note that a second dignity or living in the diocese of Lincoln, mentioned in tbe same provision, was not at present available, but that a notarial instrument was drawn up by John of Clipston, stating that one would be found. Lincoln, Mar. 26, 1296.[1]

MILTON ECCLESIA. Master Gilbert of Seagrave D.D. to the prebend of Milton Ecclesia vacant by the consecration of Master John of Monmouth as Bishop of Llandaff. Buckden, Feb. 6, 1297. Witnessed by Masters Jocelyn of Kirmington, Nicholas of Whitchurch and Robert of Kilworth, canons of Lincoln, and by Robert of Warsop, Robert of Kibworth and John de Scalleby, clerks of the bishop's household.

BUCKDEN. Master Walter of Wootton to the prebend of Buckden vacant by the death of Master Stephen of Tathwell. Buckden, the bishop's chamber. Date and witnesses as above.

The collations to Milton Ecclesia and Buckden, given above, were evidently made by proxy, though the fact is not mentioned. They were renewed to Master Gilbert and Master Walter in person, Buckden, Mar. 9, 1297, and letters to the D. and C. of Lincoln were issued on their behalf. Witnessed by Masters Jocelyn of Kirmington, Nicholas of Whitchurch, Robert of Kilworth, William of Stockton and John Maunsel,

[1] A note of the beginning of the seventeenth year of Sutton's episcopate should appear here, but does not in fact do so.

canons of Lincoln, and Robert of Kibworth and John de Scalleby, priests, and John of Clipston, notary-public.

WELTON RYVAL. Master Nicholas of Whitchurch to the prebend of Welton Ryval vacant by the collation of Master Walter of Wootton to the prebend of Buckden. Place, date and witnesses as above.

WELTON BRINKHAll. Master William of Sardinia[1] (Sarden') D.C.L. to the prebend of Welton Brinkhall vacant by the collation of Master Nicholas of Whitchurch to the prebend of Welton Ryval. London, in the house of Sir Reginald de Gray in Purtepole,[2] Apr. 4, 1297, in the morning after Mass. Witnessed by Masters Walter of Wootton, Jocelyn of Kirmington, Henry of Nassington, Robert of Kilworth, and R. of Normanton, canons of Lincoln.

QUARTODECIMO KALENDAS VIDELICET DIE SANCTI DUNSTANI ANNO DOMINI M.CC. NONAGESIMO SEPTIMO INCIPIT ANNUS PONTIFICATUS DOMINI OLIVERI DEI GRACIA LINCOLN' EPISCOPI OCTAVUSDECIMUS.

[f. 361] CROPREDY. John, son of Sir Anibaldo de Anibaldis (Anibalden'), Roman citizen, provided by Pope Boniface VIII to the prebend of Cropredy, of which Odo son of John de Colonna (Columpna) had been deprived. Admitted Louth, Dec. 30, 1297. Letter ordering his installation, in the person of Master Hugh of Langley, proctor substituted by his original proctor Philip Burgi, merchant of Florence of the Società of the Mori. Louth, Dec. 31, 1297.

LEIGHTON MANOR. Master Robert de Lacy (Lascy) D.C.L., canon of Lincoln, to the prebend of Leighton Manor vacant because Boniface VIII had included John son of John de Colonna in the general excommunication pronounced against the Colonna family. This admission was to be held null and void if it were found that the pope had made other arrangements. Nettleham, Mar. 1, 1298, in the bishop's chamber after his nap (post dormitionem). Witnessed by Masters Jocelyn of Kirmington and Robert of Kilworth and Sir William of

---

[1] I have so identified him in L.R.S. 48 p. xxxiii, but he may have come from Sarre in Kent. See Le Neve, *Fasti Ecclesiae Anglicanae, 1066–1300*, vol. III, ed. D. E. Greenway (Inst. Hist. Research, 1977) p. 39 note.
[2] 'Port Pool, or Gray's Inn Lane'. John Stow, *A Survey of London*, ed. H. Morley (London, from the edition of 1603) p. 396.

Stockton, canons of Lincoln, and Sirs Henry of Auckland, John de Scalleby, Robert of Kilworth, priests, and John of Clipston notary-public. Had letters patent (given in full). Same place and date.

———

QUARTODECIMO KALENDAS JUNII VIDELICET DIE SANCTI DUNSTANI ANNO DOMINI M.CC. NONAGESIMO OCTAVO INCIPIT ANNUS PONTI-FICATUS DOMINI OLIVERI EPISCOPI LINCOLN' NONUSDECIMUS.

———

GRETTON. Boniface son of Thomas Marquis de Saluzzo provided by Boniface VIII to the prebend of Gretton, vacant by the death of Sir Robert of Swillington and the withdrawal of Edward of St. John. The provision was forwarded by Master John de Luco, deputed for this purpose together with the Prior of Pontefract and Master Huguccio de Vercelli. The bishop sent a verbal message to the D. and C. of Lincoln by Sir Hugh of Normanton, canon, ordering Boniface's installation in the person of Berengar[1] de Quilhan (Quiliano) his proctor. Tinwell, in the manor of the A. and C. of Peterborough, Mar. 9, 1298.

[f. 361v] PROVISIO JOHANNIS LANDULPHI. Note that the bishop ordered John son of Landulph de Colonna to be admitted, in the person of Patrick of Craven, proctor substituted by his original proctor Melior de Pistoia (Pistoria) of the Società of the Ammanati, to a canonry in the church of Lincoln.[2] Liddington, Jan. 22, 1299. The pope's letter ruling that the said John was exempt from the sentence of general ex-communication directed against the Colonna family had been received at Louth, Dec. 7, 1298.

ARCHIDIACONATUS BUCK'. Sir Boniface de Saluzzo provided by Pope Boniface VIII, in a letter forwarded by Master John de Luco canon of London, to the archdeaconry of Bucking-ham. Admitted in the person of Berengar de Quilhan his proctor, Buckden, Mar. 10, 1299.

MARSTON ST. LAURENCE. Master Walter of Fotheringhay to the prebend of Marston St. Laurence vacant by the death of Master Richard of St. Frideswide, provided that it was not

[1] Here spelt *Bierlengarius*, but see below.
[2] No prebend is named.

claimed within the time-limit by a papally-provided candidate. Had letters patent. Baldock, the bishop's chamber in his lodging in the house of Henry le Parker, about noon, Mar. 18, 1299. Witnessed by Masters Jocelyn of Kirmington, Nicholas of Whitchurch and Robert of Kilworth, canons of Lincoln, John de Scalleby, priest, and John of Clipston, notary-public.

PRO DOMINO BONIFACIO DE SALUCIIS. Mandate to the inhabitants of the archdeaconry of Buckingham to obey Sir Boniface de Saluzzo as their archdeacon. London, O.T., Mar. 22, 1299.

OBEDIENCIA ARCHIDIACONI BUCK'. Note of the oath of obedience taken by Sir Boniface de Saluzzo as Archdeacon of Buckingham. London, O.T., in the chamber reserved for the bishop's clerks, Mar. 22, 1299. Witnessed by Master Walter of Wootton and Robert of Kilworth, canons of Lincoln, John de Scalleby, priest, and George de Saluzzo, precentor of Salisbury, brother of Boniface.

[f. 362v] Half folio left blank.

BEDFORD MAJOR. John de Scalleby, priest, to the prebend of Bedford Major vacant by the death of Sir William of Heanor (Hennovere). Stow Park, the bishop's chamber, October 11, 1299, after noon. Witnessed by Masters Jocelyn of Kirmington and Nicholas of Whitchurch, canons of Lincoln, and John de Clipston(e), notary public.

DISPENSATIONS OF THE YEAR 1299

f. 363	Place	Person	Time (yrs)	Purpose	Date
	Twyford R.	John of Sutton	7	Study in Arts	O.T. 28 March
	Oakley near Brill R.	William of Wrotham subd.	3	Study in Arts	O.T. 28 March
	Bletchingdon R.	Richard of Musgrave	7	Study in Arts	Buckden 5 March
	Orby R.	Robert of Reston	2	Study in Arts	O.T. 31 March
	W. Keal R.	John de Cubeldik M.A.	6	further study	Audley 2 April
f. 363v[1]	Twywell R	Geoffrey of Glinton subd.	2	study	Biggleswade 3 April
	L. Berkhamstead R.	John de Bymsted	1	study	Buckden 29 April
	Washingborough	William de la Dune	1	study for ordination	Buckden 23 June
	Bletchindon R.	Mandate to Archdeacon to reduce to 6 marks the Vicar's stipend.			No date.
	Anderby R.	William de Grendale M.A.	2	study	Nettleham 20 September
	Hanslope R.	Peter Le Blund subd.	3	study abroad	Nettleham 23 October
	Sileby	John of Somerby subd	2	study	Nettleham 23 October
	Strixton	Robert, deacon	1	study	Stow Park 26 September
	Woolsthorpe R.	Mr Simon of Threkingham	1	study	Stow Park 27 September
	Braceborough R.	John, chaplain	1	study	Stow Park 27 September
	Willingham R.	Mr Henry de la Wyle	2	study of theology	Stow Park 1 October
	Milton Bryant R.	John	1	absence in service of Princess Mary, a nun at Amesbury	Stow Park, 3 October

Mursley R.	Thomas	1	absence in service of Princess Mary, a nun at Amesbury	study
Ashby Folville R.	William of Lowthorpe	1		Stow Park 5 October

1 Mandates to archdeacons to supply suitable vicars in above cases.

INSTITUTIONS SEDE VACANTE

[f. 364v] INSTITUTIONES FACTE PER MAGISTRUM NICHOLAUM DE WYTCH' CANONICUM LINCOLN' OFFICIALEM LINC' SEDE LINC' VACANTE PER MORTEM DOMINI OLIVERI EPISCOPI EJUSDEM. PROCESSUS AUTEM CAUSARUM HABITI CORAM EO SUNT IN REGISTRO OFFICIALITATIS LINC'. CORRECTIONES ETIAM, COMMISSIONES, COMMENDATIONES ET CUSTODIE ECCLESIARUM AC DIMISSORIE LITTERE ET ALIA ACTA SINGULARIA SUNT IN ROTULIS DIVERSIS PENES CAPITULUM LINCOLN' RESIDENTIBUS.

COMMISSIO ... OFFICIALI SEDE VACANTE. Letters patent of Robert Winchelsey, Archbishop of Canterbury, appointing Master Nicholas of Whitchurch custodian of the see of Lincoln, vacant by the death of Oliver Sutton, on the nomination of the D. and C. of Lincoln. Under his seal. Chichester, Dec. 14, 1299.

Church	Incumbent	Patron	Last incumbent	Date
Croughton R.	Roger of Shilton pr.	Richard and Joan Wale[1]	Mr Richard Neyrnut dd.	Louth 31 Dec. 1299
Cottesmore R.	Gilbert of Micheldever ch.	Guy de Beauchamp kt.	Gilbert Marsh dd.	Louth 31 Dec. 1299
f. 365 Winwick R.	John of Stoke clerk	King as guardian of temporalities of see	Robert of Warsop dd.	Lincoln 13 Jan. 1300
Pinchbeck V.	Mr William of Newport ch.	P and C of Spalding	Thomas of Healing dd.	Lincoln 16 Jan. 1300
Stamford St. Peter R.	Ralph de Fulden subd.	Mr John le Flemeng, proctor of P. and C. of St. Fromund	Mr Ralph de Padgrave res.	Lincoln 17 Jan. 1300
Edmondthorpe R.	Philip de Kereby ch.	George de Charnels	Robert of Bedworth res.	Lincoln 17 Jan. 1300
Holbeach Chantry	Thomas of Wragby ch.	Laurence of Holbeach	Alan of Worlaby dd.	Lincoln 17 Jan. 1300
Shalston R.	Robert of Dunton ch.	Lady Elizabeth of Shalstone	Walter of Amersham res.	Lincoln 19 Jan. 1300
S. Kilworth R.	Alan of Kilworth pr.	A. and C. of Sulby	Mr Robert of Kilworth res.	Stamford 26 Jan. 1300
Sawtry All Saints R.	John of Boreham clerk	William le Moynge	Mr Walter de Teford res	Owston 6 Feb. 1300
f. 365v Weston in Holland V.	Walter of Rauceby ch.	P. and C. of Spalding	Mr William of Littleport	Hinkley 9 Feb. 1300
Skinnand R.	Roger of Fleet	A. and C. of Crowland	William le Constable	Stamford 9 Feb. 1300
Dinton V.	Robert of Walcot	A. and C. of Godstow	Alan of Kilworth res.	Northampton 26 Feb. 1300
Albury R.	Philip de Bachequell' subd.	A. and C. of Missenden	Mr Robert de Panteo dd.	Bradwell 28 Feb[?] 1300
Loughton R.	Geoffrey of Cosgrove clerk	Thomas of Loughton	Thomas Berard dd.	Missenden 15 Mar.
Thorpe Achurch R.	William Sturmy of Louth	Sir William Corbet kt.	Mr Thomas de Canele dd.	London 8 Mar. 1300
East Farndon	Thomas s of Alured of Dingley clerk	Hugh son of Richard, lord of Dingley	Simon dd.	London 10 Mar. 1300
Leicester St. Mary de Castro V.	Benedict of Coventry ch.	A. and C. of St Mary de Pratis, Leicester	Mr Geoffrey de Foston res.	London 10 Mar. 1300
Toddington chantry of B.V.M.	Ralph of Claxton ch.	Sir John Peyvere kt.	Ralph of Bradenham dd.	London 12 Mar. 1300
Adstock	William of Hingham ch.	A. and C. of St. Mary de Pratis, Leicester	Jordan of Withersfield res.	London 12 Mar. 1300
f. 366 Glaston	Mr Henry de Dreneshale pr. Commendation for 6 months	P. and C. of Launde	Mr Reyner Gilberti, deprived by Pope	London 11 Mar. 1300

[1] Claim established in royal court against William Wakelyn of Croughton & Miles de Beauchamp.

[*Roll VI*] The heading is now lost and the roll begins with part of an entry relating to Anderby which continues below. The rest of the roll is taken up by grants of custody (or sequestration) for the years 1298–99.

BLATHERWYCKE. R. to Mr John de Wutton clerk and acolyte p. by the P. and C. of Launde after death of Adam de Duffeld, to extend to the Michaelmas ordination. Buckden, 25 May, 1298.

TOFT to Robert de Harton chap. p. by the p. and C. of Sixhill; Robert already held a benefice in York. London O.T., 28 June, 1298.

BASSINGHAM to Hugh de Normanton, canon of Lincoln, during pleasure, and until a dispute about presentation after the consecration of Mr Henry of Newark, last incumbent, to the see of York, is resolved. Bicester, 29 July 1298.

HATTON to Mr William of Friskney, p. by Sir William Breton knight, to extend to the next ordination 31 July, 1298. *Later note*: mortuus est.

ANDERBY. Process in the court of audience in a dispute for possession of the church between Mr William de Grendale and Peter of Chichester. Hugh of Willoughby, rector of Wold Newton, appointed commissary, to hear and determine, 10 Nov. 1298.[1]

BEDFORD ST. PETER MERTON to John de Tykeshouer p. by P. and C. of Merton after the death of William, to extend to the next ordination. Buckden, 2 Sept. 1298.

CALVERTON to John de Falsham p. by Sir Hugh de Veer, after the death of William de Percy, to last to next ordination. 14 Feb. 1298.

ON DORSE: continued to next ordination owing to Bishop's illness.

KIRKBY LAYTHORPE, mediety, to Walter de Wilteshier p. by Sir Thomas Multon of Frampton after William de Folkardeby acquired another benefice: to last until next ordination. Stoke by Oundle, 27 Feb. 1298

---

[1] The entries in this cause are squeezed into existing spaces in the roll.

ON DORSE: continued, as for Calverton.

ORTON WATERVILLE to John de Husthwayt, p. by Sir Robert de Waterville after the death in Viterbo of William de Carleton, to last until next ordination. Buckden, 13 Mar. 1298.

ABINGTON to Robert de Brocton clerk p. by Mary, widow of Sir Humphrey de Bassingburn after the death of Henry de Bassingburn, to last until the next ordination. Buckden 14 Mar. 1298.

WAKELE to Stephen of Withcall, clerk p. by Walter Gacelyn of Sheldon as guardian of the daughter of Richard son of Ralph Mouche, after Ralph de Hakethorn was presented to Raithby, to last to the Pentecost ordination. Buckden, 13 Mar. 1298.

SHOBY to John de Someredby clerk after the institution of Robert Prudfot of Leicester to Little Dalby, to last to the next ordination. Buckden, 15 Apr. 1298.

FISKERTON to Mr Richard of Hertford priest p. by A. and C. of Peterborough after the last incumbent acquired Bringhirst, which has cure of souls. Gosberton, 7 Oct. 1298.

AMBROSDEN to Mr Roger de Martival archdeacon of Leicester, p. by the rector and brothers of Ashridge after the death of Mr Ralph de Martival, during pleasure. No date.

GARSINGTON to Mr Hugh de Morton, p. after the death of Mr Andrew of St. Albans. The Bishop's mandate, and Hugh's oath of obedience, are given in full. Newark, 29 Nov. 1298.

LEICESTER, ST. JOHN'S HOSPITAL to Brother Peter de Querington, elected after the removal of Thomas de Bretford, to last until Peter reaches the age for ordination. Liddington, 17 Dec. 1298.

WALMSGATE to Geoffrey of Cockerington clerk, p. by P. of Burwell after the death of Eudo, to last until ordination. Liddington, 20 Dec. 1298.

HARSTON to Thomas Thorp clerk, p. by A. and C. of Leicester after the resignation of Walter de Leicester, to last until ordination. Liddington, 29 Dec. 1298.

BUCKNALL to Thomas de Swaveseia ac. p. by P. and C. of Stixwold after William de Rasen acquired West Rasen, to last until next ...dination. Liddington, 13 Jan. 1299.

ON DORSE: sequestration extended to Palm Sunday.

WINCEBY to Robert de Silkeston p. by Edmund earl of Lancaster after the death of the last incumbent, to last to the next ordination. Buckden, 24 Apr. 1299.

EASTON by STAMFORD to Roger de Sampson p. by A. and C. of Crowland after death of Mr Henry Sampson senior, to last to the next ordination. Buckden, 24 Apr. 1299.

TANSOVER mediety, to Mr Walter de Fodringeye, priest and canon of Lincoln, p. by D. and C. of Lincoln after death of William de Clare, to last 6 months, in accordance with the Council of Lyons. Buckden, 29 Apr. 1299.

ASTON CLINTON to William Gacelyn, pr. by John de Drokenesford after the resignation of William de Wymburn, to last 6 months. Buckden, 5 May 1299.

GEDNEY to John Pickard ch. p. by A. and C. of Crowland after alleged death of John de Curiaco, to last until Lammas, unless the death is proved earlier. Buckden, 7 May 1299.

STAMFORD, ST. MICHAEL CORNSTALL Robert Homet clerk p. by John Le Flemeng proctor of St. Fromund after death of Simon de Weldon, to last until ordination. Buckden, 8 May 1299.

BROUGHTON to Hugh de Osgodeby clerk p. by P. and C. of Lenton after death of Hugh de Bezancun and renunciation of Henry de Bertelmeu who was first presented, to last until Michaelmas unless the death is proved earlier. Buckden, 21 June 1299.

ON DORSE: continued until Christmas. Stow Park, 7 Oct. 1299.

FINMERE to John de Longton clerk p. by A. and C. of St. Augustine Bristol after the death of Mr Ralph de Oxford, to last until ordination. Buckden, 21 June 1299.

OFFORD DARCY to Robert de Lafham, pr., p. by Sir John de Offord after the failure of John de Offord, his son, to take orders, to last for 6 months. Spaldwick, 28 June 1299.

HERTFORD, ST. ANDREW to William de Leycestr' p. by King Edward after the resignation of Philip de Herdewyke, to last until the next ordination. Sleaford, 26 July 1299.

COTTESMORE to Gilbert de Micheldever priest p. by Guy de Beauchamp earl of Warwick after the death of Gilbert de Marisco to last until Martinmas, when he is to be examined as to his competence.

LACEBY to John de Stratton clerk in minor orders, p. by Sir Walter de la Lynde after the death of William, to last until the next ordination. Nettleham, 20 Sept. 1299.

CLIFTON to John de Chetingdon clerk, p. by Sir Henry Spigurnel after the death of Robert Spigurnel, to last until the next ordination. Nettleham, 20 Sept. 1299.

SAWTRY, ALL SAINTS to John de Borham clerk, p. by William Le Moyne after the institution of William de Teford to an incompatible benefice, to last until the next ordination. Nettleham, 20 Sept. 1299.

STAMFORD, ST. PETER to Robert de Fuldon clerk, p. by Mr John Le Flemeng, proctor of P. and C. of St Fromund after the resignation of Mr Ralph de Pagrave, to last until the next ordination. Stow Park, 7 Oct. 1299.

WILSFORD Pr. to William de Bec p. allegedly by the A. and C. of Bec after the resignation of John de Sauvarilla, to last until Christmas, unless he produces a letter of presentation before then. Louth, 19 Oct. 1299.

THORPEACHURCH custody given to archdeacon of Stow on behalf of William Sturmy extended to Christmas. Nettleham, 5 Nov. 1299.

COLD BRAFIELD to Richard Syward of Newport Pagnell, clerk p. by Sir Ralph Pypard after the death of Walter de Wycumb, to last until the next ordination. Nettleham, 5 Nov. 1299.

INDEX OF PERSONS

Abbreviations used: a. & c.: abbot & convent; p. & c.: prior (prioress) & convent; kt.: knight; n.p.: notary public; O.F.M.: Franciscan friar; O.S.A.: Augustinian canon; canon: canon of Lincoln; s.: son of; d.: daughter of; O.P.: Dominican friar; p.: priest; D.C.L.: doctor of civil law.

INDEX OF PLACES

Carlton—*cont.*
―――, Great, Lincs., 8, 12–14
―――, Little, Lincs., 25
Caversfield, Bucks., 167
Chalfont, Bucks., 23
―――, St. Giles, Bucks., 127
Chalgrave, Beds., 114
Charlbury, Oxon., 180, 189–90, 193
Chellington, Chelvington, Beds., 99
Chenies, Bucks., 161
Chesham Bois, Bucks., 162
Chesterton, Hunts., 74
Chicheley, Bucks., 157
Chicksands, Beds., 98, 106, 113
Cholesbury, Bucks., 161
Christleton, Cheshire, 123
Churchill, Oxon., 172
Cippenham, Bucks., 137
Clanfield, Oxon., 184
Clapham, Beds., 116
Clawson, Long, Claxton, Leics., 56
Claybrook, Leics., 56
Claydon, East, Bucks., 163
―――, Steeple, Bucks., 126
Clifton, Beds., 121
―――, Reynes, Bucks., 156
Coates, Lincs., 10, 27
Cogges, Oxon., 176, 201
Cokethorpe, Oxon., 173
Coleorton, (Overton Quatermars),
    Leics., 53
Colmworth, Beds., 108
Conesby, Cuningesby, Conesby
    Darcy, Lincs., 23
Congerstone, Cuningeston, Leics.,
    69
Conington, Hunts., 83
Cople, Beds., 113
Cornwell, Oxon., 172, 179
Cosby, Leics., 55
Cosgrave, Northants., 79
Cossington, Leics., 42, 54, 59
Coston, Leics., 54
Cotes, Leics., 44, 48, 55, 67
Cottesbach, Leics., 41
Cottesmore, Rutland, 223
Cottisford, Oxon., 176
Cowley, Oxon., 201
Cranfield, Beds., 93, 102, 116
Cranoe, Cravenhoe, Leics., 52
Croft, Leics., 48
Cropredy, Oxon., 175
Croughton, Northants., 223
Crowell, Oxon., 188
Crowmarsh Gifford, Oxon., 193
Croxton, South, Leics., 42, 59
Cuckney, Derbs., 10, 27

Dalby-on-the-Wolds, Daleby, Leics., 58
―――, Great, D.Chaucombe, Leics., 36
―――, Little, 69, 71
Datchworth, Herts., 79, 84
Dinton, Bucks., 125

Diseworth, Leics., 39
Dishley, Dixle, Leics., 54, 66, 71
Deddington, Oxon., 177
Dinton, Berks., 224
Dorchester, Oxon., 184, 198
Ducklington, Oxon., 189
Duckmanton, Derbs., 10, 27
Dunton, Beds., 103

Easington, Oxon., 190
Eastwell, Leics., 36, 52, 66
Eastwick, Beds., 103
Eaton, Leics., 51
―――, Bray, Beds., 120
―――, Socon, Beds., 93, 110
―――, Wood, Oxon., 183, 201
Edgcote, Bucks., 125, 163
Edlesborough, Bucks., 138
Edmondthorpe, Leics., 38, 43, 51, 58,
    224
Edworth, Beds., 97, 114
Ellington, Hunts., 85
Elsfield, Oxon., 179
Elstow, Beds., 99
Emberton, Bucks., 170
Epworth, Lincs., 18
Etwall, Derbs., 10, 27
Eversdon, Cambs., 107
Eversholt, Beds., 107, 112, 122
Ewelme, Oxon., 173
Exton, Rutland, 44
Eynesbury, Hunts., 87
Eyworth, Beds., 106

Faldingworth, Lincs., 25
Felmersham, Beds., 123
Filgrave, Bucks., 127
Fillingham, Lincs., 11–12, 14, 19, 23,
    28–30, 117
Finmere, Oxon., 202
Fiskerton, Lincs., 2, 22, 25, 30
Flamstead, Herts., 88
Flitwick, Beds., 108Fl
Flixborough, Lincs., 28
Folksworth, Hunts., 84
Friesthorpe, Lincs., 18
Fringford, Oxon., 175
Frisby-on-the-Wreake, Leics., 38, 48–9,
    53
Fritwell, Oxon., 178
Frodingham, Froxingham, Lincs., 2,
    20, 29
Frowlesworth, Leics., 66

Gaddesden, Great, Herts., 74
―――, Little, Herts., 82, 85
Gainsborough, Lincs., 1
Galby, Great, Leics., 67
Gayhurst, Bucks., 162
Gedling, Notts., 8
Glaston, Rutland, 224

INDEX OF SUBJECTS

INDEX OF COUNTIES AND COUNTRIES

BUCKINGHAMSHIRE—*cont.*

Quarrendon
Radeclive
Radnage
Salden
Saunderton
Sherington

Simpson
Stantonbury
Stewkley
Stoke Mandeville & Regis
Thornborough
Twyford

Waddesdon
Walton
Wendover
Westbury
Wolverton
Wraysbury

CAMBRIDGESHIRE

Eversden

Morden, Gilden

DERBYSHIRE

Cuckney
Duckmanton

Etwall

Seal

HERTFORDSHIRE

Ardley
Aspenden
Berkhampstead
Bradfield
Datchworth
Flamstead
Gaddesden, Great & Little
Hatfield
Hinxworth

Knebworth
Letchworth
Lilley
Mimms, North
Offley
Rushden
Shenley
Slawston
Thurning

Tring
Wakeley
Walkern
Watton
Welwyn
Westmill
Wheathampstead

HUNTINGDONSHIRE

Alconbury
Bennington
Brington
Broughton
Buckden
Bythorn
Caldecote
Chesterton
Conington
Ellington
Eynesbury
Folksworth
Glatton
Godmanchester

Hartford
Hemingford
Holywell
Huntingdon
Keystone
Morborne
Newton, Water
Offord Darcy
Orton Longueville &
    Waterville
Paxton
Ripton, Abbots & King's
Sawtry
Somersham

Southoe
Stanground
Stanton, Fen
Staughton, Great
Stibbington
Stilton
Walton, Wood
Warboys
Washingley
Weston, Old
Winwick
Woodstone

LEICESTERSHIRE

Abkettleby
Appleby
Arnesby
Asfordby
Ashby Folville
Ashby, Great
Aston Flamville
Aylestone

Barkby
Belton
Billesdon
Bottesford
Bowden
Braunstone
Brooksby
Broughton Astley

Broughton, Nether
Burton Overy
Cadeby
Carlton Curlieu
Clawson, Long
Claybrook
Coleorton
Congerstone

LEICESTERSHIRE—*cont.*

Cosby
Cossington
Coston
Cotes
Cottesbach
Cranoe
Croft
Croxton, South
Dalby-on-the-Wolds
Dalby Great & Little
Diseworth
Dishley
Eastwell
Eaton
Edmonthorpe
Frisby-on-the-Wreak
Frowlesworth
Galby
Glen, Great
Glenfield
Hallaton
Harstone
Hathern
Higham-on-the-Hill
Horninghold
Kegworth
Keythorpe
Kibworth

Kibworth Harcourt
Kilworth North &
   South
Knipton
Laughton
Leicester
Lutterworth
Markfield
Mirabel
Morton
Muston
Nailstone
Naunton
Newbold Verdun
Norton *iuxta* Twycross
Norton, King's
Noseley
Overton, Cold
Owston
Peckleton
Ratcliffe-on-the-Wreak
Rothley
Saddington
Saxby
Sharnford
Sheepy
Shoby
Shouldby

Sileby
Skeffington
Somerby
Sproxton
Stapleford
Stathern
Stockerstone
Stonesby
Swinford
Swithland
Syston
Thornton
Thorpe Arnold
Thrussington
Thurlaston
Thurnby
Tilton
Wanlip
Walton-le-Wolds
Whatton
Wigston Magna
Willoughby Waterless
Wistowe
Withcote
Witherley
Wymeswold
Wymondham

LINCOLNSHIRE

Alkborough
Althorpe
Anderby
Appleby
Belton-in-Axholme
Blyborough
Blyton
Bottesford
Braceborough
Brattleby
Burton, Gate
Buslingthorpe
Caenby
Cammeringham
Carlton, Great & Little
Coates
Conesby
Epworth
Faldingworth
Fillingham
Fiskerton
Flixborough
Friesthorpe
Frodingham
Gainsborough
Glentham
Glentworth
Grainthorpe
Grayingham

Greetham
Greetwell
Hackthorn
Halton, West
Harpswell
Harrington
Heapham
Hemswell
Hibaldstow
Holbeach
Ingham
Ingleby
Keal
Kettlethorpe
Kirton-in-Lindsey
Lea
Lincoln
Manton
Marton
Nettleham
Normanby
Orby
Owston
Pilham
Pinchbeck
Raithby-by-Louth
Raventhorpe
Redbourne
Reepham

Risby
Rischolme
Roxby
Saxby
Saxilby
Scampton
Scawby
Scothern
Scotter
Scotton
Skinnand
Snarford
Spridlington
Springthorpe
Stainton-by-
   Waddingham
Stamford
Sudbrooke
Thornholme
Torksey
Upton
Waddingham
Washingborough
Weston
Whitton
Willingham
Willingham-by-Stow
Willoughton
Winteringham

LINCOLNSHIRE—*cont.*

Winterton   Woolsthorpe   Wroot

LONDON CITY

All Hallows the Great

NORTHAMPTONSHIRE

Cosgrave   Northampton   Thorpe Achurch
Croughton   Paston   Twywell
Irchester   Strixton   Woodford Halse

NOTTINGHAMSHIRE

Gedling   Newark

OXFORDSHIRE

Adderbury   Deddington   Noke
Albury   Dorchester   Northmore
Alkerton   Ducklington   Norton, Brize
Alvescot   Easington   Norton, Cold
Ambrosden   Eaton, Wood   Nuncham Courtenay
Baldon, Marsh   Elsfield   Oxford
Bampton   Ewelme   Rotherfield Peppard
Barton Westhall   Finmere   Rousham
Beckley   Fringford   Shiplake
Begbrooke   Fritwell   Shipton-on-Cherwell
Bix Gibwyn   Glympton   Shipton-under-Wychwood
Bletchingdon   Hampton Poyle   Shirburn
Bloxham   Hethe   Shorthampton
Brightwell Baldwin   Heyford, Lower   Somerton
Broughton Poggs   Islip   Spelsbury
Bucknell   Kidlington   Stanton Harcourt
Charlbury   Kingham   Stoke, North & South
Churchill   Langford   Stoke Talmage
Clanfield   Launton   Swalcliffe
Cogges   Lewknor   Tackley
Cokethorpe   Littlemore   Tadmarton
Cornwell   Loughton   Tew, Duns & Great
Cottisford   Marston   Wendlebury
Cowley   Merton   Weston, South
Cropredy   Middleton Stoney   Wroxton
Crowmarsh Giffard   Minster Lovell   Yarnton

RUTLAND

Cottesmore   Glaston   Ryhall
Exton   Melton Mowbray

SOMERSET

Alford

WARWICKSHIRE

Nuneaton

WESTMORELAND

Kirkby Stephen

YORKSHIRE

Adlingfleet   Bainton   Lyth

EIRE

Ballykelly

ITALY

Viterbo

NOTE: The Society wishes to record its gratitude to the Lincolnshire County Council for a grant of £300 towards the costs of this publication.